Simpson —
Cheers, amigo!
Glad to have you
reading the book and
looking forward to
making turns with
you!

AMERICAN
SNOW

The Snowsports Instruction Revolution

AMERICAN
SNOW

The Snowsports Instruction Revolution

Peter Kray

PROFESSIONAL SKI INSTRUCTORS OF AMERICA

and AMERICAN ASSOCIATION OF SNOWBOARD INSTRUCTORS

American Snow: The Snowsports Instruction Revolution

© 2011 American Snowsports Education Association
          Education Foundation, Lakewood, Colorado

PUBLISHED BY:
American Snowsports Education Association
133 South Van Gordon Street, Suite 200
Lakewood, CO 80228
303-987-9390

Cover photo by Sherri Harkin | SharkinPhoto.com

ISBN: 978-1-882409-36-5

Printed in Canada

Contents

(Photo by Dann Coffey)

List of Sidebars

Acknowledgments

To be able to record the incredible history of the Professional Ski Instructors of America and the American Association of Snowboard Instructors has been the privilege and pleasure of a lifetime. So many instructors, teachers, and coaches have contributed to the association's rich history over the past 50 years—touching millions with their knowledge, passion, and innovation—that you could fill another book with their names alone.

American Snow itself is the result of the vision and contributions of hundreds, and I am grateful to all of them for their friendship, insights, and time. To the PSIA-AASI Board of Directors who first saw the need for this book, championed it, and shepherded it through to completion, I can never thank you enough for trusting me with such an awesome production. To PSIA-AASI Executive Director and CEO Mark Dorsey and Marketing Director Andy Hawk, and the incredible team at the PSIA-AASI offices in Lakewood, Colorado, thank you for all of the resources, including the boxes of images, home-cooked meals, and personal efforts that made this such a wonderful collective effort from day one. Special thanks to PSIA-AASI staffers such as Wendy Schrupp, who helped shape the voice of the book by editing the first early articles, Erin Tulley and Kyle Hamley, who were instrumental in gathering those images, and to Earl Saline and Ben Roberts, keepers of the history and the educational stoke, every page of this book bears the stamp of your hands.

The beautiful images are thanks to the talents of Dann Coffey, Cesar Piotto, Julie Shipman, Sherri Harkin, the generosity of the U.S. Ski & Snowboard Hall of Fame and the New England Ski Museum, and dozens of individual contributions. The passion that inspired this entire project owes much to the achievements, ideas, and support of individual instructors such as Bill Lash, Doug Pfeiffer, Curt Chase, Horst Abraham, Gwen and Ray Allard, Ellen Post Foster, Juris Vagners, Max Lundberg, Jerry Warren, Mike Porter, Bruce Bowlin, Dick Dorworth, Michael Hickey, Doug Pringle, Lee Perry, Carol Levine, Dee Byrne, Randy Price, Craig Panarisi, Tony Forrest, Eric Sheckleton, Bud Keene, Lowell Hart, David Alden, Dave Merriam, Mark Anderson, John Armstrong, Katie Ertl, Michael Rogan, Bill Bowness, Geoff Krill, Ross Matlock, Scott McGee, Josh Spoelstra, Lane Clegg, and David Oliver, who have all contributed to the ongoing innovation of American instruction, helping to define their own place in time.

Thank you as well to Alan Engen, Annie Black, Bobby Murphy, Craig Albright, Dave Lundberg, Don Welch, Ingie Franberg, Karen Hollaus, Kim Seevers, Mikey Franco, Nick Herrin, Pepi Stiegler, Robert Hakkinen, Tim Petrick, Urmas Franosch, Steve Hindman, Dan Clausen, Jens Husted, Carl Boyer, Ed Younglove, Peter Donahue, John Peppler, Frederica Anderson, Hoagy Carmichael, Otto Ross,

Al Voltz, Doug Pierini, Scott Anfang, Gregg Davis, Eric Rolls, Robin Barnes, Tommy Morsch, Eric Lipton, Matt Boyd, Jeb Boyd, Jennifer Simpson, David Lawrence, Dave Lyon, Tom Marshall, Rob Sogard, Mike Hafer, Charlie MacArthur, Jim Schanzenbaker, Tim Johnson, Sara Nakon, Tom Spiess, Chip Powers, Max Felix, Karen Hagaman, Patrick Bragg, Kennon Warner, and Jennifer Johnson. Each of you represents one more reason why the deep network, camaraderie, and professionalism of the people who comprise PSIA-AASI make it such a strong and successful association.

(Photo by Dann Coffey)

(Photo by Julie Shipman)

PREFACE

THE GIFT OF FLIGHT

To teach someone how to ski or snowboard is like sharing superpowers—giving the gift of motion, freedom, and flight—it's the sensation of flying, with the world spinning beneath your feet and the wind whipping across your face.

For more than 50 years, the Professional Ski Instructors of America and American Association of Snowboard Instructors (PSIA-AASI) has carved a way of life out of sharing that gift. Since its formation in 1961, PSIA-AASI has defined itself by its unending level of innovation and insight in activities from snowboarding to alpine and cross-country skiing.

In every decade since they began teaching these snowsports, American instructors have sparked a new kind of on-snow revolution that has enriched and expanded their appeal. From the breakthrough instructional psychology of student-centered teaching and the simplified genius of the Skills Concept in the 1970s to the adaptive, nordic, and women's instruction explosions of the 1980s to the game-changing advent of snowboarding to the explosion of freestyle and the ATML Method of teaching that defined the beginning of the twenty-first century, PSIA-AASI has built an international reputation as one of the most imaginative and continuously evolving instructional organizations in all of sports.

(Photo by Julie Shipman)

(Photo by Andy Hawk)

The tale of the instructors who made it happen is as big as America itself, built on hills no bigger than a bump, blue ice and deep powder, steep-walled halfpipes, open groomers, and massive mountains with jagged cliffs. From Maine to Montana, Alaska to Wisconsin, and every hill in between, it is a tale of ideas and inspiration, of turmoil and triumph. It is the story of thousands of instructors—more than could ever be named in one place—and the millions of lives they have touched.

It is a privilege to tell their story, and to have met and skied with so many of the people who have lived it. Dreamers, doers, artists, and geniuses alike, their inspiration, energy, and friendship are the reasons this book was written. They are why somewhere right now, someone on a sit-ski or snowboard or standing at the start of a cross-country trail is beginning to stretch his own wings, preparing for flight.

(Photo by Cesar Piotto)

CHAPTER 1

THE 1960s: INTERSKI

I t was 1965 at the Interski in Bad Gastein, Austria, the international ski congress held every three years like a roving ski instructors' Olympics, where some of the greatest skiers in the world came swooping like giant birds down the slope. They made tight turns like tap dancers into the arena below, or charged through the closely set racecourse like blitzing linebackers tackling every gate.

From Austria, France, Germany, Italy, and Switzerland they had come together to dazzle and challenge and best each other with the latest ski techniques. Only the Americans were relative newcomers. The Professional Ski Instructors of America association was barely four years old and still trying to define its own national technique. But by the time the American skiers had flown home they would have signaled to the world that they were bringing a new level of energy and invention to snowsports instruction and beginning a series of on-snow revolutions that would forever change how the sport was taught.

Hochalm Pass, Bad Gastein.

(Photo courtesy of the Bad Gastein Tourism Office)

When the PSIA sent a demonstration team to the 1965 Interski in Bad Gastein, Austria, with members including PSIA President Bill Lash, Toby Von Euw, Eric Windisch, Barry Bryant, Phil Jones, and Glen Young among others, they announced their presence to the international world of ski instruction.

(Photo PSIA-AASI)

Led by the charismatic Bill Lash, a Utah businessman with a deep, gravelly voice and a singular passion for creating an American standard of skiing, the team was a hodgepodge of the hottest ski instructors from New Hampshire, Minnesota, Utah, and Idaho's Sun Valley, that first jewel of skiing in the West. Team member Willy Schaeffler was from Germany, a Bavarian skiing champion who would later lead the United States to Olympic skiing success, and Lash's good friend Paul Valar was Swiss. With such an international delegation, Lash could be understood for feeling bridled by the nationalized segregation of the event.

On the mountain, the competition between the 22 countries in attendance—there to show off who had the hottest skiers and the most groundbreaking instructional style—was particularly tense. Thousands of spectators from Munich, the nearby city of Strassburg, and little villages across the Alps had ridden up on the train and lined the fences alongside the demonstration slope, closely watching the varied styles of skiing for any hint of innovation or country-specific success. Technique was progressing rapidly, and everyone wanted to lead the way to what was next.

While that sense of experimentation created camaraderie among the national teams on the hill, down in the village it did not exist. Lash was dismayed to find that the teams all sat at separate tables for their meals; neither the venue nor the schedule allowed for informal talk. He wanted discussion and interaction. He wanted to find out what all the other countries were learning about the sport.

He said, "Paul Valar told me it was because of tradition when I asked. And when I said the Americans should host a cocktail party to bring all the teams together, he told me, 'It will never happen. Don't even think about it.'"

But Lash persisted, and he decided to use what was left of the sponsorship money from Hart Skis to host a party the following night. All of the other teams immediately warmed to the concept. The ice was broken in an instant, laughter and boasts about the best days ever on the mountain filled the room, and as Lash said, "It was a great success."

All the participants found they had a similar passion for speeding down snow-

Willy Schaeffler.

covered slopes. They found they had ideas to share, as well as insights into technology and technique. The gathering was America's first contribution to Interski, and each year thereafter the drive to outdo each other in hosting parties has become almost as important as the skiing demonstrations on the slopes. For Lash and Schaeffler, the so-called Ski Pope of the Rockies, the results were even more immediate.

After the party, the two skiers sat in their hotel room with a bottle of Scotch. Tfhe Americans were looking for a way to contribute to the sport of skiing, and they were discussing how they might make the most immediate impact. Lash remembers mentioning to Schaeffler that the Canadians would probably try to host the next Interski in 1968, and that it was a shame that the Americans were not bidding for it. When he offhandedly said, "We should—" Schaeffler jumped off the edge of his bed. "And Willy, being Willy, right away said, 'Yes! Let's do it,'" said Lash.

It was midnight in Europe, but only 4 p.m. in Colorado, when Schaeffler picked up the phone to begin calling his extensive list of well-placed contacts. He started with D. R. C. "Darcy" Brown, president of the Aspen Skiing Corporation, then called Steve Knowlton at Colorado Ski Country and Vail founder Pete Seibert. Knowlton, in turn, called Colorado Governor John Love, and by the time Lash and Schaeffler woke up (if they ever slept) nearly one dozen telegrams were waiting for them in the hotel office. Aspen Skiing said it would be honored to host the 1968 Interski, as did Vail, while Ski Industries America (now SnowSports Industries America) President Doc DesRoches and the National Ski Patrol and National Ski Areas Association indicated they would help in any way they could. The telegram from Governor Love read:

COLORADO WITH OUTSTANDING FACILITIES MOST INTERESTED IN HOSTING INTERNATIONAL SKI SCHOOL CONGRESS IN 1968 PLEASE EXPRESS MY PERSONAL INTEREST.

JOHN A. LOVE GOVERNOR

THE EVOLUTION OF TECHNIQUE

Terms, Innovators, and Books
COURTESY OF BILL LASH

Sondre Norheim the Telemark Turn ✵ Telemark Abstem ✵ Mathias Zdarsky's Alpine Technique ✵ One Pole Technique ✵ Austrian Technique ✵ Hannes Schneider's Arlberg Ski Technique ✵ Straight Running ✵ Snowplow ✵ Traverse ✵ Stem Turns ✵ Platform Turns ✵ Side Slipping ✵ Stem Christies ✵ Parallel Turns ✵ Tempo Turns ✵ Scissors Christies ✵ American Style ✵ The American Ski School of Otto Schniebs ✵ The San Moritz School ✵ The Wengen Method ✵ The Swiss Counter Rotation ✵ Otto Lang's *Downhill Skiing* ✵ Hans Georg's *Skiing Simplified* ✵

10th Mountain Division veteran Curt Chase, who was a co-founder of PSIA and also director of the Aspen Ski School, was an obvious choice to serve as coach of the 1968 Interski U.S. Demonstration Team.

(Photo courtesy of the New England Ski Museum)

Al and Betty Voltz.

(Photo PSIA-AASI)

Dizzy at the prospect of such support, Lash made an impassioned speech to the entire international delegation and wrote veritable poems about the beauty of U.S. skiing in English and German to the Austrian Interski directors. Their decision was swift. Canada would have to wait until 1987 to host Interski in Banff; Aspen would be the site in 1968. "I just wish I could remember exactly what I said in that speech," joked Lash.

ASPEN

Preparations began as soon as Lash, Schaeffler, Valar, and the rest of the team got home. A nonprofit corporation was created to host the event, with Schaeffler as president. The big, blonde, 10th Mountain Division veteran Curt Chase, who was the director of the Aspen Ski School (where his adoring instructors called him "Papa Bear"), was chosen as the U.S. team coach.

In a bit of foreshadowing for the future of the Professional Ski Instructors of America and the American Association of Snowboard Instructors (PSIA-AASI) national teams, tryouts were especially fierce. Team member Al Voltz remembers how many crestfallen skiers did not make the cut; how glad he was to be on the team with his wife, Betty; and how they all looked like alpine astronauts in their shimmering black and silver ski suits.

There were six women on the 1968 U.S. Interski team—Betsy Glen, Joan Hanna, Bonnie Pond, Jean Weiss, Carolyn Teeple, and Betty Voltz—twice as many as have been on a U.S. demonstration team since. Chase's wife, Betsy, remarked during an interview in Snowmass, Colorado, more than 40 years after the event, that Curt always strived to maintain an equal mix of male and female instructors in his ski school.

Betsy recalled wine and cheese picnics on the mountain from that time, and she realized she had been bearing witness to a demographic shift where alpine communities like Aspen began welcoming the world, with the miners and ski bums and occasional movie stars all mixed together at the bars and restaurants. She said Austrian ski instruction legends Professor Stefan Kruckenhauser and Franz Hopplicher were chauffeured down Main Street in a white convertible with a brass band and horse-mounted flag bearers to provide the 1968 Interski at Aspen with a proper sense of ceremony right from the start. "In town it had the feeling of a holiday," she said.

Buick stepped up as a sponsor, as did Colorado-based brewer Coors, which paid for a short movie to be filmed about the event. A video was shot of the opening festivities featuring Kruckenhauser in his convertible and several different teams skiing down the hill making synchronized turns in matching jackets. Travel writer Curtis Casewit helped publish a program for Interski in which he wrote, "The state is decked out with Interski posters, Interski banners snap in the Aspen air, and Interski's many languages flow along the Colorado slopes. Pride! One of skidom's most exciting events is here, thousands of miles from Zurs, Davos, Val d'Isere, Storlien, Zakopane, Monte Bodone, Bad Gastein. For the first time in seventeen years, the Congress takes place in the United States."

For Curt Chase, the proudest moment was when he saw the U.S. team at the top of the hill, preparing to perform at Interski for the first—and, as of this writing,

The 1968 U.S. Demonstration Team and Demonstration Team candidates.
(Photo courtesy of Al and Betty Voltz)

THE EVOLUTION OF TECHNIQUE

Terms, Innovators, and Books
COURTESY OF BILL LASH

Ken Syverson's ski school on Snoqualmie Pass ✎ France's Emile Allais' parallel ski instruction ✎ Allais Technique ✎ The Ruade ✎ Fritz Loosli and *Parallel Skiing* ✎ Dorothy Hoyt Nebel's *Empire State Technique* ✎ Heel-to-Toe and Around We Go ✎ Tyler Micoleau's *Power Skiing* ✎ Blocage ✎ Counter Rotation and Counter Motion ✎ Fall Line Technique ✎ Reverse Shoulder Technique ✎ The Comma Position ✎ Mambo ✎ *The New Official Austrian System* of Austria's professor Stefan Kruckenhauser

5

The Magnificent Seven

The goal of PSIA's founders was to set the national standards of American ski instruction. What they ended up with was so far-reaching and flexible that over the next 50 years it would be instrumental in generating a revolution in the mind-to-body understanding of how all sports are learned and taught.

Curt Chase was a veteran of the 10th Mountain Division who launched the Aspen Ski Patrol in 1946. He wrote the first manual for Aspen ski instructors, was head of the Aspen Ski School and Snowmass Ski School, and was coach of the PSIA delegation at the Aspen Interski in 1968.

Curt Chase was a man of many firsts. Years before he helped found the PSIA, he launched the Aspen Ski Patrol in 1946.
(Photo courtesy of the New England Ski Museum)

After co-founding the PSIA, **Max Dercum** and his wife, Edna, oversaw the design and construction of Keystone Ski Resort.
(Photo courtesy of the U.S. Ski & Snowboard Hall of Fame)

Max Dercum helped build Arapahoe Basin Ski Area in Colorado, buying up the mining claims that would become the ski area, cutting trails, teaching skiing, and running the lifts. In 1970, he and his wife, Edna, oversaw the design and construction of Keystone, built on the mountain behind the family's lodge at Ski Tip Ranch.

Jimmy Johnston created a ski school program in Minneapolis while he was still in law school, which grew to accommodate 5,000 skiers every week. As a district court judge he was a pioneer in the advent of community service and a regular writer of ski columns for the *Minneapolis Star*. He helped write the standards for PSIA and published *The Official American Ski Technique*.

PSIA co-founder **Jimmy Johnston** was the model for Mammoth Mountain's mascot.
(Photo courtesy of the New England Ski Museum)

Bill Lash
(Photo PSIA-AASI)

In 1952, **Bill Lash** wrote the nearly 30-page "Progress Report on the Certification of Ski Instructors in the United States." In 1958, he wrote *An Outline of Ski Teaching Methods*, creating an instructor's encyclopedia of topics ranging from class patter to powder technique. The galvanizing force behind the creation of PSIA, Lash was also its first president.

Paul Valar was a member of the Swiss national ski team who competed in the 1947 U.S. National Ski Championships in Utah, where he met another competitor, Paula Kann, who became his wife. In New Hampshire, Paul founded the

PSIA co-founder **Paul Valar** was the technical brains behind many of the association's first breakthroughs in technique.
(Photo courtesy of the U.S. Ski & Snowboard Hall of Fame)

Franconia Ski School at Cannon Mountain, and the pair ran ski schools at Mittersill and Mt. Sunapee. Valar also co-authored *The Official American Ski Technique*.

Doug Pfeiffer
(Photo PSIA-AASI)

Doug Pfeiffer is considered the Godfather of Freestyle Skiing for his work promoting the sport. He was editor of *Skiing* magazine; provided commentary on the *Killy Challenge*, a television show in which French Olympic champion Jean-Claude Killy raced celebrities down a mountain; and hosted radio interviews, which aired on nearly 500 stations. His high-energy freestyle competitions provided perfect programming for TV, enticing skiers on hills small and large to tackle trick maneuvers such as spread-legged Daffys, tip rolls, worm turns, and forward flips.

Don Rhinehart helped cut runs on Idaho's Mt. Baldy following his Navy stint in World War II. He became the Sun Valley Ski School supervisor, where his passion was plain to see in a remarkably fluid style of skiing. His family operated a private lodge in the Selway-Bitteroot Wilderness, and in the summers he ran kayaks down the Salmon River's Middle Fork.

Don Rhinehart
(Photo PSIA-AASI)

only—time in history on American snow. He said, "I remember it was cloudy and the Swiss team had just come down, and then the sun..." But he had to stop, as his eyes filled with tears while he remembered the blue sky bursting through the clouds and the mountains exploding into light. He looked at his wife, then waited for a moment to compose himself. "And just as the team was about to ski down," he said, "the sun came out."

"I'm sorry," he said, and waited again. "I didn't know it affected me so much."

Chase said that when Aspen's Interski was ending, he stopped to talk to Professor Kruckenhauser, who told him that the Swiss and American presentations had interested him the most. It was not the last time Kruckenhauser would say something so memorable to a member of the American delegation at Interski, as we learn in Chapter 2, and, as Chase said, "that meant a lot."

THE MELTING POT

In 1961, the year PSIA was formed, trains still outstripped planes as the predominant long-distance mode of transportation. John F. Kennedy had just been sworn in as president—it was the first inauguration broadcast in color—and in May of that year he announced that the United States would be the first country to put a man on the moon, while across the Atlantic the Beatles were just beginning to play at Liverpool's Cavern Club.

Former Aspen ski instructor Klaus Obermeyer invented everything from down parkas to early forms of high-altitude sunscreen, as well as a long-running ad campaign that promoted the mountain mystique.

(Photo courtesy of Sport Obermeyer)

Achieving Independence

As PSIA co-founder Bill Lash wrote, "The roots of the American Ski Technique (AST) go back to the 1930s. No one person created the AST as some maintained. It was the effort of many people" as well as the National Ski Association (NSA) and the US Forest Service (USFS). When special-use permits were being granted for ski areas, the USFS added a clause to protect the general public, which stated that permits for operating a ski school "would be based on the use of certified ski instructors," according to Lash. He reports that as early as 1947, W. S. "Slim" Davis, chairman of the NSA's Southern Rocky Mountain Association Certification Committee, "was looking forward to the day when a standard national certification procedure for ski instructors can be established."

It would take another 15 years for a national certification to be established, during which time ski instruction's relationship with the NSA, under whose auspices the meeting at Whitefish took place, became equally problematic. The NSA was interested in promoting racing and would become the U.S. Ski Association in 1962, parent to the U.S. Ski Team, with a competitive focus on the sport. As Doug Pfeiffer reflected on the inevitable split, he said, "Was there anger that the professionals weren't running their own affair? I think it was more that kind of resenting-your-father complex."

A 1960s ski lesson.
(Photo courtesy of the U.S. Ski & Snowboard Hall of Fame)

In skiing, equipment innovators such as American aircraft engineer Howard Head were bringing aluminum skis to market, which significantly increased skiers' ability to control and carve a turn, and former Aspen ski instructor Klaus Obermeyer was busy inventing down parkas, high-altitude sunscreen, turtlenecks, and a long-running "Obermeyer Girl" ad campaign featuring wide-eyed models who smoldered with a promise of snowy warmth.

Despite the sense of possibility sweeping across the mountains, though, ski lessons in the United States were still caught in a multicultural limbo, a confusing mix of Swiss, Austrian, and French techniques, with the likelihood of neighboring mountains offering a disappointingly different instruction experience.

"When I came to the United States in 1949, I was very surprised to find that, in the East alone, just about every technique I have ever heard of was being taught—and with all possible modifications," the Swiss-born Paul Valar wrote in the October 1961 issue of *SKI Magazine*.

In the article, entitled "Can We Have a Unified American Ski Technique?" Valar wrote, "Imagine the confusion that must have resulted among recreational skiers because of so many different techniques being taught at resorts only a few hours apart."

Skiers who took lessons at one mountain would travel to another mountain only to hear—often explicitly—what was wrong with the competing technique they had just been taught. Standardization was lacking, precisely because there was no American technique. The Europeans who had brought skiing to the United States were still waging their war of technical dominance on American slopes. And as much as those techniques were a studied series of drills to get a skier progressing toward making parallel turns—considered the Holy Grail of skiing, when you levitate down the mountain as if you were skimming the earth—they were also a source of deep national pride. Much of the core methodology had been developed training Italian, French, and Austrian mountain troops prior to each of the two world wars in the hotly contested border regions of the Alps. For many of the alpine expatriates who had fled from Europe during the pre-World War II rise of Nazism and Fascism, how they skied was as much a part of their heritage as their language, their cooking, and their writing.

Austrian ski instruction pioneer Hannes Schneider—who famously said of his plan to take the thrill of skiing to the masses, "I will put speed into everyone's skiing. It is speed that is the lure, not touring"—was the most renowned skier in the world when he immigrated to North Conway, New Hampshire, after being chased from his home in St. Anton, Austria, by the Nazis in 1939. Regarded as the father of

Known as the father of modern ski instruction, Austrian-born Hannes Schneider famously said of his plan to take the thrill of skiing to the masses: "I will put speed into everyone's skiing."

(Photo courtesy of the New England Ski Museum)

Many of PSIA's original members were veterans of the 10th Mountain Division.

(Photo courtesy of the Denver Public Library)

10th Mountain Division veteran and PSIA pioneer Herbert Schneider.

(Photo courtesy of the U.S. Ski & Snowboard Hall of Fame)

PSIA's founding fathers. Clockwise from top left: Doug Pfeiffer, Don Rhinehart, Max Dercum, Curt Chase, Paul Valar, Jimmy Johnston, and Bill Lash.

(Photo PSIA-AASI)

modern ski teaching because of his development of the "Arlberg method," whereby students started out making slow turns on gentle slopes and moved faster on steeper terrain as they progressed, Schneider became an icon in the United States as well. Many of his former instructors followed him to the United States, establishing ski schools and inspiring America's new generation of native-born ski experts.

Schneider's son, Herbert, returned to St. Anton as a member of the 10th Mountain Division, America's original alpine troops, and was treated as a conquering hero by all the townsfolk who turned out to welcome him back. Following the creation of PSIA, he would also be one of the first instructors to join the association as the news of its creation spread like a victory bulletin across the mountains of the United States.

In 1961, however, even Hannes was just one of many voices in the wilderness of American ski instruction, where the styles were as varied as the regions, the climate, and the sizes of the slopes. Not until PSIA began to integrate the best of what everyone was teaching did a single galvanizing force emerge for skiers from coast to coast.

THE BIRTH OF THE AMERICAN TECHNIQUE

On a warm day in May 1961, at Big Mountain in Whitefish, Montana, seven visionary ski instructors drafted American skiing's Declaration of Independence. They were Curt Chase, Max Dercum, Jimmy Johnston, Bill Lash, Doug Pfeiffer, Don Rhinehart, and Paul Valar, mountain men from across the country who each represented a particular region of instructors. All seven were independent thinkers who had dedicated their lives to sharing their love of the sport. Skiing was in their blood. It was in their dreams. And it was in the conviction with which they created the organization with one historic vote.

"We all raised our hands and agreed that we would do it," said Chase, who remembers the seven of them sitting together at a cafeteria table in short-sleeve shirts in the afternoon when the sun had turned the snow to slush. Like Dercum and Herbert Schneider, Chase was a veteran of America's storied 10th Mountain Division. And like them, over the next 40 years he would become a giant in the field of snowsports. He said there was a sense of inevitability when it came to finally creating PSIA—a sense that Americans were chafing at the chance to create their own style of skiing and instruction, and that they had waited long enough.

"It was just another meeting of the National Ski Association's Ski School Directors committee," Chase said, "until Bill Lash said that if we were ever going to have an organization consisting of professionals to run the business of professional ski teaching, then we needed to take charge of it ourselves."

Waiting in the main room of the lodge were dozens of other ski instructors and ski school directors who had come from across the country, including Colorado cowboys and Utah powder pilots, soft snow sliders from Squaw Valley to Seattle, and edge artistes from Wisconsin and Vermont. Doctors, lawyers, and door-to-door salesmen; expatriates from Austria and Germany; and college professors and high school dropouts who all made elegant turns on 7-foot skis in lace-up leather boots, looking like movie stars with their suntanned faces and flared ski pants. They all got that twinkle in their eyes when they talked about the feeling of the snow beneath their feet and the wind across their face, and most importantly, they all wanted to create an American standard for how to share those same sensations with everyone else.

"I am proud of that moment, because of what it meant for ski instruction in this country," said Lash, who as the architect of that meeting had the honor of walking out to the main room to announce the outcome of the vote. "It created the basis for how we would grow the sport."

What those seven instructors began to define was an American style of skiing, and an independent-minded era of experimentation emerged in the process. Lash entered the meeting as president of the Intermountain Ski Instructors Association, Rhinehart as chairman of the Pacific Northwest Ski Association, Pfeiffer as president of the Far West Ski Instructors Association, Dercum representing the Rocky Mountain Ski Instructors Association, Chase of the Northern Rocky Mountain Ski Association, Johnston from the Central

Max Dercum and Herbert Schneider on the mountain at the historic Whitefish meeting.
(Photo courtesty of the U.S. Ski & Snowboard Hall of Fame)

1958's National Ski Association Convention in Alta, Utah, drew many who would go on to be PSIA co-founders and early members. Pictured here, from left to right, are Willy Schaeffler, Paul Valar, Earl Miller, Bill Lash, Chuck Hibbard, Ed Heath, Joe Harlacher, Junior Bounous, Alf Engen, Jimmy Johnston, Kerr Sparks, and George Engle.
(Photo PSIA-AASI)

Ski Instructors Association, and Valar from the Eastern Amateur Ski Association, but to form PSIA they had to stand united and while still supporting each other as independents. It was a democracy from the start. Membership was voluntary. Anyone who did not want to join could simply say "no thanks."

"I do think we were taking control of the sport as we saw it," Lash said of the spirit of the vote. "When you think of the melting pot of people who were bringing some part of the same idea together at that time, including people like Pfeiffer, who was French-Canadian;

The 10th Mountain Division

The 10th Mountain Division was a rough-and-ready mix of displaced Europeans, Ivy League enlistees, and homegrown outdoorsmen who battled the Nazis across Italy during World War II. Recruited specifically for their ability to ski, and with a letter of reference required to enlist, the 10th was the only American combat division recruited by a civilian organization in the form of the National Ski Patrol. PSIA co-founders Curt Chase and Max Dercum were veterans, as were dozens of other instructors such as Herbert Schneider and Friedl

The 10th Mountain Division was instrumental in the development of American skiing. Many veterans of the division founded or managed U.S. ski areas, became ski patrollers, or joined the PSIA upon its creation in 1961.
(Photo courtesy of the Denver Public Library)

Pfeifer. They trained at Colorado's Camp Hale, then saw action in Italy's Apennine Mountains, gaining major victories in the capture of Mount Belvedere and Riva Ridge while also sustaining one of the war's heaviest casualty rates. Back home, former members of the 10th founded the National Outdoor Leadership School, co-founded Nike, and over the years ran more than 60 ski resorts.

PSIA's Regional Divisions

Critical to the formation of PSIA was the establishment and support of its six separate regional divisions. Each of those founders represented a specific region of U.S. skiing when they sat down at the table for the vote, and geographically oriented divisions have continued to act as localized versions of the association, supporting their local members through education and certification and acting as clearinghouses for the latest trends and innovations in both instruction and technique. As the sport grew and as PSIA, and later the American Association of Snowboard Instructors (AASI), membership exploded, the regional divisions eventually grew to nine, including the Alaska, Central, Eastern, Intermountain, Northern Intermountain, Northern Rocky Mountain, Northwest, Rocky Mountain, and Western divisions.

Valar, who was Swiss; and Austrians like Herbert Schneider and Germans like Willy Schaeffler—that created the idea to make it an independent choice. I don't know what else we could have done other than that."

"It was Lash who made it happen," said Pfeiffer, a Canadian-born skier who in the 1970s would become known as the Godfather of Freestyle Skiing—and who would become one of the most vocal critics of the very organization he helped create. "He gave PSIA its start."

And when Lash asked for a show of hands, every instructor in the room said, "YES."

A FAST START

Annual membership dues for the newly formed Professional Ski Instructors of America were $15. Membership, which was optional until 1971, included the PSIA pin, which served as proof of a national identity and of a working alpine culture—and was what most of the original wave of certified instructors seemed to want the most.

"Everyone wanted the pin," said Lash. "The phone started ringing off the hook."

Robert Hakkinen, a ski instructor from Minnesota, said he and his three best friends, "the Four Aces," have not taken a run without their PSIA certification pins on their parkas since they first earned them in 1962. "It's been there forever," said "Hak," who holds Central Division certification pin #00159. "It represents the whole aura of skiing for me. We were certainly focused on technique, and climbing the mountain of experience, but when PSIA became a national identity, it gave us a national identity, too."

Having a national body of instruction created a consistency in the quality and presentation of ski lessons across the United States while allowing for specific regional styles, which were almost as much about individual tastes as they were about terrain and snowpack.

"It settled some of the differences, if that's what you would call it," said Hak. "But everybody had idiosyncrasies about how they did things, just so a lesson at Stowe wouldn't be confused with a lesson at Indian-head, or Arapahoe Basin. The advent of PSIA helped define the terminology and teaching models—for the instructor and the student."

A PSIA Level III Certification Pin from 1976. The pins mark each instructor's level of certification. They are a symbol of accomplishment for the instructors who earn them.

(Photo courtesy of www.Robertsski.com)

Vail founder and 10th Mountain Division veteran Pete Seibert (right) surveys the mountain's famous Back Bowls.

(Photo courtesy of Vail Resorts)

A private lesson on Vail Mountain.
(Photo courtesy of Vail Resorts)

Jackson Hole Mountain Resort founders
Paul McCollister and Alex Morley prepare
for the construction of the tram.
(Photo courtesy of Jackson Hole Mountain Resort)

It also created a friendly sense of solidarity across the United States. As Hak said, "Every time I go somewhere to ski, that pin starts a conversation that I wouldn't have ever had anyway else."

In November 1961, PSIA held its first official meeting in Denver, electing Lash PSIA President, Valar Vice President, and Johnston Secretary-Treasurer, and naming as its board Pfeiffer, Rhinehart, Chase, and Jimmy Johnston.

In 1962, the United States sent its first small demonstration team and instruction contingent—composed almost entirely of instructors from the Eastern division—to Interski in Monte Bondone, Italy, officially declaring PSIA an international presence. With the Americans at the table, the International Ski Instructors Association was formed at the meeting, further highlighting PSIA's growing global identity in the sport. Meanwhile, back home, the mountain industry was expanding in hill-topping leaps. Ambitious new ski areas were being built, particularly in the breathtakingly beautiful peaks of the West, and urbanites and the quickly growing new wave of suburbanites alike were flocking uphill in their station wagons, Impalas, and Beetles for their own taste of the thrill of wintersports.

Vail Mountain opened one year after the formation of PSIA. In 1966, Jackson Hole first operated its iconic red tram, unveiling skiing in Wyoming's Tetons. And in 1971, 10 years after the meeting at Whitefish, Utah's Snowbird opened, promoting a new kind of deep snow skiing mystique.

Skiing was a ready-made symbol of the ruggedly elegant alpine panache, and other European-styled sports, such as rock climbing and bicycle touring, were also experiencing significant growth. But none of them exploded like skiing. None of them had the sense of community on the chairlifts or around the fireplaces, complete with warm drinks, waiting at the mountain's base.

The early days of après skiing.
(Photo courtesy of the U.S. Ski & Snowboard Hall of Fame)

The American Technique

In advance of that momentous meeting in Whitefish, Montana, the ski world was abuzz for any news regarding what had become an increasingly sought-after national standard—an American technique. Magazines made plans to cover the meeting in anticipation of just such a result. "The question of a unified ski technique will again be aired," the April 1961 issue of *Skiing* reported. "Also up for discussion will be the long deferred plan for a professional ski instructor's organization."

What turned those long-awaited probabilities into reality was the inescapable fact that no matter how the best skiers taught, when they skied, their styles contained the same critical elements. In the article in *SKI* in which Valar decried the lack of standardization in U.S. ski instruction, he made note of Austrian Professor Stefan Kruckenhauser's theory of "the reverse shoulder," also called counter-rotation. Americans incorporated it into their own skiing, along with *wedeln*, a series of short, aggressively unweighted turns that Kruckenhauser and his Austrian academy of ace instructors had also developed.

"A distillation of the Austrian and Swiss styles," according to Pfeiffer, it was treated as a revelation in the United States. A headline in the November 1961 issue of *Skiing News Magazine* (later *Skiing*) blared, "There is an American Technique." Publisher Bob Parker sent cameramen to Whitefish, and when they returned with "photographic evidence" of the new technique in practice, the entire staff was convinced. "American instructors were so used to teaching—and preaching—about some new variety of foreign skiing they had failed to look around them and realize they were skiing their own way!" Parker wrote, adding with a sales pitch–worthy finish, "This is the method taught coast to coast by certified ski instructors. In asking about ski instruction, ask for it by name: ask for the American Technique."

No instructor could actually deliver on such a request, but the term stuck. And the style was immortalized in a caricature of Jimmy Johnston, whose wry smile and reverse shoulder technique were the model for Mammoth Mountain, California's cartoon logo of a skiing woolly mammoth.

Paul Valar and Bill Lash with an early copy of *The Official American Ski Technique*, PSIA's "White Book," which would first set the standards for ski instruction in the United States.

(Photo courtesy of the New England Ski Museum)

"There was a whole cultural fascination with and love of the mountains," said Pfeiffer. "People were excited by the outdoor life, healthy exercise, good friends, and good times. They had left the big cities behind because they couldn't stand them, and the mountains were opening up a new world of possibilities."

With the growing demand for ski lessons, membership in PSIA was also ratcheting up. Certified instructors in the United States numbered just 1,350 at the end of 1961; by the end of 1969, there were nearly four times that many—4,264.

The new association was experiencing quick growth—so much so that it became necessary to document and market what their purpose and style of instruction were all about. The result was the bible of U.S. ski instruction, what came to be known simply as "The White Book."

THE WHITE BOOK

In 1963, PSIA published *The Official American Ski Technique*. It took the informal moniker The White Book for its almost-naked cover—completely bare except for the title and the association's logo on the lower right.

The book "was not without controversy," according to Lash. "Paul Valar felt we couldn't afford the financial risk [of printing and distributing such a large volume of books]. Doug Pfeiffer said it was premature. No one had any idea how we could undertake this costly and risky project."

With little marketing and just a grassroots sales strategy, it was still a success. The first and second editions sold more than 28,000 copies, and the third sold more than 10,000 copies. "I personally sold more than 35,000 copies of that book," Lash said. "I used to pile them in the back of the station wagon. I knew that book had to be available to the general public, because that's where ski school directors would get their new ski instructors from."

At 200 pages, it is a ski instructor's master class. Up front is a compendium of centuries of ski history by Lash, including speculation on the use of a 2,500-year-old ski found in Norway ("It is in the gliding instruments that we are interested"); awe-inspired prose regarding Dr. Fridjtof Nansen's epic 1888 adventure of frigid endurance, *The First Crossing of Greenland*; and a brief biography of Austria's Mathias Zdarsky, the Grandfather of the Alpine Ski Technique.

Sometimes dated in its deadpan earnestness—"Skis were invented to prevent sinking in the snow"—The White Book was meant to serve as much as an encyclopedia for Americans new to the whole pantheon of skiing as an introduction to the physical demands and techniques of the sport. And as Lash intended, it was also meant to be a training manual for future instructors, with essays on the history of instructor certification, ski terminology, ski exercises, and physical conditioning, as well as a chapter on how to avoid the "professional risk" of avalanche.

It worked. Whenever one of those well-thumbed copies of The White Book appears for sale on Amazon.com or eBay, almost always found penciled in the back are the mountain town address of a previous owner, some notes, and the occasional Eagles lyric or Kerouac quote. Ski instructors read it; discussed it; and, through their skiing experience and the lessons they taught, began to edit it. The sport was moving so quickly that every new edition included numerous updates.

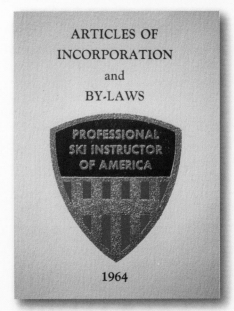

The 1964 publication of the Articles of Incorporation and By-Laws of the PSIA, printed the year after the publication of The White Book.

The White Book.

Sideslipping as depicted in The White Book.

(Illustration PSIA-AASI, from *The Official American Ski Technique*)

The Demonstration Forms

The demonstration forms were built around seven "basic concepts" of skiing:
1. Natural positioning
2. Total motion
3. Unweighting
4. Axial motion
5. Edge control
6. Weight transfer
7. Leverage

(Illustration PSIA-AASI, from *The Official American Ski Technique*)

Certification

As early as 1937, the U.S. Eastern Amateur Ski Association began certifying qualified ski instructors in an attempt to differentiate the professionals from the "phonies" trying to hustle lessons on the slopes, and also to begin to standardize instruction as a whole. Each of the other six existing divisions established their own certification standards in the coming decades, and in 1947 the US Forest Service (USFS) added a clause to the special-use permits being granted for ski areas requiring the use of certified ski teachers at those areas. The process quickly became a way for instructors to validate their teaching skills while also providing a series of benchmarks in regard to their own ongoing educational process. There are currently three primary categories of certification in ski and snowboard instruction, including Level I, Level II, and Level III. PSIA and the American Association of Snowboard Instructors (AASI) also offer credentials in specific areas such as instruction for children, seniors, and freestyle.

(Photo PSIA-AASI)

But if there was one aspect of *The Official American Ski Technique* the new breed of teachers saw as a clearly unnecessary nod to the original influence of the Austrian style of instruction, it was the extensive focus on Finished, or "Final," Forms, a series of compulsory exercises that instructors, as well as their students, had to master before advancing to the next task.

The purpose of Final Forms was to drill into students the mechanics of a ski turn through an endless repetition of snowplows, sideslips, and stem christies. The aim was to achieve the ultimate skier's silhouette, with the locked knees and the stiff, straight back.

Teaching Carson

Ski writer John Fry called it "the Most Famous Ski Lesson of All Time," referring to the evening in 1964 when Johnny Carson learned to ski on NBC's *Tonight Show*, beaming the burgeoning sport out to millions of viewers in an instant. Carson, who was already a skier, wore a suit and tie and skied on a plastic ramp of chips, hamming it up as an erstwhile beginner while Hunter Mountain ski instructor Kitty Falger beautifully and effectively "corrected" the talk show host's technique.

(Photo courtesy of Hunter Mountain)

As Ray Allard, a longtime Eastern Division instructor and examiner who served two terms as the PSIA-AASI board president, said, Final Forms did little to reflect what was actually happening on the slopes. "The big thing we talked about was that they weren't real anymore," he said. "We were already so beyond that technically that it became unreal to try and make the student perfect a Finished Form. The idea was already that you were teaching for fun, and for the student."

"There was definitely the sense of a deep difference between how we skied and how we taught," agreed Pfeiffer. "When you went to other mountains to ski with other instructors, you would go ski the backside of the mountain so that the ski school director wouldn't see you skiing in a way that was so decidedly different."

The seeds for the next revolution were already being planted but would take until 1969 to bear fruit. First, Bill Lash and Willy Schaeffler would make their bid to host Interski, and Aspen and the United States would enjoy their moment in the spotlight with the world speeding down their slopes. It was only afterward, when everyone could have been basking in the accomplishment, that a bitter dispute over the very nature of what constitutes good skiing would threaten to tear the young organization apart.

PSIA co-founder Doug Pfeiffer was an early critic of the direction the association took in the late 1960s, arguing that "Final Forms" in particular were holding instruction back.

(Photo courtesy of the New England Ski Museum)

THE FEUD

The argument would come down to the difference between skiing how you wanted to and skiing how you were told to. It was fun versus the fundamentals, or more appropriately, Final Forms versus freestyle. And how PSIA would first struggle with, then work to merge, those two concepts set the stage for everything that happened next.

Rapid improvements in grooming, lift service, and especially the quality of skis and boots at the end of the 1960s were creating higher speeds of skiing and allowing more freedom of expression on the slopes. "Freestyle" skiing, so named to convey direct opposition to the technical formalities of ski racing, and especially Final Forms, with its flips, tricks, and great floating 360s, was rapidly gaining converts. And many of the new instructors coming into the sport felt that if PSIA could not help them incorporate that sense of freedom into their teaching, then they would have to find a way to do it by themselves.

At the same time, French instructor Georges Joubert's book, *How to Ski the New French Way*, was being heralded as a breakthrough in "advanced skiing" as soon as the English translation became available in the United States. Written with fellow Frenchman Jean Vuarnet, Joubert's innovative use of photomontage made it immediately clear what he was proscribing, while his cutting-edge understanding of new techniques such as the tuck and *avalement*—a way of absorbing the terrain by bending the knees—resonated with racers and freestylers alike.

Just as American instructors were struggling with the limitations of their own teaching style, Joubert presented them with a technique that reflected how their own skiing really looked—which only added fuel to the fire already burning on the slopes. PSIA's board of directors, including Valar, Johnston, and Lash, were under increasing pressure to either embrace the new techniques and styles of skiing or give the job to someone else. Revolutionaries in 1961, they were now increasingly seen as the old guard, and it was their old partner Doug Pfeiffer who helped lead the charge to push them out.

Pfeiffer had become editor of *Skiing* magazine and was one of freestyle skiing's leading proponents. He thought the Austrian-centric methodology of PSIA was holding the sport back, and he took dead aim on Final Forms as the primary target of the free-skiing resistance.

In the November 1969 issue of *Skiing* he wrote, "I have not followed the how-to-do-it dogmas of the PSIA's American Technique. Like many other certified ski teachers, I have felt that its emphasis on Final Forms was keeping ski teaching in this country in the Dark Ages." Like the revolution-minded audience of young instructors he was speaking to, Pfeiffer readily employed the anti-establishment language of the day, labeling Lash and Valar "obstructionists" and, in an op-ed titled "Power to the Ski Instructors," wrote, "Down on dogma! Death to the Final Form!"

Lash was so stung by the accusations that, as late as 1994, he was still mounting his defense. In a paper titled "The PSIA Beginnings," he wrote, "This concept of finished forms caused confusion. Many instructors failed to even read the book. Yet, they wanted no part of anything that hinted of a universal teaching system. The American Technique was not fixed methodology. Ski instructors today claim that this book was an attempt to unify teaching methodology. It was not."

By then, of course, it was far too late. Final Forms became the symbol of what many instructors saw as the rigidity and over-institutionalization of the organization, and one month after Woodstock electrified Max Yasgur's farm in Upstate New York, at a general member-ship meeting of PSIA—held in conjunction with the Canadian Ski Instructors Alliance in Toronto—the American instruction establishment was equally rocked. Willy Schaeffler, who would later become coach of the U.S. Alpine Ski Team, was elected to succeed Bill Lash as PSIA president. Paul Valar resigned as chairman of the Technical Committee, and Jimmy Johnston was replaced as secretary by Herbert "Herbie" Schneider. At least symbolically, a change was taking place, and after nearly a decade of running PSIA, three of the association's founders had been replaced.

At least another three years would pass before real changes were seen in the way U.S. instructors taught ski lessons, but the restructuring of the board opened the door for a new generation to begin to lead the way to one of the greatest breakthroughs ever seen in any sport. As Curt Chase said, "What came next, the Skills Concept, or rather the idea of teaching certain skills rather than specific drills and maneuvers, was one of international ski instruction's most significant developments."

Herbert Schneider, Bill Lash, Peggy Frost, Paul Valar, and Willy Schaeffler enjoying an après ski moment. As the decade ended, Schaeffler and Schneider would be voted in to replace Lash and Valar on the PSIA board.
(Photo courtesy of the New England Ski Museum)

The advent of plastic boots such as the Lange Banshee greatly increased the abilities of skiers in terms of speed and control.　(Photo courtesy of Lange Ski Boots)

(Photo by Dan Coffey)

CHAPTER 2

THE 1970s:
REVOLUTION TO RENAISSANCE

The November 17, 1975, issue of *Sports Illustrated* (*SI*) featured a full-blown hockey melee on the cover under the headline "A Violent Sport Turns Vicious." Inside, though, the content was almost exclusively about skiing. It focused in particular on the team of U.S. ski instructors who had delivered a historic presentation at the 1975 Interski in Strbske Pleso, Czechoslovakia, the previous winter, forever altering the instruction of snowsports.

After five years of experimenting and innovating, American instructors had created two ground-breaking concepts, both of which bore the distinctive "fun first" stamp that would continue to define ski teaching in the United States. Inspired by the rapid progress of some of his staffers after just a few hours on-snow with the U.S. Demonstration Team, *SI* chief Jack Meyers marveled at the new "American Technique"—which actually did exist by this time—in his Letter from the Publisher, writing, "The American Technique is so easy to follow and master that he [Alpine Team Coach Max Lundberg] never doubted it would pass our staffers' test. Lundberg's system offers solace for skiers everywhere. Anyone who has ever despaired of skiing well should give it a try. It works."

The November 17, 1975, issue of *Sports Illustrated* was a celebration of U.S. ski instruction, including a Letter from the Publisher, several pages of illustrations depicting the U.S. Demonstration Team in action, and a full-length feature all celebrating the new "American Technique."

(Images courtesy of *Sports Illustrated* magazine)

PSIA Alpine Team Coach Max Lundberg (right) and team member Mike Porter were instrumental in preparing the 1975 Interski team's presentation.

(Photo PSIA-AASI)

A several-page collage of Leroy Neiman-esque caricatures of U.S. Demonstration Team members performing high-speed maneuvers followed. Under the title "Easy as One Two Ski," it argued that "the tyranny of one slavish technique or another" was killing skiing, until "to the rescue came the U.S. demonstration team, 10 easy riders showing off the wide-stance, hang-loose style that promises to revitalize the sport around the world."

The feature article, "Back to the Basics," by Anita Verschoth, was just so much powder on top of that praise. Smitten by the sense of freedom the skiers conveyed, Verschoth brought the hopes of the student into the picture, writing, "they are skiing easily. Their legs are apart.

They swing along in a natural, wide stance. Their arms are out. They are loose. Seeing them in action, one cannot help but think, *'I can do that. Anyone can.'"*

Even *Skiing* magazine, a regular source of criticism of PSIA in previous years, was ebullient in its praise of the Czechoslovakian presentation. Editor-in-Chief Al Greenberg wrote in the September 1975 issue of the magazine, "For this reporter, the most profound contribution made at the meeting was that of the U.S. Demonstration Team."

As Greenberg noted, the underfinanced Americans were only able to attend the event because of the generosity of family members, a handful of ski areas, and an anonymous donation "rumored to have been from a well known skiing actor." The donation tally included $1,000 from Winter Park in Colorado, $1,000 from Mt. Mansfield in Vermont, $5,000 from an anonymous donor, and $1,500 from a source listed only as "Redford" (presumably Robert Redford, considering team member Jerry Warren was the ski school director and then operations director at the actor-director's Sundance ski area in Utah). The contributions totaled $14,685, which the team raised for training and the trip to Europe. The fund stood in stark contrast to the big budgets of the European teams, especially the Italians, who had been provided with a half-dozen Lancias for personal use.

But the nature and amount of fundraising was irrelevant compared to the veritable buffet of brave new ideas the Americans presented on the demonstration slope—ideas the world continues to develop. As Greenberg wrote, "From a theoretical point of view, the U.S. presentation was remarkable. If it is ever fully understood, its effect on ski teaching everywhere could be significant."

Robert Redford, with Jerry Warren to the right, was an early supporter of U.S. ski instruction.
(Photo PSIA-AASI)

As serious as America's ski instructors were about technique in the 1970s, they knew what they were really selling was the mountain lifestyle, and found plenty of time to enjoy it for themselves.
(Photos PSIA-AASI)

THE WINTER OF DISCONTENT

The Americans' achievement in Czechoslovakia is nothing short of epic. When the decade began, generational disputes, regional divisions, financial issues, and the continuing argument over just what good skiing was were ripping at the open-minded sense of unity PSIA had been built to foster. In *Skiing* magazine, Pfeiffer argued that Final Forms had created "a whole breed of ski instructors who ski like automatons—rigid, artificial, stereotyped and awkward." He said that by not embracing freestyle skiing, PSIA was alienating younger instructors as "the generation gap hit the PSIA smack in the middle of its credibility gap."

Even the articles praising ski instructors never missed a chance to take the association itself to task. In the December 1970 issue of *Skiing*, in an article titled "The Sit-In at the Ski School Bell," the late author John Jerome vividly described a ski instructors' après party as a gyrating mix of "Hard muscles and trim bodies, suntans and teeth. Brilliant styles. Smashing clothes—bell-bottom whatsits and foulards and ascots, magenta and chrome yellow and cerulean. Gorgeous men, stunning women, dancing so hard, drinking so gaily. So bloody beautiful."

Writing that "Any teenage girl will tell you that a convention of ski instructors *has* to be the best place in the *world* to be, right after, maybe, front row center at a rock concert," he had painted a picture of a unique population of teachers, coaches, and independent thinkers—equal parts Zen master, athlete, and artist. But he said that very sense of independence was creating deep fractures within PSIA, which "is currently in the throes of a revolution which affects everything from its administration to its ideology."

It *was* an incredibly innovative time for skiing in the United States, with equipment and technique evolving so rapidly it was hard for anyone to keep up. Plastic ski boots and fiberglass skis vastly improved control at increasingly higher speeds, while antifriction devices in ski bindings dramatically reduced the number of broken legs on the slopes. In 1971, the International Freestyle Skiers Association was formed and held its first National Championship of Exhibition Skiing at Waterville Valley, New Hampshire. Herman Goellner was performing forward flips on skis in Vermont, and ski instructor Bill Briggs boldly signaled one of the high-water marks in the emerging sport of ski mountaineering when he made the first ski descent from the summit of Grand Teton in Wyoming's Teton National Park.

A sense of possibility was pulsing through the mountains, even if no one was sure exactly what to do with it. "There was an energy in this country then that I haven't seen since," said Dick Dorworth, a former speed skiing record holder and ski instructor certified in both the United States and Chamonix, France. "Skiing wasn't just our business, it was what we were doing with our lives. We skied it, argued it, and debated the techniques of everything we did on the mountain all day together. We were totally engaged in it."

The white-capped slopes and warm-bodied camaraderie were also working their spell on popular culture, and the very term "ski instructor" was becoming a password for independent individuals with sun-kissed sex appeal and the ability to soar down the slopes. "It was still so much harder to ski well, so the people who *could* ski well really stood out," said Karen Hollaus, a Wisconsin ski instructor who was one of the

Freestyle skiing was an exciting new part of the alpine world in the 1970s, and across the country, ski instructors were integrating it into their own technique.
(Photo courtesy of Waterville Valley Resort)

Powder skiing, and the search for winter's untouched slopes, was also becoming increasingly popular in the 1970s among instructors and their clients.
(Photo PSIA-AASI)

The Ski Cine

Warren Miller's annual barnstorming ski movie tour was already nearly 20 years old as 1969 drew to a close—the same year Neil Armstrong became the first person to walk on the moon—and famed Sun Valley ski instructor Otto Lang had already appeared in the film *Ski Flight*, which premiered at Radio City Music Hall in 1938. But skiing hit the mainstream media harder than ever as the decade ended, with *Downhill Racer,* starring Robert Redford and Gene Hackman, and skiing filmmaker Dick Barrymore's *The Last of the Ski Bums,* both enjoying a widespread theatrical release. A contrasting presentation of the tensions and ticking-clock drama of ski racing and the hedonistic appeal of ski bumming, the two movies presented a compelling mix of the different disciplines that ski instructors were eager to discuss.

"Comparisons with the recently opened *Downhill Racer* can be instructive," film critic Roger Greenspun wrote of *The Last of the Ski Bums* in the November 11, 1969, edition of *The New York Times*. "*Downhill Racer* deals with the competition of ski racing, with the mystery of the downhill race, demonstrated but unexplained, at its center. *The Last of the Ski Bums* explores skiing itself (though it also has some fine downhill race footage), and because it is about human accomplishment rather than human ambition it means to describe a quality of life rather than an action. *Downhill Racer* is much the better movie, but *The Last of the Ski Bums* is, at least occasionally, more beautiful, more terrifying, and more profound."

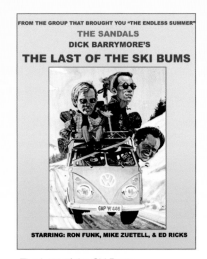

The Last of the Ski Bums.

(Image courtesy of Marina Zuetell and the Barrymore family)

first female certification examiners and the wife of former PSIA President Otto Hollaus. "There was a lot of glamour involved with skiing then, and I think that was matched by how passionate ski instructors were about the sport."

Gripping turns on blue ice, sliding over moguls, or plowing through powder, those ski instructors went out on the snow each day, whether they had a class to teach or not. They studied how people learned, and they noticed how some skiers focused on what they had seen while others talked about what they had felt. They realized that no one learned in the same way. And that realization more than anything else gave them an idea of what they could accomplish next; they could see the possibilities ahead on the horizon like an eagle dropping off the peaks.

"It was certainly in the air," said Dorworth.

GLM and the Short-Swing King

Clif Taylor was a 10th Mountain Division veteran and certified ski instructor who began experimenting with short skis—also called "goon skis"—at Mad River Glen, Vermont, in 1948. Taylor said his "shortees" made it easier for beginners to learn, and he guaranteed he could teach anyone to ski parallel in "two turns." As more ski areas began to adopt his idea, he even earned a mention in *Newsweek*. The Colorado Ski and Snowboard Hall of Fame, which inducted Taylor in 1999, notes he was asked to coach a PSIA Graduated Length Method (GLM) demonstration team in Garmisch, Germany, at the World Congress of Instructors in 1971. Shortees fell into obscurity, though, and did not return until the 1990s as an integral aspect of the shaped ski introduction.

Clif Taylor, king of the short ski.
(Photo courtesy of the U.S. Ski & Snowboard Hall of Fame)

THE GOLDEN AGE

John Armstrong was born in New Zealand, but like so many other ski instructors from around the world, he moved to California to tap the energy of the United States in the early 1970s—the long hair, rock-and-roll, and golden sunsets—and was immediately blown away by the culture of cliff-jumping skiers, high-mountain hospitality, and nonstop interest in advancing the sport. An instructor, examiner, trainer, and former president of PSIA-AASI, Armstrong was especially keen for all of the locker room-, chairlift-, and bar stool-based discussions about how to better explain ski technique.

"It was pretty intense," said Armstrong. "I once saw a shoving match that almost turned into a full-blown fight in the locker room because two guys were arguing over what Warren Witherell had really meant in his book."

After *How to Ski the New French Way*, Witherell's *How the Racers Ski* was the next great ski instruction sensation to appear in print. Witherell, who founded

The dispute over just what good skiing was, and how to teach it, got heated in the 1970s. Former PSIA-AASI President John Armstrong remembers seeing a shoving match break out over the meaning of Warren Witherell's *How the Racers Ski*.
(Photo by Dann Coffey)

While technique was rapidly changing, so were the ways in which lessons were taught. Many skiers chose private lessons for a more personalized instruction experience.

(Photo courtesy of the U.S. Ski & Snowboard Hall of Fame)

With all of the changes going on, some instructors were still having trouble translating all of the new ideas to their students.

(Photo PSIA-AASI)

Burke Mountain Academy in Vermont and was its headmaster from 1970 to 1984, created a pipeline of young talent for the U.S. Ski Team. His coaching and writing focused less on style and more on a skier's mechanics.

Economy of motion, optimum balance, and the physics of a turn were his fortes, and the result of his approach was a simplified language of fundamental needs that outmatched the extended rehearsals of Final Forms and that technique's mannequin stances. Like Joubert, Witherell gave a new language to all the young instructors trying to strip skiing down to only those factors that affected a turn the most.

"There were a number of young people who came into the sport between 1967 and 1972, who started to ask a lot of questions," said Michael Hickey, a former PSIA Alpine Team member and former president of the Northern Rocky Mountain Division of PSIA-AASI. "There were still a lot of old Austrian systems around, and the progression in the way you taught was still incredibly defined. There wasn't a lot of room for creativity, or personality, and a lot of us were asking why that was."

Despite those first claims made with the announcement of the American Technique in the 1960s, instructors across the country could still choose to be certified in the French, Swiss, or Austrian style. And in terms of achieving standardization, all except the deeply influential Eastern Division had agreed to accept a secondary "associate" classification of ski instructor certification, while the East continued to draw the line at "full cert."

Hickey grew up in New Hampshire around many of ski instruction's most revered pioneers. However, already teaching at age 17, he aligned himself with the next generation of young turks eager to change the world. He remembers how strained the conversations between the new and established instructors could become regarding the differences between established teaching systems and emerging techniques. "If you keep pushing, it can create some animosity,"

Freestyle's Serious Influence

When it comes to how skis perform and how technical maneuvers can be taught, ski racing remains one of ski instruction's primary sources of insight. From Steamboat, Colorado's Buddy Werner to White Pass, Washington's Phil and Steve Mahre to Cannon Mountain, New Hampshire's Bode Miller, with each new great ski racer comes a corresponding leap in technology and technique. But in the 1970s, in the United States especially, freestyle created its own influence. The level of invention and energy, of backscratchers and screaming 360s, was also important to the instructional discourse. Waterville Valley "became the first [ski] area to offer freestyle instruction," according to author Grace Bean's history of Waterville Valley, *The Town at the End of the Road*. A freestyle program was started in 1969–70 with classes for adults and kids. PSIA co-founder Doug Pfeiffer organized the First National Open Championships of Freestyle Skiing there in 1970, which immediately attracted substantial TV coverage, as well as freestyle skiing sensation Wayne Wong. By 1972, Sun Valley and Vail were also hosting events.

Waterville Valley was one of the key sites in America's freestyle skiing boom. Regular competitions brought national television coverage to the New Hampshire ski area, and also helped launch the career of U.S. free-ski legend Wayne Wong.

(Wayne Wong photos courtesy of Waterville Valley Resort)

Hickey said. "I remember once we literally had a meeting where the old guard was sitting across the table and Herbert Schneider said, 'So this is how it's going to be then?' And I said, 'Yes.'"

That pattern of obstinacy and invention, of resistance and evolution, would become as regular as the seasons for ski instruction in the United States. The template for change was set that day in Whitefish in 1961 and, according to Hickey, "became a kind of cycle of discovery how everything new created a lot of excitement and controversy in the beginning. But that would come with its own restrictions, and those restrictions would dictate where the next breakthrough would start."

The patterns of complacency and renewal work their way into the fabric of every sport. Only in American skiing do they seem to progress at a faster rate. For PSIA, the next great revival was already coming. It just needed two instructors born an ocean apart—Max Lundberg and Horst Abraham—to find a way to steer all that wild energy that was buzzing around the slopes.

Ski instructors were continually challenging themselves to improve their own level of skiing in their on-snow clinics.

(Photo PSIA-AASI)

FROM AUSTRIA TO ALTA

Max Lundberg's five uncles were all ski instructors at Alta, in Utah, in the 1950s, and every Saturday he rode with them to the ski area in the family station wagon. Only nine years old at the time, he remembers how lucky he felt to be asked to tag along. "I have some real choice memories of those times," Lundberg laughed. Weathered by so many winters, his wide smile and the way his blue eyes burn with curiosity still make it easy to imagine how ecstatic he must have been for each day on the slopes.

On 7-foot-long wooden skis that took all his strength to turn, he entered a world of deep-snow skiing that was being defined by powder pioneers such as Alta founder Alf Engen. At the time, avalanche scientists Ed Chappelle and Monty Atwater were explaining the nature of snow and friction. And every weekend kids from Salt Lake City, Ogden, and Provo flocked to the mountain—kids who Lundberg, at age 12, was asked to help teach.

"It was for the *Deseret News* school program," he said, naming a kids' ski program that has been in existence since 1956. "And even though I was a little nervous, of course I said yes." That moment marked the beginning of a career older than PSIA itself, during which he served as a member of the Aspen Interski Team in 1968; as captain of the team in Garmisch-Partenkirchen, Austria, in 1971; and as coach in Czechoslovakia in 1975, where the team made its groundbreaking presentation.

Ego-free in an era when alpine gods were beginning to sprout like dandelions from the snow, Lundberg was the perfect antidote to PSIA's early conflicts. His greatest desire was to promote what he calls "the family of skiing"—that same extended community his uncles first welcomed him into while driving to the lifts. "When I think of all the people I

Max Lundberg, who would help steer the development of PSIA's revolutionary Skills Concept, began teaching at Utah's Alta Ski Area at the age of 12.
(Photo courtesy of the New England Ski Museum)

have met and been influenced by along the way," he said, "it's nice to think of how my own family introduced me to the family of skiing."

Of course he didn't do it alone. No one could. And the same way Lash had worked so well with Valar in creating PSIA, Lundberg would need his own visionary counterpart. That visionary was Horst Abraham. A product of the rigid Austrian instruction method that was also stifling the new breed of free-skiers on the other side of the Atlantic, Abraham was especially succinct about his reasons for moving to the United States: "I came to the States to align myself with the rebel thinkers," he said.

In the same way Americans were chafing at their own rules of on-hill engagement, Austrians were experiencing even more confinement. "In Austria, where I worked for Professor Stefan Kruckenhauser, he had said, 'I don't want to recognize you by your profile,' and all of your ideas were annihilated and repackaged into a very regimented style of how you dressed—especially how you skied—and even how you looked."

Just like the Americans he had come to join, Abraham was fascinated by the distinct difference between what he was told to teach and how weightless and windborne he felt when he skied with his friends. "We skied in the way that bodies should move," he said. "It was easy to feel how much freer we felt on the snow when we were on our own, and in terms of the Austrian method, from the start that began to create a lot of doubt."

In Aspen, he worked for Curt Chase, and his reputation as an innovator quickly spread, so much so that Vail stole him away, hiring him as its technical director, before PSIA hired him as education director in 1971. There his love for experimentation set the template for what came next in American skiing. "I was with Horst at Vail and we tried a lot of experimenting, sometimes to the dismay of the ski

Horst Abraham was an Austrian-born ski instructor who came to the U.S. to "align myself with the rebel thinkers."
(Photo courtesy of Horst Abraham)

Abraham at Alaska's Alyeska Ski Area.
(Photo courtesy of Horst Abraham)

33

school director, because not all of it worked," said Jens Husted, who would also be a key member of that demonstration team in Czechoslovakia. "But you needed a guy like Horst who really did want to push it, because someone needed to become the driving force."

With Lundberg, Abraham began assembling a group of inquisitive ski instructors from across the country who were more than willing to shake things up: skiing blindfolded, with freezing water spritzed into their ears to disrupt their equilibrium, with their boots unbuckled, to different kinds of music, or with their arms held out as

The Family of Snow

Through those first years of instructing other kids, from the formation of PSIA to the introduction of snowboards and shaped skis, Max Lundberg's thrill at being part of the on-snow community only grew. It was that deep satisfaction to ski and provide snowboard instruction, knowing that a new friend, new story, or new idea could always be waiting on the next chair, that drew him in. And he passed it on to one of his sons, Dave Lundberg, who also made the PSIA-AASI Alpine Team and created a career on snow all his own.

"It wasn't until high school that I realized what a great, unique childhood I really had, running around in the locker room and having Alf Engen asking me how my soccer game was," said Dave Lundberg, one of Max's eight children. "That's when I realized how many great friends my dad had made teaching, and from all over the world."

As the training coordinator at Park City Mountain Resort, Dave says a genuine interest in other people is what sets the great instructors apart, no matter how advanced their abilities are on snow. "I think the timeless element to instruction—what separates people I think are great, like my father and others—is the quality of the personal relationships that you build," said Dave. "The way you expose someone to a lifestyle they otherwise might not have known."

Max and Dave Lundberg on the hill at Snowmass, Colorado, during PSIA-AASI's 50/50 celebration in April 2011.
(Photo by Cesar Piotto)

if they were held up by balloons was just the beginning; anything was fair game as long as it improved instruction. Abraham wanted to be surprised by the instructors he rode the chair with and to work with the people whom he thought had the best questions to ask.

"We always knew there were very smart people throughout the ski instruction ranks, and they were integral to what happened," Abraham said. "From the start we wanted to reach out and make the members of PSIA an extension of what we were trying to accomplish."

AMERICA'S ANSWER

To channel the heightened level of dialogue, PSIA created the National Education Committee, a think tank tasked with synthesizing all the new styles of skiing that had become as ubiquitous as fad diets. The committee members were asked to be curious and to extensively test different techniques to see what really worked. Culling from the best new ideas in ski methodology that followed, they created what would become known as the American Teaching Method (ATM) and, later, the American Teaching System. Combining breakthrough elements of both the mental and the physical side of instruction, it was developed as an approach both *of* and *from* the United States. And from the outset it was meant to represent the individuality and independence of skiing in the United States.

"The idea that we depended on Europeans for the thinking and methodology of skiing was distasteful to us, and we thought that if Europe was not the answer, then what was?" said Abraham. "We had this great group of people like Jerry Warren, Max Lundberg, and Juris Vagners—who worked for Boeing and brought a very sobering perspective on the mechanical level—and so many others who all thought in such wonderful ways in terms of seeing the possibilities of skiing.

Jerry Warren was one of the first instructors Horst Abraham and Max Lundberg contacted when they began to rethink ski instruction in the United States. Warren, a longtime friend of Robert Redford, is the director of mountain operations at the actor's Sundance Ski Resort.
(Photo PSIA-AASI)

Mike Porter was influential in ski instruction from an early age, and helped steer the PSIA through four decades of growth.
(Photo PSIA-AASI)

Whether it was slalom skiing on a race course, or using the same techniques in powder, Horst and Max's "think tank" was trying to boil ski instruction down to its most basic ingredients. Shown here is PSIA Alpine Team member Joe Waggoner.

National Education Committee members such as Chris Ryman (left) and Jerry Warren pushed each other in creating new ideas, and also improving their own technique.

Everyone was spreading their wings, and it was an honor to be in the middle of that."

As he had hoped, in their conversations and their skiing, the sky was the limit. Heated arguments were a regular occurrence, as were days when they all stayed out on the lifts run after run, trying to see who would be the last skier standing on the slopes. But the process was based as much on ideas as on ego, and the conviction was ever present that, mentally and physically, they were redefining the sport.

In psychological terms, W. Timothy Gallwey and Robert Kriegel's book *Inner Skiing* (part of a series that also included *The Inner Game of Tennis* and *Inner Golf*) was enormously influential in PSIA's growing understanding of skiing's more cerebral aspects. Abraham was fascinated with the many roles the mind plays in affecting physical performance, and he was immediately attracted to how Gallwey's understanding of "healthy fear" and "breakthrough runs" could work their way into the vernacular of glisse.

As the left-brain balance of the new creative spirit was explored, the technical methodology of the Skills Concept was also taking shape. Featuring a focus on a triumvirate of technical aspects—a skier's rotary movement, edging, and pressure control—with balance as the core, it gave instructors real-time teaching tools to work on particular aspects of each student's skiing, on any kind of slope. Light years ahead of Final Forms, even today, skills-based teaching remains one of ski instruction's most critical elements.

"I think the most important thing is still how you teach, and then what you teach. But Skills let us focus on *where* people wanted to ski, and *how* they wanted to ski it," said Mike Porter, who was part of the demonstration team that put the two new theories together so famously in Czechoslovakia, and was team captain when the team refined the message and did it again at Interski in Japan in 1978. "You have to remember that this was a time when university studies and the instruction of sports were crossing over—whether it was in ideas like how stretching or lifting weights could prepare the body for physical activity—and the role the mind plays was a large part of that."

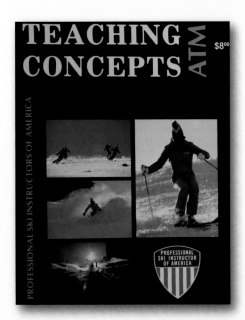

The American Teaching Method (ATM), which became the American Teaching System (ATS), was the result of years of hard work.

(Photos PSIA-AASI)

The focus on Skills is both deceptively simple and decidedly exact. But that's not how it started out. "It was Horst who took the lead on the humanistic areas, and I took the lead on the mechanics," Juris Vagners said. "I remember the original list was born in a basement tavern in Alpental, Washington, and we had something like 100 Skills, including how to plant your poles, which obviously got parsed down to the final result."

Informed by studies in gymnastics and diving, Vagners was thrilled to be testing biomechanical laws in relationship to skiing, especially because of the speed of the sport. "Skiing is not static," he said. "It's very dynamic. And the whole focus was on how the body interplays with the physics."

ATM's twin-barreled approach to technical and student-based ski instruction was as much about sensation as it was about science, and it would wow the world when the Americans first presented it.

Inner Skiing

By 1979, the study of how mental focus affects physical performance was well under way. It is especially relevant in skiing, where a healthy sense of fear informs the moves of almost every participant. *Inner Skiing,* by W. Timothy Gallwey and Robert Kriegel, was written with the intention of getting skiers into the right headspace. As much about visualization and mental preparation as it was a self-help book for athletes, the book trumpeted a new era of sports psychology, bringing terms such as "visualization" and "self 2"—that happy, confident, uninhibited self—into vogue (as well as the idea that "Inside us all is a mountain with no top and no bottom. The skiing there is perfect"). Inspired by the work, Horst Abraham invited Gallwey to a series of on-snow sessions and said, "We invited each other into our different camps to validate what we were working on." The sensibility of teaching first to the mind of each student, then to the body, was the lasting result.

Bruce Bowlin (above) and Scooter LaCouter (below) were two of the hot-skiing instructors the U.S. Demonstration Team brought with them to the 1975 Interski in Czechoslovakia.

(Bowlin photo courtesy of Bruce Bowlin. LaCouter photo courtesy of the New England Ski Museum.)

PUTTING THE SHOW ON THE SLOPES

Porter remembers that the team used Alta Ski Area's old ski instructor jackets for uniforms, and each sewed his own American flag on the back. Everyone bought matching black pants before heading to Stowe, Vermont, for a final practice session. According to Porter, they were still finalizing their presentation on the plane to Europe.

Taking a demonstration team that included such emerging instructional icons as Porter, Chris Ryman, Bruce Bowlin, Jerry Warren, Jens Husted, Scooter LaCouter, Jim Hinman, Steve Bratt, Billy Duddy, and Paul "P. J." Jones, with Lundberg as coach, to Interski was the skiers' first chance to really put their show on the slopes. Knowing that the other countries had rehearsed for similarity and synchronization for years, the Americans focused on their uniqueness. Their individuality was their strength.

"It didn't feel like it was coming from the seat of our pants, because we felt very much that we were presenting our belief system, and when we looked at each of us skiing, we really recognized our levels of talent," said Porter. Himself the epitome of a ski instructor, with the swept-back hair and eternally tanned face, he said, "We really had a lot of different personalities and different strengths, and we wanted to develop and demonstrate that."

What nerves there might have been came more from the sense of expectation and relief for finally having a creative outlet and the opportunity to show the world of skiers that they really had developed something different. "We used to call the Austrians the Lipizzaners because of the way they skied so rigidly and perfect," said Husted. "We took a lot of heat because we didn't look the same in our presentation, but it was all part of the free-thinking American way of looking at things, and the Skills Concept was really intertwined with that."

Once they got on the snow, with their loose style of efficient skiing, their infectious energy, and their obvious joy at barreling down the hill, they still initially earned a decidedly mixed response. While many instructors were complimentary, even emotionally so, others were politely dismissive. It was a breakthrough, some of them said, while others said it did not look how skiing is supposed to look. To their surprise, the Americans discovered that they were the only presenting country that actually skied the same way they taught.

"Instructors from all the other countries came up and said, 'You guys are so lucky,

Before heading to Europe, the 1975 Demonstration Team got one last training session in on the slopes of Stowe, Vermont.

(Photo courtesy of Bruce Bowlin)

you got to ski. We had to demonstrate,'" said Porter. "And the French did 20 minutes of progression, then 10 minutes of how they actually ski at the finish."

In regard to the Skills Concept in particular, the Europeans may not have been completely sure of where the Americans were heading with their new methodology, but they were moved by it. "They didn't know exactly what the hell we were doing," said Bruce Bowlin, who performed freestyle tricks such as royal christies and tip rolls while wearing a black cowboy hat. "But they liked it because it made movement analysis obviously easier. You could look at a skier and see what they were weak in, and design a program just to fix that."

THE EVOLUTION OF TECHNIQUE

Terms, Innovators, and Books
COURTESY OF BILL LASH

Natural Method ✦ Knee Angulation ✦ Hip Angulation ✦ Angulation of the Spine ✦ Ankle Angulation ✦ The Perfect Turn ✦ Outcome Based Learning ✦ Mastery Learning ✦ *Sybervision Learning* ✦ The Wedge ✦ Gliding Wedge ✦ Easy as One Two Ski ✦ Teaching for Transfer ✦ Exchange of Weight ✦ The Ski Teaching Network ✦ Filter Up and Flow Downward ✦ Correct Technique ✦ Automatic Turn ✦ Early Tip Pressure ✦ Push the Feet ✦ Roll the Ankles ✦ Step over Swoosh ✦ Milestones ✦ The Red Line & Common Threads ✦ Uphill Ski Turn ✦ Two Step Turn Stem ✦ Two Turn Balanced Turn ✦ Inside Pressured Giant Slalom Turn ✦ Diagonal Hip Extension Turn

For some team members, it was the first time traveling overseas.
(Photo PSIA-AASI)

Lundberg's notes at the closing were clear on what the demonstrations had meant for American instruction of the sport: "We have expressed an idea, not a system. Our understanding of skills development will undoubtedly broaden as we increase our understanding of the mind, body and equipment of the skier. The skills we develop will remain the same."

And as word of the presentation spread, and more people began to realize its impact, the Demonstration Team became a year-round entity as PSIA moved to capitalize on its success. A kind of ongoing, on-snow research and development center for the cutting edge of instruction techniques, the team grew to include nordic, adaptive, and snowboard teams as well, with the best instructors from across the

The European demonstration teams looked thoroughly outdated in their presentations.

(Photo PSIA-AASI)

country coming together every four years to try out for a spot. "Before that there was no way to share the information that came out of Interski," said Husted. "We wanted to carry that energy and inquisitiveness forward. We wanted to professionalize it."

Creating a year-round team gave PSIA more opportunities to refine its message. By the time the team participated at Interski in Japan in 1978, it had developed a color-coded Skills presentation, with instructors in red sweaters demonstrating rotary movements, those in dark blue sweaters showing edging, and those in royal blue showcasing pressure control, all in presentations, according to Porter, based on "What does the consumer want?"

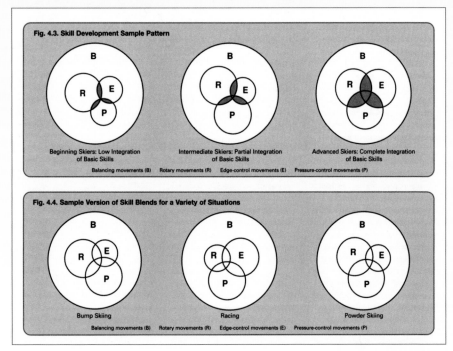

The Skills Concept Venn Diagram

Fig. 4.3. Skill Development Sample Pattern

Beginning Skiers: Low Integration of Basic Skills

Intermediate Skiers: Partial Integration of Basic Skills

Advanced Skiers: Complete Integration of Basic Skills

Balancing movements (B)   Rotary movements (R)   Edge-control movements (E)   Pressure-control movements (P)

Fig. 4.4. Sample Version of Skill Blends for a Variety of Situations

Bump Skiing

Racing

Powder Skiing

Balancing movements (B)   Rotary movements (R)   Edge-control movements (E)   Pressure-control movements (P)

Examples of how the basic tenets of the Skills Concept easily adapt to varying terrain and snow conditions.

(Illustration PSIA-AASI)

Skiing Right was the culmination of more than a decade of breakthrough ski instruction, both in technique and in the psychological element of how people learn a sport.

(Photos PSIA-AASI)

SKIING RIGHT

By the time the Demonstration Team arrived in Zao, Japan, in 1979 for Interski, the Skills Concept and the student-centered teaching system were becoming state of the art. Even the few countries that had been dismissive of the 1975 presentation were sold by the Americans' 1979 program, with many of their representatives actively taking notes. For Abraham, one of the most lasting images from the U.S. Demonstration Team's triumph in Japan was when Professor Stefan Kruckenhauser—the same man who complimented Curt Chase in Aspen in 1968—pulled him aside, "and with a little smile on his face, told me, 'I like your disobedience.'"

Abraham was greatly honored, and shocked.

"I wondered how he could continue to stick with his regimented ski school after he had seen the possibilities," Abraham said. "I think that once your convictions are economic ones, then you have lost your right to sit at the helm. It should never cease to be about artistry—especially in sport."

He felt they were just scratching the surface of what was possible and could not wait to create the next innovation. "We had a fragmented idea of what we wanted to achieve," Abraham said. "We had to have the courage to reexamine everything that was on the table and see what belongs and what does not. We wanted to be on a joyous adventure, and we wanted to create a divergent, learning environment."

Like Lash before him, Abraham wrote a book that synthesized the sense of that joyous adventure, titled *Skiing Right* and published in 1983. The title refers to skiing correctly as well as to engaging the right hemisphere of the brain while on the slopes. In a section titled "A Turn to the Right," while discussing right-brain activity such as dreams, "drawing, craft works, and creative

By the time the U.S. Demonstration Team reached the 1979 Interski in Japan, they had dialed in their presentation of the Skills Concept, color-coding their sweaters to reflect who was demonstrating balance, who was demonstrating edging, and who was demonstrating rotary motion.

(Photo PSIA-AASI)

thought," Abraham adds sliding on snow to that list of ethereally focused tasks, writing, "In skiing we draw on the right brain capabilities of holistic perception, rhythm, spatial relationships and simultaneous processing of many inputs."

Most noticeably, the skiers depicted in the book's line drawings are much more fluid and athletic than those in the images in the last revised edition of *The Official American Ski Technique*. From basic fall-line tactics to powder to moguls to freestyle to ski racing, the advanced technical presentations are still relevant, while the level of personal narrative and thought-provoking philosophies of learning reflect as much of the give-and-take of an actual ski lesson as anything presented in print previously— all while summarizing a wildly inventive period in American snowsports.

"It wasn't our quest when we set out to best other nations. It was more about finding our own American way," Abraham said when remembering how completely the United States had tailored and edited its message by the time the team had arrived at Interski 1979. "'Coming to America' [recorded by Neil Diamond], that was our song. It meant to us that we Americans are here to ski free, rhythmically and joyfully. That song sort of carried our spirit in our presentation, and as we looked around at our audience, we saw how they had caught the fever, too. That was the greatest part."

After the 1979 Interski, many U.S. Demonstration Team members were able to capitalize on their success back home in the States.

(Photo courtesy of Michael Hickey/Head Skis)

At the 1979 Interski, Mike Porter experiments with chopsticks.

(Photo PSIA-AASI)

Michael Hickey enjoying the thrill of the 1979 Interski in Japan.

(Photo courtesy of Michael Hickey)

The "Lipizzaners" in action.

(Photo PSIA-AASI)

Dee Byrne (right) and Nancy Oakes earned their way onto the PSIA Alpine Team in the 1980s and 1990s, respectively, contributing deep technical knowledge and incredibly strong skiing.

(Photo PSIA-AASI)

CHAPTER 3

SKIING, IN ALL ITS FORMS

Every decade a new revolution emerged in snowsports, from the equipment being used to the terrain being skied to how skiing and snowboarding were taught. In fact, for the half century since that day in May in 1961 when the Professional Ski Instructors of America was formed in a sunlit cafeteria in Whitefish, Montana, it has become a pattern that every 10 years another quantum leap forward will occur in snowsports instruction across the United States.

By the time the 1980s dawned, another development was emerging in American snowsports, one deeply rooted in skiing's past: breakthrough ideas of *who* could ski, combined with historical ideas about *how* to ski, were firing the imaginations of ski instructors from coast to coast.

Nordic skiing, the original form of winter glisse, experienced a boom from the advent of skate skiing and an especially passionate revival of that graceful swoop of a turn, the telemark.

Adaptive skiing, first popularized by wounded 10th Mountain Division veterans who refused to let injuries and amputations keep them from the slopes, welcomed a new wave of instructors and instruction styles, as well as incredible improvements in the quality of equipment.

Diana Golden (shown here with the PSIA Alpine Team) was a pioneer of adaptive skiing, winning 10 gold medals at the World Adaptive Ski Championships and 19 gold medals at the U.S. Adaptive Alpine Championships over the course of her career.

(Photo by Tom Lippert)

Telemark, skiing's original turn, enjoyed a rebirth in the late 1970s and early 1980s as hardcore skiers looked to free-heel equipment as a means to get further into the backcountry.

(Photo courtesy of Craig Dostie)

Nordic track skiing also experienced rapid growth, thanks to a fitness craze that swept the country in the 1980s.

(Photo PSIA-AASI)

In addition, snow-sliding women, who had been on the snow just as long as any men, started skiing their way onto the PSIA Alpine Team, taking more leadership roles in the hierarchy of the association, developing breakthrough women's ski programs, and writing new instructional books.

In mainstream America, it was the era of MTV, Live Aid, *The Simpsons*, Michael Jackson, Molly Ringwald, Indiana Jones, and rap music. But on the country's slopes, asking "What's Next?" was overtaken by finding out "What have we missed?"

THE NORDIC BOOM:
THE NEW TECHNIQUE

In *Skiing Right*, the compendium of skiing and ski instruction written by Horst Abraham and published by PSIA in 1983, PSIA co-founder Bill Lash wrote, "The word 'ski' is the Norwegian name for a snowshoe that was used by the northern nations of the Old World. . . . it is found in the English words skid, skip, skiff, slide and skate."

At its beginning, skiing was a means of survival, transit, and touring—sliding across the snow on a hunt or on the way to a battle—more than it was a way to experience the thrill of descent. But Hannes Schneider had been so effective in marketing speed as the primary pursuit of skiing that, even into the 1970s, nordic skiing was still regarded as a form of winter hiking or deep snow strolling in the United States.

Ski Racing

As the 1980s began, U.S. ski racing was riding an incredible string of dominance. With the emergence of Tamara McKinney, a ski racing phenomenon from Squaw Valley, California, who shocked the alpine world when she won the overall World Cup Ski Racing title at age 20 in 1983, and the dominance of Phil and Steve Mahre, the turbo-thighed, gate-bashing twin brothers from Yakima, Washington, the U.S. Ski Team rolled like a wrecking ball across the World Cup—contending only with the genius skiing of Sweden's Ingemar Stenmark. Phil Mahre won the overall World Cup title for an astonishing three years in a row, from 1981 to 1983, and he grabbed a silver medal at the 1980 Winter Olympics at Lake Placid in the slalom (Stenmark won the gold)—the same games at which the U.S. Men's Hockey Team achieved the Miracle on Ice, famously defeating the Soviet Union before beating Finland in the gold medal game.

Phil Mahre.
(Photo courtesy of the U.S. Ski & Snowboard Hall of Fame)

The U.S. Men's Hockey Team's 1980 Miracle On Ice at the Lake Placid Winter Olympics.
(Photo courtesy of the U.S. Ski & Snowboard Hall of Fame)

The PSIA was quick to adapt the instructional methodology it developed for alpine skiing to nordic skiers, providing a baseline by which proper teaching could help grow the sport.
(Photo PSIA-AASI)

American nordic skier John Caldwell helped give the sport a heart-rate-raising push when he published *Cross-Country Ski* in 1964, the first official "how to" book on cross-country skiing in the United States. The Vermont native and Dartmouth College graduate competed in the 1952 Winter Olympics, finishing twenty-second in the Nordic combined event, a highlight at the time for North Americans in a Scandinavian-dominated sport. But his most lasting legacy to the history of nordic skiing may have been as a coach at Vermont's Putney School, where one of his students was a young, phenomenally focused skier named Bill Koch.

West Yellowstone, Montana, remains a hotbed for cross-country touring and nordic competition, and is a favored PSIA Nordic Team training spot.
(Photo PSIA-AASI)

A cross-country innovator who grew up in the windblown winters of Vermont, Koch made history as the first North American to win a medal in cross-country skiing at the Olympics when he took silver in the 30-kilometer race at Innsbruck, Austria, in 1976—a feat that went unrepeated for 34 years, until the U.S. Nordic Team's multi-medal performance at the 2010 Winter Olympics in Whistler, British Columbia.

"When Bill Koch won the silver medal in Innsbruck, by skating instead of striding, he started the whole skating craze," said Urmas Franosch.

An instructor, a patroller, and a cross-country shop owner in the 1970s, Franosch skied his way onto the PSIA Nordic Team in 1996. He said the rise of Koch and the athleticism and technique required for skating created a new generation of cross-country skiing students, and new opportunities for instructors from Minnesota to Montana to teach.

Even now, Franosch marvels at how a lone American such as Koch had such a significant impact on the deeply rooted traditions of nordic. "By the late 1980s, skating had

Even dressed for skating, some free-heel skiers can't resist the lure of telemark.
(Photo PSIA-AASI)

surpassed track skiing as the most popular style, and there was more pressure on cross-country ski centers to prepare the track," he said. "It's ironic that Koch is an American, and yet he's one of the most pivotal figures in the sport."

FROM THE PODIUM TO THE PINES

In 1987, the International Ski Federation finally officially endorsed Koch's athletic skiing style and split World Cup Nordic skiing's two main events into freestyle, or skating, and classic, five years after Koch had amassed enough points to win the 1982 World Cup title using the skating technique.

Partially in response to Koch's success (and a booming fitness craze), and partly because of the increasing desire of many skiers to get back to nature—away from the new quad chairlifts and singles-bar mentality being promoted at some resorts—nordic ski sales soared. And in response, a new, aerobic, athlete-friendly kind of resort—the cross-country touring center—with groomed tracks, warming huts, and lodges began to spring up.

At Royal Gorge, near Lake Tahoe; Yellowstone; Steamboat Springs, Colorado; and all across the Northwest, Midwest, and Northeast, the cross-country community was suddenly flocking to little free-heel meccas where they could learn, practice, and celebrate the sport.

At the same time, competition, à la ski marathons, long traverses, and kilometer-paced races styled after running events—cross-country skiing's warm-weather counterpart—also came into vogue, with an increasing emphasis on time, technique, and fitness.

Launched in 1973, Wisconsin's Birkebeiner race, known as the "Birkie," was the New York Marathon–style equivalent of U.S. Nordic skiing's cross-country renaissance. Developed by Tony Wise, a ski resort operator from Cable, Wisconsin, the race became a key facet in the creation of the Worldloppet, a series of internationally staged cross-country races that remain must-do events on the worldwide free-heel circuit. Participating skiers receive a passport that is stamped for each race they complete.

At the apex of cross-country's resurgence, in 1985 PSIA published *Cross-Country Skiing Right*. From ski technology to the specific mechanics of each style of nordic skiing to methods of ski touring to appropriate clothing and even pre-season conditioning, its contents represented the increasing breadth of the association's involvement in the proper instruction of every form of snowsports.

Cross-country innovator Bill Koch made history as the first North American to win a medal in cross-country skiing at the Olympics when he took silver in the 30-kilometer race at Innsbruck, Austria, in 1976.

(Photo courtesy of the U.S. Ski & Snowboard Hall of Fame)

Building on the competitive allure of nordic skiing, PSIA developed the Nordic Star Test for enthusiasts to rate their skills.

(Photo PSIA-AASI)

49

THE EVOLUTION OF TECHNIQUE

Terms, Innovators, and Books
COURTESY OF BILL LASH

Broken Wing Turn ❧ Diagonal Hip Extension Movement and Hip Cross Over ❧ Ankle Turns ❧ First Day Turns ❧ "L" Shaped Turns ❧ Square Turns ❧ C Turns ❧ U Turns ❧ S Turns ❧ Swoop Turn ❧ Up-hill Ski Turns ❧ Lateral Cross Over ❧ Lateral Extension ❧ Momentum/Anticipation ❧ Holistic Perspective ❧ Simultaneous Leg Rotation ❧ Diagonal Extension ❧ Ski Steer ❧ Open Track/Narrow Track ❧ Inside Leg ❧ Outside Leg ❧ Terrain Caused Pressure Control ❧ Proven Principles ❧ Diverging Parallel ❧ Step Turns ❧ Skating Turns ❧ Wedge Christies 1 & 2 ❧ The Universal Ski Technique ❧ Ethereal Dynamics

Written by Bill Hall, an original member of the PSIA Nordic Team and a Rocky Mountain–based PSIA Nordic chief examiner, the book followed the lead of Horst Abraham's *Skiing Right*, focusing first and foremost on the needs of the student.

As far as the cerebral aspects of cross-country skiing were concerned—cold running through winter's woods in a kind of meditative silence—Hall felt that PSIA's dual focus on the mental and physical elements of the sport was especially apt. "The sport is much more than simply sliding around on 'skinny' skis. It is a fulfilling exercise for mind and body," he wrote.

Hall also included a chapter titled "Telemark Turns," in which he commented that "the essence of cross-country skiing is captured in the graceful beauty of the telemark."

Developed by Norwegian Sondre Norheim in the mid-1800s, the telemark is skiing's oldest method of changing direction while descending a snow-covered slope. With its albatross wide stance, bent back leg, and myriad ranges of motion, it was a precursor of the stem christie, which became the basis for alpine skiing. A century after its first recorded practice, the telemark turn, in both its aesthetic and athletic aspects, ignited the passions of expert skiers at many of the country's most difficult slopes.

Centerline

With so many new images of skiing developing, PSIA was hard pressed to set a model for what "good skiing" looked like. A skill-specific baseline of needs for skiers at every level—from absolute beginners to World Cup–ready experts—emerged in the form of the Centerline instructional method. A mainline of technical fundamentals for whatever tributaries of style or focus a lesson might take, Centerline's strength was its adherence to the Skills Concept basics of balance, rotation, edging, and pressure, or "the highway," as Centerline creator Jerry Warren called it. Its weakness was its resemblance to Final Forms in some ski instructors' eyes, and these teachers rebelled at the idea of a new "perfect skiing" blueprint. Warren maintains Centerline was intended to create a diagnostic tool and constant reference point for where each lesson should start. Asked if it just meant that you had to know the rules before you broke them, Warren said, "That's exactly what it was all about."

THE FREE-HEEL REVOLUTION:
THE BALLET OF TELEMARK

As if triggered by a sense of mass ski intelligence, in the late 1970s and early 1980s the telemark turn seemed to be appearing everywhere at once. "Telemark skiing in the 1970s was re-invented independently in a half dozen scattered, isolated mountain towns that at first were not in communication with each other," Jeffrey R. Leich, director of the New England Ski Museum, wrote in the organization's 2010 spring journal.

He said that "the Crested Butte pioneers were the first revivalists," adding that soon after, "telemark skiing began to evolve in places like the Adirondacks of New York, Whitefish, Montana, Alta, Utah, and the White Mountains of New Hampshire."

At first, telemark's new wave emphasized using lightweight cross-country equipment to get to the fresh powder in winter's snow-laden forests, as celebrated in books such as Steve Barnett's *Cross Country Downhill*, published in 1978.

But enthusiasts soon found their way back to the ski areas, where they increasingly pushed for the right to ride the lifts and faced a reluctance that would

Hardcore skiers flocked to telemark in the 1980s, because it was a more difficult turn to learn, and also for the ease of backcountry access.
(Photo courtesy of Craig Dostie)

Norwegian Amund Ekroll (far right) was the coach of the PSIA Nordic Team that famously took the telemark turn back to Europe at the 1983 Interski in Sesto, Italy. Telemark ski innovator Paul Parker is on the far left.
(Photo PSIA-AASI)

Tony Forrest, who succeeded Ekroll as coach of the PSIA Nordic Team, once said, "It's a festival, not a stress-stival," of the sport of telemark.
(Photo PSIA-AASI)

Former PSIA Nordic Team Coach Craig "Pando" Panarisi airs it out.
(Photo PSIA-AASI)

Putting the fun in free-heel.
(Photo by Tom Lippert)

foreshadow the difficulties that snowboarders would experience when they first tried to gain acceptance on the slopes.

"Either the ski areas didn't think you could control that skinny gear, or they thought that you were going to go jump off the nearest cliff as soon as you got off the lift," said Tony Forrest, a member of the original PSIA Nordic Team who later became captain. "I remember *Powder* and *Outside Magazine* covering it, probably mainly because it was so much about really being in the mountains, but also because they could see all of these little tribes of good skiers across the country picking it up."

Telemark practitioners called themselves "pinheads" and "pinners" because they used three pins on their toe piece that fit into the fore-flap of the boot. They printed counterculture slogan T-shirts and bumper stickers with Zen-like sayings such as, "Free your heel, and your mind will follow." Forrest remembers how they used to hand newly certified nordic instructors three brass safety pins with their PSIA pin, saying, "You earned your pins," as a joke.

The PSIA Nordic Team putting on a show at the 1983 Interski in Sesto, Italy.
(Photo PSIA-AASI)

"That gear was so flimsy then that we were cutting up pickle buckets just to try and build a sturdier ankle cuff for our lace-up leather boots," said Craig Panarisi, a former member and two-term captain of the PSIA Nordic Team.

Panarisi said the obvious low-tech difference to the gear was key to the allure, hearkening back to the original professional skier's pleasure of being good at something that was hard to execute.

He said, "It was a different trend at first, with all of the locals at ski areas getting into it, dressing up in costumes and holding these bump skiing events on skinny little skis just because it was harder, and because they wanted to be different. It wasn't the kind of crowd that took a lot of group ski lessons at first, but if you called it 'a festival,' then they'd all show up."

In Crested Butte, Colorado, in particular, a retro ski turn revivalism took root, led by the region's strong history of guides, patrollers, and instructors looking for the next challenge.

"The men who brought the modern-day telemark out of its icy-flamed deathbed, like a Phoenix rising from the cold fire of winter, were young men, the majority of whom were in their early 20's," wrote Molly Murfee in *Telemark Skier Magazine*, in an iconoclast-tracking story of Crested Butte's telemark posse called Contri-Buttians.

THE EVOLUTION OF TECHNIQUE

Terms, Innovators, and Books
COURTESY OF BILL LASH

Active Inside Leg Skiing ✺ Two O'clock Turn ✺ The "J" Turn ✺ Mathematically Pure Parallel Turn ✺ Divergent Step ✺ Dynamic Parallel ✺ Open Parallel ✺ Hierarchy of Movement Analysis ✺ Rail Riding ✺ Inward Rotating of Legs and Feet ✺ Outward Lateral Tipping of the Feet and Ankles ✺ Problem Solving Style ✺ Guided Discovery Style ✺ The Service Model ✺ Balanced Ski Flex and Unbalanced Ski Flex ✺ Lower Hip Push, Counter Steered Up Stem ✺ Lower Hip Push ✺ Steer Countering Wedge ✺ Diagonal X-Over Movement ✺ Hip Diagonal X-over Movement ✺ Tip Turns ✺ *Inner Skiing* ✺ The Invisible Ski Technique ✺ Belly Button Turn ✺ Double Carving

The PSIA Nordic Team in Italy, just prior to the 1983 Interski.
(Photo PSIA-AASI)

Paul Parker's Free-Heel Skiing

Amund Ekroll, the first coach of the PSIA Nordic Team, said that he told team member Paul Parker, "Do something with yourself." That something was the publication of *Free-Heel Skiing: Telemark and Parallel Techniques for All Conditions* in 1988. Perhaps more than any other instructional manual written, it allowed telemark skiers all over the world to teach themselves. Clear, concise, and filled with images of a hot-skiing Parker tearing up the slopes tele-style, *Free-Heel Skiing* is still referred to as the bible of telemark.

"There gathered a convergence of people with an independent, adventuresome spirit who were looking to drop out of society and into the next powder cache.

"They became certified instructors when the certification process was only a few years old," she added. They were mixing the roots of the desire to professionalize the basic brushstrokes of that telemark turn with a discipline based on how it works. "These men took an unquenchable desire for the backcountry and stirred it with the athletic determinism and experimentation to create a turn that has become a phenomenon."

PSIA had certainly seen the potential—and the need for standardized instruction. In 1979, the association created the first PSIA Nordic Demonstration Team, with members from each of the nine regions representing their own local flavor of the quickly reviving sport. Rather than being known as the U.S. Demonstration Team, the national teams also began to be identified by the discipline they were formed to represent.

Team member Paul Parker went on to publish *Free-Heel Skiing: Telemark and Parallel Techniques for All Conditions*, often referred to as the bible of telemark skiing. And in short order the team adapted PSIA's American Teaching Method to nordic skiing, creating a baseline for teaching free-heel skiing in all of its many forms. Then finally, at the 1983 Interski in Sesto, Italy, it took the telemark turn right back to Europe.

"I remember when we got to Interski in Italy in 1983, and we basically did an all-telemark demonstration," said Forrest. "All of the other countries were making group tracks, and we were the only country that asked to use the lifts. And when we were done, there were a lot of Norwegians and Scandinavians coming up to us saying, 'We remember that turn. We did that turn first.'"

Amund Ekroll, a tall, hawk-nosed Norwegian who was the coach of that first nordic team, said, "We were way ahead when it came to telemark." He said he had warned the team members that the Europeans would want to buy their equipment—Phoenix skis and Asolo boots—when they were done, and he said that while they would not sell their gear, "We did let other skiers try the equipment, while we waited for them in our socks."

THE ADAPTIVE EXPANSION:
GRAVITY CREATES FLIGHT

While the telemark turn helped revive the interest of expert alpine skiers, adaptive skiing emerged to provide a transformative experience for wounded soldiers back from Vietnam as well as physically and cognitively challenged skiers from all kinds of backgrounds.

After Doug Pringle lost a leg in Vietnam, he remembers sitting in a bed in Letterman Hospital in San Francisco when some World War II 10th Mountain Division veterans came in and showed a movie of a one-legged skier. A West Point graduate who failed horribly the one time he tried skiing while at the academy, Pringle said his first response had been, "I couldn't ski on two legs; how am I ever going to do it on one?"

But when his fellow wounded Vietnam veterans returned from their first trip to the slopes with the 10th Mountain Division veterans, talking about bars and girls and that gravity-fed feeling of freedom, he said, "Well, where do I sign up?"

That sense of energy, of possibility, inspired adaptive ski instruction's new wave of converts. Once they realized how the slip of the snow and the pull of the planet could expand the world of any adaptive skier—be they blind, autistic, paraplegic, or even quadriplegic—they were hooked.

"It literally changed my life," said Pringle, president of Disabled Sports USA Far West. "I had no choice but to spread the message once I first felt that sense of mobility, freedom, speed, and exhilaration that can't be duplicated in any other sport. It became my life's work."

As with the telemark resurgence, throughout the 1970s a groundswell of adaptive ski chapters grew across the United States. Adaptive skiers slept on friends' floors; traveled from resort to resort; and, like those first free-heelers, had to prove again and again that they were not a liability on the chairlifts. "We became the apostles, the emissaries of adaptive skiing," Pringle said. "Many took it as a mission to see what they could get going in their own community, and that's how the chapters sprang up."

But even as the number of instructors grew, the equipment was struggling to catch up. In 1970, Swiss electrician Hans Schmid, inspired by watching skiing amputees, demonstrated his mono-ski design. Until then, almost any adaptive skier had to master the ability to merely stand up on a ski before balancing on it. And Pete

Vietnam veteran Doug Pringle (back) became a zealot for adaptive skiing after experiencing the thrill of gravity's pull for himself.

(Photo courtesy of Disabled Sports USA Far West)

Shown here in 1980, the Disabled Sports USA Far West team continues to be an integral factor in getting adaptive skiers and riders on the slopes.

(Photo courtesy of Disabled Sports USA Far West)

Snow and gravity allow adaptive skiers a chance to experience a sense of freedom that they can't find anywhere else.
(Photo PSIA-AASI)

Axelson, an engineer who had sustained a spinal cord injury in a climbing accident, would later develop his own mono-ski designs, making it possible for virtually every level of adaptive skier to enjoy the experience of the slopes.

"At the beginning, the state of instruction was just awful. We were duct-taping people into boots and throwing them onto chairs, and really just trying to achieve that sensation of sliding with anyone who had the cojones to keep trying to stand up," said Katherine Hayes-Rodriguez, who, with Pringle in California, became a pioneer of the adaptive descent.

With Pringle leading the way after he earned his Level III ski instructor's certification on one leg, Hayes-Rodriguez helped develop the methodology and standardization of adaptive instruction that they presented to PSIA. They wanted to prove the method to their madness and to be recognized as professional instructors themselves.

"It became important to me to have PSIA endorse what Doug and Katherine had done because they had worked so hard to prove that they were professional ski instructors, and educators of the industry," said Gwen Allard, who as the executive director of PSIA's Eastern Division had been an early champion of bringing adaptive instruction under the PSIA umbrella. "And to me, that was what PSIA was formed to represent."

Allard said one of the greatest rewards for incorporating adaptive programs into PSIA occurred at Interski in St. Anton, Austria, in 1991, when the late Diana Golden, who amassed an astounding 19 gold medals in the U.S. Adaptive Alpine Championships, led the PSIA Alpine Team down the slope.

"From a distance people couldn't tell that

Lee Perry

Lee Perry, of Oregon, is the Pied Piper of adaptive skiing. A Korean War veteran who saw several comrades suffer life-changing wounds, in 1958 he started figuring out ways to get amputees on the snow and then began building their equipment. He developed the first ski school for amputees at Mt. Hood's Government Camp in cooperation with Pat McPhail and Hal Schroeder, and he shocked the families of amputee children by knocking on their doors and asking if he could take their kids to the slopes. "These kids only had one leg, and their parents thought I was going to break it." He published an instructional manual in 1964 to help others teach and said, "That feeling of going downhill with the wind in your face is something that's understood by all of us."

Lee Perry, the Pied Piper of Adaptive Skiing.
(Photo by Dann Coffey)

she had only one leg, but as they got closer you could hear the murmur beginning," Allard recalls. "And when she finished with the crispest turn that just threw snow into the air, well, the crowd just exploded after that."

Former Disabled U.S. Ski Team member Kirk Parkhurst.
(Photo courtesy of Disabled Sports USA Far West)

Member of the U.S. Ski & Snowboard Hall of Fame, Diana Golden was an inspiration to skiers around the world.
(Photo PSIA-AASI)

Hal O'Leary/Bold Tracks

In 1987, Winter Park ski instructor Hal O'Leary published *Bold Tracks: Skiing for the Disabled*. Other adaptive instruction manuals and books had been written before it, but O'Leary's obvious passion for teaching and his straightforward style made his an immediate classic. "When you consider the problems we have to overcome, we're all skiers with disabilities," O'Leary wrote in the foreword. As it interwove the American Teaching System, it was also very particular about specific adaptive practices such as "protecting the stump" for students with above-the-knee amputations. Originally a volunteer with the National Sports Center for the Disabled at Winter Park, by 1970 O'Leary was its director. Working with kids, veterans from Fitzsimons Army Medical Center in Denver, and a range of volunteers and professional instructors from across the state, he was instrumental in creating an international standard for adaptive instruction.

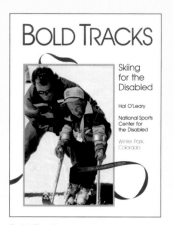

Bold Tracks.

MAKING THE SAME TURN:
SKIING'S EQUAL RIGHTS

The airborne Ellen Post joined the PSIA Alpine Demonstration Team in 1980 along with Carol Levine, marking an obvious rise in the influence of women in the field of instruction, and also on the sport.

(Photo courtesy of Ellen Post Foster)

Of course, women in the United States have been on the snow as long as men have been, and competitively they had more of an impact on the international scene much earlier than the men had in the United States. American Gretchen Fraser won medals at the St. Moritz, Switzerland, Winter Olympics in 1948, and Andrea Mead Lawrence won two gold medals at the 1952 Winter Olympics in Oslo, Norway, while the men waited for their first breakthrough at the 1964 Games at Innsbruck, Austria.

On the instruction front, women were earning their U.S. Eastern Amateur Ski Association certification as early as the 1938–39 ski season, and, according to E. John B. Allen's book *Teaching and Technique*, in 1949, New York State Professional Ski Instructors Association President Dorothy Hoyt Nebel was already arguing for a standardization of American teaching technique.

The 1980 PSIA Alpine Team, which included Carol Levine and Ellen Post.

(Photo PSIA-AASI)

Women were on the U.S. Demonstration Team at Interski in Aspen in 1968, but at the time the team was still disbanding after each event. Karen Hollaus in the Midwest and Elissa Slanger in California—both PSIA examiners—were influential through the 1970s and into the present, though in ski lessons, men were still teaching all of the advanced classes and almost all of the adult lessons on the slopes. But in the 1980s that imbalance changed for good.

One benchmark was reached in 1980, when Carol Levine and Ellen Post (now Post Foster) made the PSIA Alpine Team, and they were joined by Dee Byrne in 1984. All three had worked hard to earn a spot.

"When I made the team in 1980, I had to deal with more than being a female trying out for a previously all-male team. At 4' 10" tall and 95 pounds, I didn't come close to the stereotypical stature of a Demo Team member," Post Foster said. "After I was chosen, I was told that I qualified using the same criteria that [were] used for the men."

When giving clinics to other instructors across the country, Post Foster always had to ski harder than the men and be spot-on with her methodology to earn respect. But the student-centered instruction method at the core of U.S. ski teaching meant that focusing on how women learned and excelled was as relevant as any other topic considered in ski instruction. For Levine, "women could ski strong and not have to ski like [a] guy, or like their husband, but just by skiing for themselves."

In 1979, Slanger, with former *Ski* and *Skiing* magazine writer Dinah Witchel, published *Ski Woman's Way*, based on a series of ski-week seminars Slanger was hosting at Squaw Valley. The book helped establish recognition of the different psychological and physical aspects of female skiers

Deb Armstrong (seated), who won a gold medal in giant slalom at the 1984 Winter Olympics in Sarajevo, became a certified ski instructor and also a member of the 2004–08 PSIA Alpine Team.
(Photo PSIA-AASI)

The 1984 PSIA Alpine Team included, front row: Shawn Smith, Ellen Post, Dee Byrne, Carol Levine, Walt Chauner. Back row: Chris Ryman, Jerry Warren, Paul Jones, Kent Stevens, Mike Porter, Dave Merriam, Tim Petrick, and Victor Gerdin. (Photo PSIA-AASI)

and inspired teaching seminars and equipment innovations that continue to develop.

What is interesting to note is how many of the women who helped build the standards for ski instruction in the United States felt less like pioneers and more like winter athletes who were just helping their sport follow its natural course.

"Regarding growing up in this business as a 'woman,' I'm thankful not to have a story illustrating how I 'broke through the glass ceiling.' Yet I know it is not very dramatic," said Byrne, who is director of skiing at Squaw Valley. "It was more about doing a good job and taking pride in having the skills to be effective. That was always the point."

Ski Woman's Way

Based on Elissa Slanger's breakthrough Squaw Valley, California-based ski seminars, *Ski Woman's Way*, the book she co-authored with Dinah Witchel, created a template for identifying the ways in which women learn best. Equal parts psychology, physiology, and philosophy lesson, the book's pictures and conversational prose also celebrate the natural beauty of the sport. Paired with the works of pioneers such as Jeannie Thoren, who started an equipment revolution when she realized she could drastically increase the control of her skis just by moving her bindings forward, the combination triggered a growing category of new women's gear and classes.

Ellen Post Foster leads the way in training for Interski. (Photo PSIA-AASI)

Together, cross-country skiing, adaptive skiing, and the new focus on women's instruction programs substantially increased the number of ways professional ski instructors could teach snowsports—and especially the number of people they could teach. After yet another 10 years of incredible innovation, it might have seemed that the pace would slow.

But snowboarding was already on the way. And if the passion for snowsports burned like a woodstove in the winter, then the one-board revolution would land in the fire like a can of gas.

The JETs

Tim Gallwey said that the book he co-authored with Robert Kriegel, *Inner Skiing,* was inspired by the natural, unconscious way children ski. As the American Teaching System grew, it revealed that kids needed more than just a watered-down version of what the adults were being taught. The result was a flurry of creative new ways to inspire the next generation of riders, including PSIA's publication of *Captain Zembo's Ski Teaching Guide for Kids* and *Child-Centered Skiing,* and the

Kids on snow.
(Photo PSIA-AASI)

Captain Zembo.
(Photo PSIA-AASI)

Child-Centered Skiing.
(Photo PSIA-AASI)

creation of a demonstration team focused on children known as the Junior Education Team, or the JETs. The team was instrumental in implementing the CAP (cognitive/affective/physical) Model for teaching children and in preparing the instructional community for the advent of teaching in terrain parks and halfpipes. The legacy of the JETs is they saw teachers of children become respected as snowsports instructors and paved the way for a national credential in this area of teaching.

Snowboarding mega-
star Shaun White won
two Olympic gold
medals while being
coached by pioneer
snowboard instructor
Bud Keene.

(Photo by Oliver Kraus, courtesy of the
U.S. Ski and Snowboard Association)

CHAPTER 4

THE ONE-BOARD REVOLUTION

S nowboarding hit skiing like a runaway train, speeding the entire sport onto a faster track. American born, built on skate culture and surf style, it pulsed with the exuberance of youth and freedom—two of the country's most consistent exports—and fat skis, halfpipes, and shaggy-haired Olympic gold medal shredders sprang up in its wake.

It began with a simple question—"Why not one board instead of two?"—that spread like wildfire across U.S. ski resorts, creating a blaze of excitement and conflict and launching a new era in activities from slope preparation to the design of equipment. One joke among snowboarders goes, "Hey skiers, you never thanked us for saving your sport," because snowboarding arrived at the exact moment when many skiers were beginning to bristle against skiing's increasing sameness and lack of access—its focus on perfect turns, stretch pants, and real estate and the sense that the mountains were being run by risk managers doing all they could to prohibit fun on the slopes.

Ski filmmakers such as Greg Stump were already showcasing cliff jumping and steep chute skiing far beyond the area boundaries in extreme ski movies such as *Blizzard of AAHHH's,* which openly called out the lack of innovation by the resort establishment. Stump created new ski heroes out of the bigger-than-life personality of Glen Plake, as well as Montana-bred soul skier Scot Schmidt, who in *AAHHH's* says to the camera, "Insurance companies won't let us ski things that are totally within our ability," while Plake adds that he especially likes skiing steeps, "and cliffs go automatically from steeps."

Snowboarding exploded onto the wintersports scene in the 1980s and 1990s, creating a new snowsports culture, as well as events such as the U.S. Open of Snowboarding, and also the X Games.

(U.S. Open photo by Hubert Schriebl)

It seemed a particularly ripe environment had emerged in which to introduce snowboarding—especially with the promise of all the new kids the sport could bring to the slopes—but the ski areas were terrified of it. Most immediately banned it, as much in reaction to the rebellious attitude of the sport's early participants as to snowboarders' primitive wooden boards, rubber bindings, bulky Sorels, or surplus army store-bought boots.

"It certainly had a bit of the outlaw image at the start, coming as it did from skate and surf culture. But the intolerance in the beginning just helped push that through the roof," said PSIA-AASI member Bud Keene, who was one of the country's first snowboard instructors and who later coached the two-time Olympic gold medal performances of U.S. superstar Shaun White. "That ready-made conflict gave the sport a kind of romanticism that just pushed the needle up a lot."

Because of their sideways riding stance, the lack of steel edges, and surfboard-style rudders and skegs still attached to the tails—both first-generation design elements that were quickly made obsolete—the earliest snowboarders lacked the control of skiers and often dropped a hand into the snow like an oar to make a turn, which led to them being labeled as "knuckle draggers" by skiing's purists.

That perceived lack of control was another reason insurance companies would not underwrite snowboards as "directional devices" and why resorts were able to bar snow-boarders from that one aspect of on-mountain infrastructure that they most wanted to access—the chairlifts.

But being locked out of the playground only strengthened the resolve of the rapidly growing group of converts who were inspired by the simple grace of snowboarding and who helped build the sport. Said Keene, "As soon as you saw someone else with a snowboard you had something to talk about. You immediately had something unique in common, and there was a bond that came from that."

Before he became the first snowboarder to serve as Chairman of the Board for PSIA-AASI, Eric Sheckleton was a hard-riding instructor.
(Photo PSIA-AASI)

Building the Boards

The snowboard revolution altered skiing in a way that no other established sport has been changed before or since. But it was a slow-growing success. The catalyst was born just a few years after PSIA itself, in Muskegon, Michigan, in 1965 when Sherman Poppen invented the "Snurfer," a snow surfing toy, by fastening two skis together and attaching a guide rope. Poppen refined, then licensed, the idea to sports giant Brunswick, which manufactured and sold about one million Snurfers from 1966 to 1976. Early fans included Jake Burton Carpenter, who in 1977 started building his own snowboards in Londonderry, Vermont. Skateboarder Tom Sims had also begun to produce his namesake boards in California, Dimitrije Milovich was building Winterstick in Utah, and together, Mike Olson and Pete Saari started both Gnu and Lib-Tech in the Northwest. In 1982, the first national snowboard race was held near Woodstock, Vermont, at Suicide Six, and the next year, at Soda Springs, California, Tom Sims hosted the first world championship competition in halfpipe.

Jake Burton Carpenter rides one of his earliest big-mountain designs.
(Photo courtesy of Hubert Schriebl)

California snowboard icon Tom Sims.
(Photo courtesy of Hubert Schriebl)

THE EARLY YEARS

Keene, who was first introduced to snowboarding in Stowe, Vermont, by another pioneer of snowboard instruction, the tall, blonde, perpetually inspired Lowell Hart, said the perception that snowboarders lacked technique only made him want to perform even better, whether in the moguls, the steeps, or on the ice. His naturally competitive persona made him want to beat the skiers at their own game. It was Hart, he said, who saw that working within the existing structure of skiing would be the fastest way to open the doors for the widespread acceptance of the sport.

"Lowell understood from the beginning that if we wanted snowboarding to succeed, we needed to go to the resorts with an instruction plan, and an equipment plan, and most importantly, a way to make it profitable," Keene said.

"Ski areas had a huge concern about liability," added Hart. "But in those early years the people who were snowboarding had a very high inner level of motivation, so we would keep doing things like hiking up under the chairs on powder days, sometimes having confrontations with the ski patrol, and then going into the management offices all covered in snow to ask if we could ride the lifts."

Bud Keene learned how to snowboard by hiking up the mountain at Stowe, Vermont, with Lowell Hart, for years before the ski areas began to open the chairs for them.

(Photo by Monte Isom/Sportschrome)

Lowell Hart has long been a source of inspiration for snowboard students and instructors alike.

(Photo courtesy of Lowell Hart)

In an effort to prove they were just as skilled as skiers, early snowboard contests often resembled ski competitions. Here, Andy Coghlan crashes the gates.

(Photo by Hubert Schriebl)

In the evenings, they went in search of instructional insight. Borrowing as much as they could from PSIA and other existing sports programs—"Even diving," Hart said, echoing Juris Vagners' 1970s-era biomechanical research—they were trying to create an instructional progression for the sport's ever-expanding groundswell of surf-snow acolytes. Both Burton and Sims Snowboards, two of the sport's original brands, were early supporters of instruction, providing snowboards; stoke; and, most importantly, connections to like-minded riders around the country, all just as passionate about proving to those old-school resort managers that snowboarding belonged on the slopes.

"We kept finding these little pockets of forward-looking people who were all out there developing the equipment, and the technique," Keene said. "And they all wanted to share how great snowboarding felt."

Riders such as Ray Sforzo, David Alden, Jeff Grell, Randy Price, Kerri Hannon, and Jane Mauser—the "Johnny Appleseeds," as Keene calls them—were all working on getting snowboarding accepted at their home resorts.

The same way telemark and adaptive skiing had grown, like little cults across the country, snowboarding was gaining momentum. And it was the smaller areas, such as Soda Springs, California; Berthoud Pass, Colorado; Mt. Baker, Washington; and Snow Valley, Vermont, where snowboarders first found independent-minded owners who were willing to give them a chance to prove the new sport could provide an economic impact.

Snowboarding stood skiing on its head, in both its sense of fun and invention.
(Photo PSIA-AASI)

Randy Price, one of the "Johnny Appleseeds" of snowboard instruction.
(Photo by Scott Markewitz)

David Alden, who was instrumental in writing the first official snowboard instruction manual, was the original snowboard instructor at Berthoud Pass.

(Photo by Tom Lippert)

Several ski areas across the country, including Soda Springs, California; Mt. Baker, Washington; Snow Valley, Vermont; and rugged Berthoud Pass, Colorado, led the way in allowing snowboarders on the slopes.

(Photo courtesy of Tom Winter)

THE ONLY SNOWBOARDER
IN THE WORLD

"In 1981 I was working as a kind of ambassador at Berthoud Pass just to talk to the people who were starting to show up with snowboards," said David Alden, a tall redhead from Colorado who at the time may have been the only official snowboard ambassador on earth. "Ike Garst, who owned Berthoud with his wife, Lucy, came from a farming family in Iowa and was very much a pragmatist. I don't think it ever occurred to him that one way of sliding on the snow might be better than another. He just saw people who wanted to ride the lift."

Berthoud was ground zero for the snowboard scene in Colorado in the 1980s. Anyone who wanted to ride would eventually end up there, dropping into the trees and hitchhiking back up the highway with carloads of skiers on their way to Winter Park, or riding the T-bar or chair where Alden worked. Everyone was making it up as they went along, he said, as "people showed up on Burton 'Woodys' or Sims or Wintersticks—or even boards they made on their own— and my job was just to make sure their gear was set up right and find out if they even knew the difference between riding regular or goofy foot. Then I might give them a couple pointers after that."

Alden lived in what he called the "prehistoric" Berthoud Pass Lodge at 11,000 feet, a wooden, wind-blasted remnant of the 1950s that the US Forest Service tore down in 2005, two years after the removal of the chairlifts. A series of owners and a subsequent bankruptcy eventually shuttered the ski area, though it remains a popular backcountry spot. Alden said it felt like being on a ship at sea when snow control or an avalanche closed the pass.

Every morning he hiked out to ride the bare peaks and steep chutes, often in sub-zero conditions, and was back at the base by the time the lifts were running to high-five the next wave of riders as they were heading up. In 1982, Lucy Garst made him a nametag that said "snowboard instructor"; Alden found himself increasingly thinking about the basic skills of snowboarding and, more

An early handcrafted halfpipe on Berthoud Pass.

(Photo courtesy of Lucy Garst)

importantly, how to make it less painful to learn for the people just being introduced to the sport.

"Learning how to snowboard then was kind of a personal discovery experience, where everyone fought their own battle with the mountain," Alden said. "To me, learning how to do it properly was as much about pain avoidance as anything else."

In southern Colorado, at the Purgatory ski area, snowboard instructor Randy Price was also looking for less of a full-contact experience in teaching the sport, an approach that went beyond the male-dominated, sink-or-swim mentality being offered in the earliest variations of snowboard classes. "The first three or four years that I taught, I rarely had a woman in any class," said Price. "They were all men, all fit and fairly athletic, and every one of them wanted to go straight up the lift to the top."

Price said falls were so common that a catalog of the most popular wipeouts quickly came into use, from the "Scorpion," where you catch an edge with speed and the board whips you on the back of your head, to the face-planting "Flyswatter" and the all-encompassing "Schwack!" For those new riders who immediately fell in love with the sport, half the fun was wiping out. But as Price said, "You got so you could tell pretty quickly who was going to stick with it. By the time you got to the bottom of the mountain, they were either snowboarders forever or they were never coming back."

THE EVOLUTION OF TECHNIQUE
Terms, Innovators, and Books
COURTESY OF BILL LASH

Ski School ✦ Keep It Simple Ski Instructor ✦ The Centered Skier ✦ *A Ski Instructor's Guide to the Physics and Biomechanics of Skiing* by Juris Vagners ✦ Hip-Hip, Knee-Knee Short Ski Technique ✦ Technical Logic ✦ Whole Body Skiing ✦ Bill Briggs's Great American Ski School ✦ Countering Curve ✦ Split-Rotation Foot Push ✦ Royal Carve Rebound ✦ Pedal Hook Rebound ✦ Mind over Skis ✦ Skidding vs Carving ✦ Peter Brinkman's System of Radical Pure Parallel Natural Turning Radius (NTR) Turns ✦ Duncan Reid's *Skiing the New Way* ✦ Super Carve Turn ✦ Transcendental Skiing ✦ Edge Lock Traverse ✦ Railroad Track Turns ✦ Early Edge Change ✦ Early Lead Change ✦ Dynamic Ski Balance ✦ Jet Rebound ✦ Cowboy Turns ✦ Rock and Roll Turns

Halfpipes

Invented when California skateboarders first started sessioning empty swimming pools in the 1970s, halfpipes were one of the first innovations snow skaters brought with them when they hit the slopes. Part coliseum, part snow-fed space program, halfpipes could be built by anyone with snow and good grooming equipment; they have developed into a consistent center of youthful excitement and energy at snowsports areas from coast to coast—as well as a creative forum for a new generation of winter heroes and a new series of competitive events. After enjoying early success at the X Games, where it continues to be one of the highest-drawing spectator events, in 1998 halfpipe snowboarding debuted at the Nagano, Japan, Winter Olympics. On April 6, 2011, the International Olympic Committee announced that halfpipe skiing would also be added at the 2014 Winter Olympics in Sochi, Russia. "Today is the beginning of a chapter in the history books," U.S. Ski and Snowboard Association President Bill Marolt said at the time of the announcement.

Skiers appreciate how snowboarders brought halfpipes and twin tips to the mountain.
(Photo courtesy Jake Paulsen, U.S. Ski and Snowboard Association)

THE THINK TANK

When Colorado's Breckenridge Ski Area opened the lifts to snowboarders in the spring of 1985, Alden was hired as the first instructor. As other areas followed suit, he began to hold informal clinics with the other new snowboard instructors. Through daily trial and error, he made a list of best practices for learning, and in the same vein as Lash, Abraham, and O'Leary before him, in the summer of 1986 he wrote an instruction manual for snowboarding in a first attempt "to create a really definable process by which it could be taught."

"I felt like I had become a kind of clearinghouse of information by that point," he said. "I started to envision the process from that moment you are first handed a board to when you're really snowboarding, and to break down all the motions in between in a way that really works."

He typed up his manual on an old typewriter, "published" it in three-ring binders, and presented it to the PSIA Board of Directors in Lakewood, Colorado, that fall, along with another snowboarder named Marvin Christianson, who had already made a presentation on snowboarding to ski instructors in the Pacific Northwest.

Not everyone was receptive. And Alden was not sure just what kind of impression he and Christianson had made until two instructors in particular led him to believe that everything would work out. "I think Max Lundberg and Jerry Warren saw the whole picture," Alden said. "I remember they came up to me later and kind of gave me a sense like 'Yeah, we'll talk some sense to these knuckleheads.'"

But PSIA had already been doing plenty of its own research. And, despite resistance from many instructors in its own ranks, by the next fall the association was ready to act. Alden, Price, Hart, and several of Keene's other Johnny Appleseeds were invited to Copper Mountain, Colorado, for a snowboard think tank. Their task was to take all the insights they had gleaned from their time on the cutting edge of the sport, combine them with PSIA's collected breakthroughs in teaching, and in one week set the template for snowboarding's own instructional renaissance.

The fact they actually did so is a tribute to the snowboarders who were on the hill, and to PSIA itself. From the slopes to their condos and back each day, those riders embarked on a massive idea dump and shred fest, unleashing years of pent-up insights into how they were growing snowboarding at their home mountains. Brainstorming and bonding from the lifts to the bars, they kept the conversation going as long as they had strength, often falling asleep right where they sat as they hammered out a live-action storyline for their sport.

"I can't remember who it was, but at one point we had a guy strapped into his snowboard on a glass table so we could all get underneath it and look up and see how every move he made affected the board's edges and flex," said Price. "We were looking at everything and arguing about everything, but that was just because of our egos. What we were accomplishing was a way to make learning very simple and movement based."

The obvious connection in spirit to the innovations of the 1970s was made real by the presence of Juris Vagners, who was instrumental in keeping the opinionated and eclectic group of riders on task. The same technician of sliding who had been so important to establishing the actual science of skiing, he kept returning the conver-

A draft copy of the first *Snowboard Ski Instruction Manual*, which PSIA produced following a snowboard think tank at Copper Mountain, Colorado.
(Photo PSIA-AASI)

Randy Price has mentored hundreds of other riders as a longtime instructor and former AASI Snowboard Team coach.

(Photo PSIA-AASI)

The first snowboard instructor certification pin.

(Photo courtesy of Robertsski.com)

Members of the 1988–1992 AASI Snowboard Team Ray Sforzo, Brian Dunfrey, Dave Alden, Jane Mauser, Kerri Hannon, Jim Sechrist, and Paul Naschak.

(Photo by Tom Lippert)

sation to focus on which elements worked the best. "Whether it's two edges or one, fundamentals are fundamentals," Vagners said.

"Juris was a real inspiration. He was a very important presence, and why so much was initially accomplished that week," said Hart. "He was a great unifier," Keene concurred. "He had 10 people in the room who had developed the sport on their own in 10 different places, and he calmed them and kept them focused. He had the right personality for it."

Together, they created the material that would form the basis for the official *Snowboard Ski Instruction Manual*, which PSIA published in 1989. By matching the movements of snowboarding with the success of the American Teaching System, it was a template for snowboard instruction that could be applied across the country, and it was a foundation for the sport's next wave of growth. PSIA also certified the first class of snowboard instructors at A-Basin that year: 12 riders in all, Vagners said, "They sort of formed the core for the national organization, and they took off from there."

After more than a decade, snowboarding seemed to explode overnight. "It all happened so quickly," Price said. "If you were a snowboard instructor then you were booked all day, and barely had time to come off the lifts."

THE TIPPING POINT

In 1991 in St. Anton, Austria, David Alden and Jane Mauser recorded another milestone for U.S. snowsports by providing Interski's first snowboard presentation on the demonstration slope. The sport was beginning to take off around the world by then, but as far as instruction was concerned, all the other countries were still far behind the United States. The following winter, in a clarion call of just where American instruction was heading, the 1991–92 issue of *The Professional Skier* featured a gorgeous cover shot of Ray Sforzo arcing his snowboard down Vail Mountain with nothing but a classic, clear blue Colorado sky overhead.

That one beautiful image graphically marked the strengthening partnership between PSIA and snowboarding—a relationship that continues to develop to the benefit of both. As snowboarding's inevitable growth accelerated as a result of PSIA's vast instructional experience and its incredible network of instructors, the sport brought several gifts of its own to the slopes. The most obvious was the energy of youth, which is almost synonymous with freestyle, and a whole new generation of kids who just wanted to go spin 360s and jump off stuff.

"Snowboarding is all about going out every day to hit some jumps and find new things to play on," said Shaun Cattanach, an AASI Snowboard Team member in the 1990s who now works for Burton Snowboards in its resort development department. "That's still what I think about when I go out. So did almost everyone who came to a lesson. The challenge was how quickly you could help people do that."

That freestyle future was already emerging by the time the issue of *The Professional Skier* with Sforzo on the cover came out. In an article titled "Shredding 101: A Snowboard Primer," John Schinnerer noted, however awkwardly, that "some aspects of snowboarding are quite different from skiing. This is most obvious in 'freestyle,' which snowboarders perform primarily in a halfpipe," and later that "the freestyle moves made in a halfpipe come from the surfing and skateboarding roots of the sport."

Though Schinnerer was prescient in his awareness of freestyle's looming impact, he probably could not have imagined how big it—or snowboarding—would get. By the mid-1990s, snowboarding was America's fastest-growing sport. In 1990, there were more than one million riders in the United States, and that number quadrupled by the end of the decade. Halfpipes and terrain parks, which could be built anywhere there was snow, suddenly bloomed from the East to the Midwest to the West. Ride, a

THE EVOLUTION OF TECHNIQUE

Terms, Innovators, and Books
COURTESY OF BILL LASH

Rotary Skills ✣ Rotary Edging ✣ Rotary Movements ✣ Balancing Movements ✣ Pressure Control ✣ Edge Control ✣ Lateral Adjustment ✣ Automatic Turns ✣ Javelin Turns ✣ Due Line ✣ Stork Turns ✣ Let Nature Take Its Course Turns ✣ Open Stance Parallel Wedge Turns & Christie I and II Turns ✣ Open Stance Parallel ✣ Dynamic Parallel ✣ Gliding Wedge Turns ✣ Edged and Guided Turns ✣ Karl Gamma's *The Handbook of Skiing* ✣ Functional Skiing ✣ *Ski Mechanics* by John Howe ✣ *The Way to Ski: The Official Method* by Stu Campbell & Max Lundberg ✣ Lito Tejada-Flores's *Breakthrough on SKIS* ✣ Flex Turns ✣ Instant Parallel Skiing ✣ Pure Carved Turns ✣ Counter Punch ✣ Simultaneous Steering ✣ Diagonal Pelvis Move ✣ Active Flexing Motion ✣ High Power Turns ✣ Billy Goat Turn ✣ Gliding Wedge ✣ Lateral Weight Transfer ✣ No Techno Babble ✣ Fly Away Turns

Jane Mauser would make history with David Alden as the first two snowboarders to demonstrate at Interski in St. Anton, Austria, in 1991.
(Photo PSIA-AASI)

Ray Sforzo carving powder beneath a deep-blue Colorado sky.
(Photo PSIA-AASI)

publicly traded snowboard company, was one of the hottest stocks on Wall Street for a brief, shining moment, and the sports world buzzed as snowboarding anticipated making its grand competitive entrance at the 1998 Nagano Winter Olympics.

For PSIA, after watching membership stall throughout the 1980s, in the 1990s the association began to experience massive growth. Adding thousands of instructors over just a few short seasons, by 2004 more than 29,000 snowsport instructors across the United States were members of PSIA-AASI. PSIA's embrace of snowboarding brought its own new wave of recruits, but more skiers were joining as well, inspired as much by the energy of the association as by the open-minded approach to snowsports in general that the association continues to represent.

In response to its own swelling ranks of snowboard instructors and the rapid evolution of snowboard instruction, PSIA embarked on one more move that would create deep resistance from across the country, especially at many resorts but also throughout its own instruction ranks. In 1997, PSIA created the American Association of Snowboard Instructors (AASI), the world's first integrated snowboard instructional division, aimed solely at improving the on-snow riding experience. While other countries continue to treat snowboard instruction as a kind of secondary aspect to skiing, PSIA, which then became PSIA-AASI, was the first to give the sport equal footing. It was also the first to recognize the need to further facilitate the growing educational aspects of the sport.

According to PSIA-AASI Executive Director and Chief Executive Officer Mark Dorsey, it was his predecessor, Stephen Over, who was critical to establishing snowboarding's instructional independence. While many diehard ski instructors and resort managers were still loath to accept snowboarding's increasing level of influence and instructional insight, Dorsey said Over was instrumental in working with resort managers, as well as his own membership, to convince them the association could not survive with just an alpine focus.

"Had AASI not been formed, had we not won out, it is likely that snowboarding would not have the education clout it enjoys in the United States today or be effectively mainstreamed as part of the consumer experience," Dorsey said.

"Two of the great advantages to instruction in America are the levels of diversity and that we don't have a long trail of tradition, so we can focus on what is happening as it happens," Over said. "Creating AASI was a prime example of that. We weren't setting it up as a landmark, but more because it reflected our current needs. It was only later that we realized what we had accomplished."

Dorsey added that in the United States, because of the creation of AASI, it is no surprise to see skiers and snowboarders in the same class, while in other alpine countries the mere mention of such an idea would create immediate conflict. By establishing a platform for snowboard instruction to have an equal voice in the U.S. teaching process, the United States had again put itself in the instructional passing lane, as the increasing exchange of information on both the educational and technological aspects of skiing and snowboarding would continue to spur the evolution of both.

Former PSIA-AASI Executive Director Steve Over (left) and former PSIA-AASI President Mark Anderson were two of the key architects of the American Association of Snowboard Instructors.
(Photo PSIA-AASI)

Bud Keene in his element.
(Photo courtesy of Bud Keene)

The Y Model

One of snowboarding's earliest contributions to instruction was the Y Model (also known as the Martini Model for the Y's cocktail glass shape), a method of teaching that showed the relationship between everything from carving to freestyle before focusing on more specific elements of style and technique. Freestylers, free-riders, and carvers—the respective left, center, and right side of the Y—could learn their turn and then master whatever halfpipes, deep powder, or hard arcs most caught their interest. "The idea was that there are some steps until you learn to turn, but once you can make that turn the world is open to you," said Eric Sheckleton, who was part of the snowboard team that created the Y Model and who became the first snowboarder to be named PSIA-AASI Chairman of the Board in 2010. "After that you can really just focus on what direction you want your riding to take."

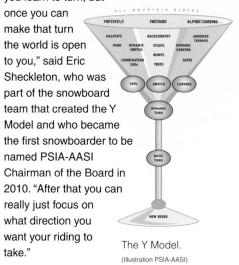

The Y Model.

(Illustration PSIA-AASI)

SKIING HOLDS ITS OWN

Even as snowboarding was exploding, skiing continued to undergo its own next-step revolution. In the uber-technical world of ski racing, standout American Olympians such as Tommy Moe and Picabo Street were achieving the ultimate success. Moe won a gold medal in the downhill and silver in Super G at the 1994 Winter Games in Lillehammer, Norway, and Street won silver in downhill at those same games, then a gold in Super G at Nagano in 1998.

At the same time, big-mountain ski stars such as Glen Plake, who himself would become a certified ski instructor, and Scot Schmidt were pushing the new strain of "extreme" skiing over cliffs and down steep chutes. And PSIA's Demonstration Team—the "D-Team," as it came to be known—had become a kind of royalty of the American ski set. James Tabor called it "the Dream Team" in the February 1991 issue of *SKI Magazine,* and in the December 1996

PSIA-AASI Teams Manager Katie Fry (now Ertl) flying off a cliff in the yellow "Dream Team" jacket.

(Photo PSIA-AASI)

issue, editor Andrew Bigford published a story called "The $100,000 Parka," in which he referred to trying out for the team as "the ski instructor's equivalent of the Olympics."

"Besides the prestige, the bright-yellow D-Team uniform translates into media exposure, product endorsements and career opportunities," Bigford noted. "The most successful team members can approach six figures in endorsement deals over a four-year term. More significant is their increased status in the job market."

Citing the success of former D-Team members such as Chris Ryman and Tim Petrick, who contributed to the teaching breakthroughs of the 1970s and went on to run several U.S. ski resorts and ski companies, Bigford painted a picture of the D-Team as a kind of finishing school for not only some of the hottest skiers on the hill but also its future executives.

For Dave Merriam, who was interviewed for the *SKI Magazine* article and who coached the PSIA-AASI team until 2004, the experience was as much a culmination of his goals as a reward for his own particular ski instruction-based career path.

"I've always been an active learner, which is why the traditional educational environments never worked well enough for me—because there isn't enough doing," said Merriam, who became mountain recreation director at Stowe Mountain Resort.

Dave Merriam enjoying the active elements of a snowsports instruction career.
(Photo PSIA-AASI)

Dave Merriam (left) and Lowell Hart at the 1995 Interski in Nozawa Onsen, Japan.
(Photo PSIA-AASI)

"Once I hooked up with the whole ski teaching thing, there was no lack of role models or ways in which you could actively work to develop yourself."

By the time Merriam became coach, the precedent of innovation established by the likes of Petrick, Mike Porter, Max Lundberg, and Jerry Warren had already been well set. To his great joy, however, rather than resting on their laurels or touting their accomplishments, all of the previous innovators remained happily involved, encouraging and even contributing to his success.

"I remember when I went to my first national academy and met guys like Shawn Smith, Jerry Warren, Jens Husted, and Chris Ryman, and they all exuded this energy and excitement about going out and trying to better your best," said Merriam. "They all shared that sense of possibility that's so addicting every time you jump on the lift. It's the real sense of promise that this could be the best run of your entire life—the breakthrough run when all of the variables come together into this seamless whole, and you absolutely get it. That's the engagement that they shared. And I still get tingles up and down the back of my neck just thinking about it."

After several years on the PSIA Alpine Team, Tim Petrick began a new career as an executive for some of skiing's most storied brands.
(Photo PSIA-AASI)

Stu Campbell

Stu Campbell may have been the most well-known—and most prolific—ski instructor in the United States. Campbell started out teaching in Stowe, Vermont (where he continued to spend his summers), before heading west to Heavenly to serve as director of skier services. A talented instructor and examiner, Campbell discovered that his greatest contribution to the sport was in the way he wrote. As the instructional editor of *SKI Magazine* for 30 years beginning in 1976, he maintained a steady pace of tips columns, feature articles, and essays that reached millions of skiers with a regular dose of humor, wonder, and instructional insight. He also authored ski instruction books, including *Ski with the Big Boys*; *The Way to Ski*; and, along with former Alpine Team member and good friend Tim Petrick, *Good Things to Know about Gliding on Snow*. Of the sport itself, he once wrote, "The art of skiing is, ultimately, the search for sensation."

Skiing's most prolific instructor, Stu Campbell.
(Photo courtesy of the U.S. Ski & Snowboard Hall of Fame)

THE CROSS-CULTURAL INFLUENCES START

Merriam oversaw that first real interdisciplinary mix of snowboarding and alpine, adaptive, and telemark skiing that comprised the Demonstration Teams throughout the 1990s. He said the energy among the team members was palpable as the first real breakthroughs in shaped skis, powder skis, terrain parks, and halfpipes took off.

"Everything was happening so quickly, but at the same time there was the sense that we were steering it," said Merriam. "You could see how we needed to integrate the voice of the teacher, the voice of the student, and especially the voice of the sport. It's only through instruction that all of those voices come together at once."

After absolutely changing the culture and style of snowsports, the one-board revolution was also having a deep impact on the way skis were built. Mimicking the benefits of the snowboard's wide body, ski companies began widening the tips and tails of their skis to improve the ease of turn initiation on hardpack and especially to enhance the skis' ability to float in powder snow.

Initially envisioned to be used by intermediate skiers and World Cup racers, the wider skis were eventually adopted by experts, who found they not only allowed them to turn more easily in powder but also provided more stability and confidence in the steeps. When turned-up tails—twin tips—were added to skis such as the category defining Salomon 1080, skiers were suddenly charging into what had previously been the exclusive domain of snowboarders, the halfpipe.

As the cross-disciplinary influences began to expand, more instructors sought certification in more than one on-snow pursuit. Beginning in 1991, Mike Shaw of Mt. Hood Meadows in Oregon became the first person in the United States to earn the

Mike Shaw was the first snowsports instructor in the United States to earn Level III certification in alpine, snowboard, nordic downhill, and nordic track.
(Photo PSIA-AASI)

Shaped Skis

When shaped skis were first introduced, some experts ridiculed them as "cheater" and "grandmother" skis and were the last people on the mountain to strap them to their feet. Their pride in the ability to make a long, straight ski turn and their distrust of any activity based on snowboarding were at the root of the ridicule. When brands such as Elan, Kneissl, Head, and K2 started building shaped skis for mainstream skiers in the early 1990s, "many of the dealers didn't want anything to do with them until we started getting them on people's feet," said Bill Irwin, an Elan executive who was teaching skiing in Killington, Vermont, when the brand's oversized SCX skis first came out. Easier turns on powder; easier turns for older legs; and the amazing results of an up-and-coming American ski racer named Bode Miller, who took three firsts and one second while skiing on a pair of shaped K2 Fours in the 1996 Junior National Ski Championships at Sugarloaf Mountain, Maine, finally helped turn a lot of heads.

PSIA-AASI launched *The Pro Rider* magazine in response to the growing ranks of snowboard instructors.

(Photo PSIA-AASI)

The Professional Skier magazine reflected the new energy and attitude sweeping across the slopes.

(Photo PSIA-AASI)

highest-level certification pins in alpine, snowboard, nordic downhill, and nordic track. He would not be the last. In a story about the accomplishment, written by Juris Vagners for *The Professional Skier*, "If anyone can talk about the common elements of the alpine sliding sports from experience, Mike is the one!"

Although a testament to the ongoing sense of self-improvement that fuels so many snowsports instructors (as well as the addictive quality of the educational environment), Shaw's accomplishment was still most closely tied to his passion for all of the sliding sports. As he responded when Vagners asked him how he ever found the time to obtain full certification in so many different disciplines, Shaw just said, "It's easy if you love it."

By the beginning of the twenty-first century, that level of cross-pollination accelerated, from ski and snowboard design to best practices in teaching lessons. Whether because of the constant interaction between the instructors who were both teaching and learning from the rapidly evolving sports, or because of the increasingly rapid pace of innovation on the manufacturing side, in the next 10 years, snowsports again evolved at a staggering rate. During its fiftieth anniversary celebration at Interski 2011 in St. Anton, Austria, the home of modern ski instruction, PSIA-AASI had yet one more series of on-snow breakthroughs to unleash.

Randy Price drops in.

(Photo PSIA-AASI)

PSIA Alpine Team member Jim Schanzenbaker prepares for a practice run down the St. Anton demonstration slope.

(Photo by Cesar Piotto)

CHAPTER 5

THE HOMECOMING

More than 35 years after that landmark presentation by the Americans at the 1975 Interski in Czechoslovakia, there was a sense of déjà vu as the U.S. team headed to the 2011 Interski in St. Anton, Austria, because even they were not quite sure whether they had much of a breakthrough technique to present.

A security scare had kept the U.S. team from the 2007 Interski in South Korea, and it had been more than a decade since all of the teams—alpine, adaptive, nordic, and snowboard—had taken the international stage together. The fact that the congress occurred in the spiritual birthplace of ski instruction, the hometown of the great Hannes Schneider, as well as on the eve of PSIA-AASI's fiftieth anniversary, sent the sense of drama through the roof.

"The entire team worked so hard over the previous year to put their presentations together—they actually prepared twice as many topics as they got to present," PSIA-AASI Education Manager Ben Roberts said of the nonstop preparation leading up to the event. Long nights of spirited brainstorming and action-packed days of athletic on-snow sessions across the United States had become the standard by then, most notably at the annual Team Training event in October 2010 at Copper Mountain, Colorado, where the team had been quietly amazed at the number of ideas they felt could hold special significance.

AASI Snowboard Team member Eric Rolls shares some freestyle instruction tips at Interski 2011.

(Photo by Cesar Piotto)

Once again, the pace of innovation in equipment had altered the on-mountain landscape. At home, the Americans were working against a backdrop where the development of "rocker" ski and snowboard design had, as if on cue, irrevocably altered the sport. Meanwhile, internationally, the legacy of U.S. instructors, who for the previous 50 years had found a way to surprise and inspire the world, meant the Americans almost felt it was their duty to continue to bring something new to the snow just to sustain the trend.

"Instructors from other countries certainly look to the U.S., whether it be because they expect us to present something that is innovative, thought-provoking, or contrary to popular thinking," said PSIA Alpine Team Captain Michael Rogan, who seemed quietly assured that at least in that regard, the 2011 Interski would be no different from Interskis of the past.

So often seen as a kind of ski instruction shootout, where countries come just to prove who has the hottest feet, as far as the exchange of information was concerned, the 2011 Interski *was* more than ever an open symposium of free-flowing give and take. Of course there were nights under the lights when huge crowds filled the bleachers at the base of the slopes to watch the Slovenians (tuxedo-clad, skiing to the James Bond theme song), techno-synced Japanese, hard-rocking Swiss, Argentines, Italians, Americans, and teams from 38 other countries reaching ridiculous speeds in tight formations as they rocketed down the slopes. But that was more the après portion of each day, allowing the instructors to unwind with a massive sound system, impromptu Lady Gaga sing-a-longs, and fireworks. On the hill it was more like a fast-moving science fair for snow geeks, all skimming across the endless white acres of the Arlberg region, looking for powder and speaking in a dozen different languages about teaching and technique.

"There is always an interesting clash between some of the national teams at Interski," said Rogan, standing on a street papered with blockbuster movie-style posters of the Norwegian and Slovenian teams that had been produced especially for the event. "Some teams are completely focused on what they are going to do in the demo, while a lot of others are here more for sharing, completely ready to be surprised by something they didn't expect."

On the day of the presentation, the sky was gray and overcast. Ski instructors from around the world hurried uphill in bright green and yellow parkas to indoor

"Is there a group rate?" The PSIA-AASI teams line up for lift tickets.
(Photo by Cesar Piotto)

workshops conducted by the Americans, Austrians, Kiwis, Germans, and Dutch. The sound of their ski boots clattered on the cobblestone as their voices echoed off the white walls of St. Anton, and the smell of hot coffee and fresh-baked bread lingered in the streets.

The sun burned away the clouds by noon, setting fire to the snow-capped peaks. And inside the auditorium where presenters Rogan, Adaptive Team Coach Bill Bowness, Snowboard Team member Josh Spoelstra, and Nordic Team member Ross Matlock sat waiting for an audience, they realized that even with several rows of chairs and a little balcony for over-flow, very quickly they were going to run out of seats.

PSIA-AASI Adaptive Team Coach Bill Bowness and PSIA-AASI Adaptive Team member Geoff Krill on the demonstration slope.
(Photo by Cesar Piotto)

The Ongoing Influence of the Skills Concept

With obvious nods to PSIA-AASI's own Skills Concept of teaching, as well as the focus on the customer experience, at Interski 2011, Sweden unveiled the Will-Skill-Hill way of teaching. Beginning with "will," the Swedes focus on what each rider wants to do and his main objective in taking a lesson. "Skill" is the element that focuses on rotary, edge, pressure control, and balancing. And "hill" is the weather, terrain, equipment, and dynamics of the lesson. The Swedes made a point of continually adjusting expectations, repeating the mantra, "Predefined progression is Stone Age." What emerged was a holistic approach that kept all three elements at the forefront, rather than focusing on any single element.

THE FOUR-PART HARMONY

It was, in fact, a standing-room-only crowd; all in attendance were breathlessly waiting for some new math of sliding the Americans might bring, or some revival of a beautiful turn they had all but forgotten. So when Rogan began by focusing on a community of "culture and connection" instead, it nearly knocked them off their feet.

"Our focus is on a partnership of learning. It's about building a relationship," Rogan said, and across the mountains you could have heard the collective gasp.

While all of the other teams were still adding on to America's earlier contributions to the science and psychology of teaching, the United States had leapt ahead again, by focusing on the global community of snowsports instead. The mechanics of making turns were suddenly secondary to the pure pleasure of soaring down the slopes. As much as instruction was about improving, it was foremost about sharing the love of the sport. You still taught the turn, but only after you built the trust.

America's secret weapon was "The Four-Part Harmony," a mission statement that summarized the past 50 years of innovation and, in particular, where U.S. ski and snowboard instructors were headed in their quest to steer the sport. At its core, The Four-Part Harmony celebrates the reason so many vibrant people get out on the snow to teach in the first place: they want to get people excited about skiing and snowboarding. That culture of connection, to the mountains and to each other, is the way they share that joy, opening doors to what are life-enhancing, and sometimes even life-changing, experiences. Through their passion for the sport and their instructional skills, PSIA-AASI members are the hub of the sport, providing both information and experiential contact. No matter who the student is, what equipment he brings to the mountain, or what he wants to accomplish, U.S. instructors are his primary source of stoke and access.

PSIA-AASI Executive Director and Chief Executive Officer Mark Dorsey had literally set the stage for that message with a riveting keynote address to a packed house of 2,000 international snowsports instructors and ski school directors the day before the U.S. national team presentations took place. Touching on an array of topics from the nearly 100-year potential age span between people taking classes to the multitude of different skis, snowboards, and abilities they might bring to the mountain to their various desires for social interaction or heart-pounding adventure, he said the association would thrive by doing what it has always done best—focusing on

PSIA Alpine Team Captain Michael Rogan presents to a packed house on U.S. instruction's focus on fostering a community of "culture and connection."

(Photo by Cesar Piotto)

the people first. Painting a picture of a country where wintersports continue to thrive despite challenges posed by climate change, time management, and other factors, just as Rogan would do in the team presentation, Dorsey blew away the assembly of experts. Or, as one European audience member loudly proclaimed as he stood to cheer, "Now that was a keynote!"

"It's always been all about the people," Rogan said as the national teams prepared to take their message to snow, readying to head up the lifts. Square-jawed, with searching brown eyes, Rogan spends the entire year in the mountains, heading from

PSIA Nordic Team members David Lawrence (left) and Ross Matlock celebrate the intangible aspects of snowsports instruction.

(Photo by Cesar Piotto)

Tahoe to South America every summer when the deep Sierra snowpack starts to melt, always immersed in the culture of skiing from continent to continent.

It was people, he said, who represented the final breakthrough, even though their joy of belonging has *always* been at the center of the sport. Echoing Dorsey, he said all the achievements the Americans had worked toward were based on sharing each individual's sense of exhilaration. They wanted people to be better skiers and snowboarders, but they wanted to be together more than anything else. That was at the heart of the ideas the United States first began to address with its humanistic focus and with the Skills Concept.

Ski instruction had grown and expanded in response to every form of snow sliding to come down the slope. As Rogan said, "Alpine skiing is one pinnacle, but it isn't the only pinnacle. It isn't always the same, where and how you enter the sport."

Giving Back to the Sport (Daron Rahlves and Glen Plake)

As recognized a brand as U.S. ski and snowboard instruction has become, nothing in the sport can match the worldwide awareness of Glen Plake's trademark two-foot-high mohawk. Like some rare bird of paradise, it was on full display when Plake and his wife, Kimberly, came to support the teams at Interski 2011. PSIA-AASI Chairman of the Board Eric Sheckleton, who dared to go out on the streets of St. Anton with them one night, joked, "I think it took us an hour just to walk two blocks."

A U.S. Ski Hall of Fame inductee in 2011, Plake, along with Kimberly, also joined PSIA that year, and the two achieved their Level II instructor certification before the season was out. Joining Plake in the 2011 Ski Hall of Fame Class, and also as a member of PSIA, was Daron Rahlves, America's most decorated male downhill and Super G ski racer. Bringing equal doses of the freestyle and ski-racing heritage that has guided the twin influences of American ski instruction, Rahlves and Plake together also brought a strong belief that teaching skiing was the best route for them to keep innovating in the sport.

"One of the messages that I like the most about ski instruction is that this is one of the best avenues for anyone who really wants to have a career in skiing," Plake said. His father taught skiing for 20 years at the Sierra Ski Ranch (now Sierra-at-Tahoe), and Plake regularly crisscrosses the country in an RV with Kimberly as part of his Down Home Tour, an annual grassroots road trip celebrating skiing's widespread stoke. "It's the teachers who have the most impact on the next generation of skiers," he said.

ON THE SNOW

At the base of the mountain where the United States team sent its clinics out, the crowds were so deep in some places you could barely see their little handwritten signs: small sandwich boards advertising an on-snow revolution that read, "Freestyle for Everyone Skiing," "Freestyle for Everyone Snowboarding," and the "Evolution of Teaching Ski," all addressing new ideas and new equipment.

There was that electric buzz of a new ski day in the air, with the feeling that something exciting and unstoppable was about to start. As David Oliver, the lanky, blonde freestyle specialist on the PSIA Alpine Team, grinned at the crowds, he summed up the excitement of those about to hit the snow when he said, "Let's do this!"

In every direction they went speeding off. On the nordic trails, they went kicking and poling across perfectly groomed piste. Snowboarders rode up the Galzig Bahn gondola in clusters of bright parkas that spread out like flowers across the mountain, arcing off the groomed runs and dropping into the terrain park. The telemarkers and alpine team members led little United Nations-style groups of skiers from Japan, Argentina, Norway, and Australia from lift to lift. And everywhere they went, and in everything they presented, whether it was how rocker technology was accelerating the learning curve, how freestyle in beginner's classes would bring more kids to the mountain, or how adaptive riders just wanted to celebrate the board sport culture, their message was the same: This is about *more* people having *more* fun on the slopes.

From Canada to Korea, that joyful concept came beaming back. "This is information I'm excited to take home"; "Adding freestyle makes it more fun"; and "Rocker really is for everyone" were just some of the comments the PSIA-AASI team members heard as they went chasing from run to run like little flocks of birds in a lilting flight.

It was the most interactive presentation the Americans had ever given at Interski, where rather than just demonstrating they were actually out on the mountain skiing and breathing it. It had been so long since the United States had sent such a strong force of instructors—and such a strong message—to an international snowsports instructor's congress that it was only at the end of the day when they all began to realize the uniqueness of what they presented. And they also came away with a deeper feeling of kinship with all of the instructors who had preceded them, building as they were on the innovations of the past.

PSIA Alpine Team member David Oliver gets ready to greet the world for his freestyle skiing clinic.
(Photo by Cesar Piotto)

THE
EVOLUTION
OF
TECHNIQUE
Terms, Innovators, and Books
COURTESY OF BILL LASH

Victor Gerdin's Functional Tension ✍

Powerfully Relaxed Movements ✍

Preloads ✍ Overflexing ✍

Automatic Thoughts ✍ Move In

Balance ✍ Expanded "S" Concepts

✍ Radically Revised Way of

Analyzing Movements ✍

Radical Pole Planting Procedure

✍ Early Release to Energize the

Next Turn ✍ Ed Kreil's Parallel

Three Foot Ski Technique ✍

Weems Westfeldt's *Brilliant*

Skiing Everyday ✍ The Bull

Fighter Circle Step Turn ✍

Keeping the Shins Against the

Tongues of the Boots ✍ Stay

Centered ✍ Movement Analysis

✍ "Stand up and let the ski do the

work." (An old Swiss saying)

France and the Art of the Off-Piste

The French demonstration team warms up for the powder with a fast lap on the Interski demonstration slope.
(Photo by Cesar Piotto)

No one has the art of the off-piste down like the French. And at Interski 2011, French Team member Alexis Mallon's presentation on out-of-bounds instruction mixed Yoda-like phrases such as, "Experience is not what you have done, but what decisions you will make based on your past," with a straightforward assessment of the very real costs of screwing up.

The thrust of his presentation was that the information gathering and decision making involved in off-piste instruction never ceases—whether you are teaching "a bunch of 25-year-olds that just want to eat powder" or "a couple of supermodels." The weather may change, the snowpack may be wildly different than what was forecast, and a student's mental attitude and fitness will present its own variable, so the success of instructors depends on how well they can manage those aspects. As American ski areas increasingly push the boundaries and more instructors are asked to provide a wild snow experience, among the U.S. delegation in particular, Mallon's remarks found a rapt audience. "More and more people are demanding instruction and guiding in the backcountry," said John Armstrong, former PSIA-AASI President and current International Vice President. "As with any kind of instruction, safety and terrain selection are what you have to focus on first."

Adaptive Team Coach Bill Bowness—who paired with Adaptive Team member Geoff Krill to lead the United States down the demonstration slope at warp speed in their sit-skis during those evening show-off runs—was grinning from ear to ear as he hoisted a giant bottle of Wiesse bier in the Sporthotel, where the American teams were staying. He said it was the pure thrill of sharing what had taken the Americans so long to perfect that gave him more pleasure than anything else. "My highlight was presenting," he said. "It [felt] great to finally get out and do what we do so well."

As for Rogan's prediction that the other countries expected a surprise from the United States, they got it—even more than they expected, perhaps. And from America's latest inspirations, they would go home and evolve their own techniques. That much became apparent throughout the 2011 Interski, as earlier benchmarks such as the development of student-centered teaching and the Skills Concept kept appearing as key elements in other countries' presentations, particularly in a Swedish presentation titled "Will, Skill, Hill," which just reworked the existing framework of the Skills Concept. Even as the 2011 PSIA-AASI teams debuted their own new ideas, the innovations of earlier American teams were still echoing around the sport.

THE SESSION LESSON

To see the fat skis floating over the snow at any ski area, and all the kids like happy chipmunks spinning through the halfpipes and terrain parks, is to witness the overwhelming impact of snowboarding on snowsports. Turn on the television and note the way it has affected popular culture, from advertisements for video games modeled on the sport to broadcasts of the X Games to coverage of the Winter Olympics, where boarding has increasingly taken the spotlight. But in the past 20 years, has it also changed the way ski *and* snowboard lessons are taught?

According to Professional Development Manager and former AASI Snowboard Team member Earl Saline, "Without a doubt."

The biggest impact, Saline said, is the element of freestyle, which is present the moment someone decides to strap a board to his feet. That sense of possibility—and freedom of expression—seems to snowball the moment gravity starts pulling him down the slope. Saline summed it up this way: "In a beginner ski class, if you accidentally spin a 360, the impulse would be to correct that. If a student accidentally spins a 360 in a snowboard class, everyone would cheer."

Coaching Freestyle

PSIA Alpine Team member David Oliver takes freestyle skiing to new heights.
(Photo by Scott DW Smith)

More than just an alternative to racing or carving, freestyle skiing and snowboarding are sports unto themselves. And in the early 2000s, PSIA and, in particular, AASI began to offer freestyle credentials for instructors who were most interested in teaching riders who want to ride the parks and pipes. PSIA-AASI Professional Development Manager Earl Saline said the development was based on not just the growth of freestyle but also establishing a quality of riding to accompany that growth. Focused on riding features and man-made elements, calling tricks and stomping jumps, being able to do it as well as coach it, this new program created a clearinghouse of freestyle information and best practices. In 2005, it also resulted in the *PSIA-AASI Park and Pipe Instructors Guide*.

Snowboarding, he said, had inspired a style of teaching he called the "session lesson," and it represented more of a change in attitude than technique—a shift to a kind of lesson where the instructor is less of an assignment-giving taskmaster than an encouraging and supportive coach. Saline said, "There's this level of mutual inspiration that you find out snowboarding with your friends, that I don't think you can find in too many other sports."

Mark Dorsey said that, in the United States especially, the session-lesson style was the result of snowsports schools being the first place skiers and snowboarders joined forces, before anyone else on the slopes. "The first place skiers and snowboarders ever really came together was in snowsports schools," Dorsey said. "As far as learning from each other and perfecting technique was concerned, snowboarding just breathed new life into that whole process."

At Interski, the session-lesson mentality was presented as the most immediate ingredient for any snowboard student, even in an adaptive class. AASI Snowboard Team member Josh Spoelstra stressed that everyone who comes to a snowboard lesson wants to tap into the feeling of freedom as much as the sense of culture associated with it. "Those in the adaptive community are just as inspired to try snowboarding as able-bodied people," he said. "Amen to that!"

At the same time, the popularity of slopestyle and halfpipe skiing in the X Games had created a cycle of serious consideration for the 2014 Winter Games as well. Just days after the PSIA-AASI teams returned home from Interski, the U.S. Ski and Snowboard Association announced the launch of the US Freeskiing brand. And the International Olympic Committee's announcement that halfpipe skiing *would* premiere as an event at Sochi came the same week PSIA-AASI was celebrating its fiftieth anniversary in Colorado at Snowmass.

"The sport is going where the kids want it to go," said U.S. Ski and Snowboard Association President and Chief Executive Officer Bill Marolt. "You go to any mountain in America and see all the kids in the halfpipes and it's obvious, and both the USSA and the IOC have recognized that."

Despite cracking some ribs early in the week, David Oliver continued to represent skiing's interpretation of the session-lesson mentality at Interski, throwing skyscraper-sized airs in the demonstration runs and skiing backward at impossibly high speeds like a man calmly looking over his shoulder as he jumped off a cliff.

A modern-day equivalent of PSIA co-founder Doug Pfeiffer, Oliver is adamant that freestyle is as necessary to the future of skiing as snow and chairlifts—especially because it ties so directly to one of PSIA-AASI's original guiding concepts: that the student is the center of every class. "This is the next big step in student-centered teaching," he said. "The fact it comes from the roots of what U.S. teaching is all about only makes it that much cooler for me. It's really just taking it to the next level in the whole experience."

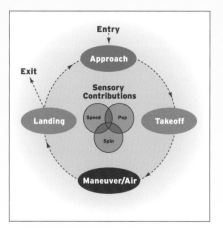

The ATML Method

A Skills Concept for the freestyle-minded crowd, the ATML Method Progression was designed specifically for hitting the parks and the pipe. With "A" for approach, "T" for takeoff, "M" for maneuver, and "L" for landing, it covers the four main aspects of hitting, styling, and landing tricks.

The ATML Method.
(Illustration PSIA-AASI)

THE ROCKER REVOLUTION

With all the new ideas presented at Interski, the Americans were surprised to be the only team to include the emergence of rocker technology in its clinics. Only the French and a few members of the Swiss team were even skiing on rockered skis in St. Anton. Otherwise, rocker seemed to have escaped the attention of everyone except the United States, though it may prove to be the greatest technological breakthrough since snowboarding.

Characterized by an exaggerated pre-flex of the tip of a ski or snowboard, and often the tail (think of a rocking chair), the technology makes it substantially easier to turn and pivot, most dramatically in deep snow, where the technology has flourished. For beginners and intermediates, the easy direction change accelerates the learning process so quickly that, as one ski instructor said, "It looks like the equipment has finally caught up with what we've been trying to teach."

In snowboards, rocker channels a rider's energy to the edges, creating a giant sweet spot that greatly enhances the surfing sensation so central to the sport. "I've seen three revolutions in my career—snowboards, shaped skis, and now this," said Craig Albright, managing director of the

Rocker Glossary

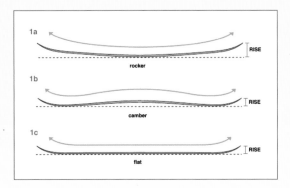

1a

rocker

RISE

1b

camber

RISE

1c

flat

RISE

Rocker is, quite simply, an exaggerated rise in the tip of a ski or snowboard that creates easier turn initiation and more float in mixed conditions and deep snow. Full rocker includes an exaggerated rise in the tail as well. Also called "early rise" because of the gradual raising of the shovel height at the front of a ski, designers can fine-tune the pivot point for an almost butter-like turning experience while also maintaining strong edge hold.

(Illustration PSIA-AASI)

Mammoth Mountain Ski and Snowboard School in California, where the region's Pacific-fed snowfalls made it one of the new technology's early takeoff points. "And just like how the old school guys said that shaped skis were cheating, or that snowboards wouldn't last, the same people were pooh-poohing this.

"Until they try it," Albright laughed. "Then they become great advocates."

For skiers in powder, instead of deflecting snow, a rockered tip rides above it. The relaxed tip also has tremendous advantages on hardpack and has been incorporated into everything from beginner boards to skis for the World Cup. "It's really an extension of what most people have been trying to accomplish since they first detuned their tips," said ski instruction guru Mike Porter, who helped test several of the early rocker prototypes. And at that Copper Mountain training session when the teams were dialing in their presentations (and a wave of early storms foreshadowed an epic winter to come), Adaptive Team member Geoff Krill was fascinated by how much easier rocker made it to turn a sit-ski just with lateral motion, saying, "It really is changing everything at once."

The late freeskier Shane McConkey (who in 2011 was inducted into the U.S. Ski Hall of Fame) was the design's earliest advocate. As famous for his sense of humor as for speeding down sheer faces and throwing great arcing backflips (sometimes in the nude) off giant cliffs, he reasoned that snow was simply frozen water, so the best skis for deep powder should be designed in the same fashion as the hull of a ship. He even put a pair of alpine bindings on water skis and proceeded to rip down giant ridges in Alaska on them to prove his point.

McConkey developed the category-busting, catamaran-style Spatula ski with Volant in 2002, and the appropriately named Pontoon with K2 in 2006, when he told the media, "Over the next few years, all the companies out there are going to start making rockered skis. It just works too well."

That was five years before Interski 2011 in St. Anton, by which time ski companies were predicting rocker design would be used for the majority of skis and snowboards sold in the North American market. Yet even at

America's rocker ski clinic, the many Norwegians, Croatians, and Swedes who showed up were still on slim-shaped carving skis that in the powder were pushed around like skinny sticks. "I thought it was just for helicopter skiers," one participant said, shocked at the idea the technology could so greatly improve the experience for beginners and intermediates.

As PSIA Alpine Team Coach Rob Sogard said after the clinic, the United States certainly did its part to give its instructional brethren a heads-up. "It's industry-changing technology," Sogard said. "Given that we have kind of a reputation for being innovators at Interski over the years, how rocker is going to make that happen was a perfect message to come from us."

THE FUTURE STARTS NOW

The idea of American ski and snowboard instruction has always been built on the vast diversity of the United States. From the family-owned community hills with rope tows and hot chocolate to the proud powdered mountains with tram and gondola access, just as many young kids as retirees, as many mothers as fathers, and as many injured veterans just home from overseas as able-bodied civilians wanted nothing more than to move through that wintry world, skimming across the snow as if they had wings beneath their feet.

For half a century, through generations and presidential administrations, fashion trends, and music and hairstyle changes, PSIA-AASI has continued to celebrate that diversity, happily awaiting the opportunity to share with anyone and everyone its passion for the sport. If there is a past-is-present moment in 2011, it is the emergence of yet one more glorious on-snow renaissance brought on by the new technology available to skiers and snowboarders combined with the potential number of new riders in the United States.

Record or near-record snowfall across much of the country saw skiers and snowboarders swarming to ski areas in 2011, while the next new wave of riders was filling up children's ski school classes. Generations Y and Z, also known as millennials and the net generation, respectively—estimated at between 70 million and 100 million strong—are beginning to make their on-snow presence felt. What's more, their parents and grandparents are joining them on the slopes. Despite the recession

Tele-rocker

With its exaggerated lead change and steady rhythm of turns, telemark has always looked like an elaborate dance step. Involving every part of the body, telemarkers can ride up to 300 centimeters of effective edge at each turn's depth. As far as turning is concerned—especially in deep powder—telemark also has the greatest likelihood of falling apart. That is why when telemarkers are skiing deep snow, they typically try to balance the back leg enough to keep from flipping over the handlebars should the front leg sink. Not anymore, PSIA Nordic Team member Ross Matlock said, precisely because of rocker's forgiving tip. "Telemark skiers can go on the offensive in powder now," he said. "They ski powder now just like they ski anywhere else."

PSIA Alpine Team Coach Rob Sogard (foreground) and PSIA Alpine Team member David Oliver introduce themselves to one of the Austrian students in their Interski ski school class.

(Photo by Cesar Piotto)

that still gripped the United States in 2011, the U.S. snowsports industry enjoyed record ski and snowboard sales, while American mountains recorded their best season ever in terms of skier or rider visits.

Welcoming them all to winter were more professional ski and snowboard instructors across the United States than ever before as well, with nearly 32,000 PSIA-AASI members in 2011 compared to nearly 20,000 in 1991. "There are four to five generations on snow right now," Mark Dorsey said in his keynote lecture at Interski 2011, noting not only how the diversity of the potential ski and snowboard student population continued to expand but also how seamlessly the sport's future was being inspired by its past.

The Austrian hosts of Interski had also identified connecting the various generations on snow as a priority of the 2011 instructor's congress. Every day they ran a kind of volunteer ski school, bringing up kids on the trains from all over Austria to ski

PSIA Alpine Team member Nick Herrin stops for a photo with his class of fast-skiing Austrian girls.

(Photo by Cesar Piotto)

The skiers of tomorrow are on the snow right now, building the future for another 50 years of snowsports instruction.

(Photo by Sherri Harkin)

with instructors from around the planet. Lunch and the lift tickets were paid for, and for at least a day, each country sent someone from its team to ski with a class. The only team that continued to send instructors every single day was the United States.

Nick Herrin, a member of the PSIA Alpine Team from Crested Butte, Colorado, who served as a volunteer instructor, was happily surprised to be paired with a group of teenage girls who could speed across the snow like descending hawks. After tiring

PSIA Alpine Team member David Oliver takes his class of young skiers into the powder.

(Photo by Cesar Piotto)

of trying to chase them down the groomed runs, he took them into the steep powder bowls to try and wear them out. After a second such run, he was asked on the chair why, at Interski of all places, when he could have only spent his time talking to other instructors, he had wanted to take out a class.

Amiable and energetic, with a smile that spread all the way across his face, Herrin laughed. The better question, he said, would be why wouldn't he? It was what he loved. "Writers write. Painters paint. And teachers teach," he said. "When I heard Interski was hosting a kid's ski school, I couldn't wait to sign up."

He talked about the history of ski and snowboard instruction, and how many people he kept meeting who inspired him with what they had contributed to the sport. Pioneers, mentors, and renegades, they had built a strong foundation in the past, and the most appropriate gesture he could make was to keep paying that culture of connection forward, and try to inspire someone else.

At the top the girls were all ready to rock. They were going back to the groomed run, they declared with their Austrian accents. While Herrin, standing there for a moment, was asked what, after 50 years of innovation, might the next 50 years hold for PSIA-AASI. What did he think—was it rocker, all the new kids hitting the snow, freestyle, or the session lessons—would impact the future the most?

"All of it," he laughed. "It's already happening. You say the future, but we're already living it."

Then "Hey!" Herrin called to the girls, who had stopped to wait below, and he went skiing after them, all of them speeding away together then, soaring down the mountain with the wind in their faces and their arms outstretched.

EPILOGUE

A MOUNTAIN FULL OF STOKE

I n April 2011, the Professional Ski Instructors of America and the American Association of Snowboard Instructors held a fiftieth anniversary party in Snowmass, Colorado, to celebrate what had begun on the fateful day in May 1961 in Whitefish. Hundreds of instructors came from across the country to celebrate, from Alaska, Minnesota, California, New York, Colorado, Oregon, Arizona, Maine, and every other state with ski trails, snow, and chairlifts. Fifty-year members and instructors who had only been teaching skiing or snow-boarding for a few years alike all wanted to honor their history and begin to define where the sport was going next.

PSIA-AASI Executive Director and CEO Mark Dorsey at the PSIA-AASI 50/50 Celebration with instruction legends Gwen and Ray Allard. Ray served two terms as the PSIA-AASI President and Chairman of the Board, and Gwen is a former PSIA Executive Director and founder of the Adaptive Sports Foundation.

(Photo by Patrick Brigg)

Frederica "Freddie" Anderson was there, the grand dame of East Coast skiing, as were Dee Byrne, Carol Levine, and Ellen Post Foster, those three hard-skiing athletes who keep pushing the importance of women on snow to the forefront. There were Max and Dave Lundberg standing side by side, with their arms over each other's shoulders as they talked, and Mike Porter, Dave Merriam, John Armstrong, and Michael Rogan all standing outside at the end of the day, watching the sunset as the

The timeless Frederica "Freddie" Anderson.

(Photo by Dann Coffey)

alpenglow flooded the deck. Bill Lash was sitting for insight-filled interviews, while Doug Pfeiffer appeared like a man just down from the mountains, his face like a folded trail map and a silver ponytail flowing down his back. There were Tony Forrest, Lee Perry, Bud Keene, Randy Price, and dozens of young instructors from across the country who were raring to do their part in defining the next step.

Every night they stayed up until the stars got sleepy, making plans for the future and toasting the past. But early every morning they were on the chairlifts, skiing and riding just as hard and happy as they could, as weightless as birds on the wind.

In giving the keynote address, Bud Keene told the crowd that what he learned as a member of PSIA-AASI directly contributed to his Olympic coaching success. "It was the same tools and philosophy that I learned from PSIA that helped put an athlete on the top of the Olympic podium," Keene said. "So thanks for that."

But it was Curt Chase who summarized all of the excitement, pride, and passion that was at the heart of that week. In accepting his PSIA-AASI Lifetime Achievement Award—which honored not only his role as one of the co-founders of the Professional Ski Instructors of America but also his 80 years in snowsports—Chase told the more than 500 people in attendance, "When I grow up, I want to be a ski instructor!"

He received a standing ovation in response. There were cheers, and there were tears. And for everyone in the room, there was the happy conviction that there could never be a better job in the entire world than to teach people how to ski and snowboard. There was the sense that even after half a century of breakthroughs, every instructor in the room couldn't wait for the next 50 years to start.

There was plenty of time at PSIA-AASI's 50/50 Celebration for catching up with old friends and hitting the slopes.

(Photo by Cesar Piotto)

Appendix

PSIA-AASI Presidents
(Title was changed to Chairman of the Board in 2010)

1961–1968	Bill Lash	Intermountain
1968–1969	Willy Schaeffler	Rocky Mountain
1969–1971	Jimmy Johnston	Central
1971–1973	Jerry Muth	Rocky Mountain
1973–1975	Jim Riley	Rocky Mountain
1975–1976	Keith Lange	Intermountain
1976–1978	Werner Schuster	Western
1978–1979	Loren Prescott	Northwest
1979–1981	Otto Hollaus	Central
1981–1982	Einar Aas	Eastern
1982–1983	Norm Burton	Intermountain
1983–1987	Randy Short	Western
1987–1994	Bill Hetrick	Eastern
1994–2000	Mark Anderson	Central
2000–2006	John Armstrong	Western
2006–2010	Ray Allard	Eastern
2010–	Eric Sheckleton	Northern Rocky Mountain

PSIA-AASI Board Members

1971–1978	Jim Sandberg	Alaska
1979–1984	Laural Peterson	Alaska
1984–1988	Betty Emerick	Alaska
1989–1998	Bruce McCurtain	Alaska
1998–	Bill Ellis	Alaska
1961–1971	Jimmy Johnston	Central
1971–1979	Otto Hollaus	Central
1979–1980	Victor Chigas	Central
1980–1994	Mark Anderson	Central
1994–	John Peppler	Central
1961–1969	Paul Valar	Eastern
1963–1973	Herbert Schneider	Eastern
1970–1973	Jon Putnam	Eastern
1973–1976	Kerr Sparks	Eastern
1976–1979	Charlie Rockwell	Eastern
1979–1981	Einar Aas	Eastern
1981–1987	Bill Hetrick	Eastern
1987–1991	Einar Aas	Eastern
1991–1997	Sherman White	Eastern
1997–2006	Ray Allard	Eastern
2006–	Bill Beerman	Eastern

1969	Lou Lorenz	Intermountain
1970–1972	Clark Parkinson	Intermountain
1972–1977	Keith Lange	Intermountain
1977	Ed Pond	Intermountain
1977–1979	Robin Clark	Intermountain
1979–1982	Norm Burton	Intermountain
1982–1983	Duane Vigos	Intermountain
1983–1987	Doug Harmon	Intermountain
1987–1993	Gene Palmer	Intermountain
1993–1994	Craig Pearson	Intermountain
1994–2000	Stewart Marsh	Intermountain
2000–2009	Jerry Warren	Intermountain
2009–2011	Carl Boyer	Intermountain
2011–	Kent Lundell	Intermountain
1979–1980	Carl Wilgus	Northern Intermountain
1980–1983	John Michael Brassey	Northern Intermountain
1983–1987	Jack Colvin	Northern Intermountain
1987–2001	Harold Stanger	Northern Intermountain
2001–2006	Martin Rood	Northern Intermountain
2006–	Walt Coiner	Northern Intermountain

PSIA-AASI Board Members

Through 1976	Royal Johnson	Northern Rocky Mountain		1974–1975	Bob Dorf	Rocky Mountain
1976–1982	Bud Ridenour	Northern Rocky Mountain		1975–1979	Pam Ammons	Rocky Mountain
1982–1988	Jerry Hinman	Northern Rocky Mountain		1979–1982	Bob Dorf	Rocky Mountain
1988–1989	Jean Mills	Northern Rocky Mountain		1982–1988	Ruth McClelland	Rocky Mountain
1989–2002	Joan Rostad	Northern Rocky Mountain		1988–1991	Jim Isham	Rocky Mountain
2002–2010	Eric Sheckleton	Northern Rocky Mountain		1991–1998	Ruth McClelland	Rocky Mountain
2010–	Eliza Kuntz	Northern Rocky Mountain		1998–2003	Tom Long	Rocky Mountain
				2003–2006	Jeff Patterson	Rocky Mountain
1971–1974	Bill Lenihan	Northwest		2006–	Peter Donahue	Rocky Mountain
1974–1977	Loren Prescott	Northwest				
1977–1982	Mike Brassey	Northwest		1961–1967	Doug Pfeiffer	Western
1982–1983	Lenore Lyle	Northwest		1967–1971	Nic Fiore	Western
1983–1990	Lou Lenihan	Northwest		1971–1973	Dick Kun	Western
1990–1993	Tim Koger	Northwest		1974–1980	Phil Kerridge	Western
1993–2002	Kathy Hand	Northwest		1981–1984	Randy Short	Western
2002–2008	John Weston	Northwest		1984–1990	Stu Campbell	Western
2008–	Ed Younglove	Northwest		1990–2000	John Armstrong	Western
				2000–2002	Mike Iman	Western
1965–1967	Curt Chase	Rocky Mountain		2002–2010	Craig Albright	Western
1967–1968	Charles Patterson	Rocky Mountain		2010–	Neil Bussiere	Western
1968–1969	Hank Emery	Rocky Mountain				
1969–1970	Jim Riley	Rocky Mountain				
1970–1972	Jerry Muth	Rocky Mountain				
1972–1974	Jim Riley	Rocky Mountain				

PSIA-AASI TEAM ROSTER

2008–2012

Scott Anfang	Rocky Mountain		David Lyon	Northwest
Robin Barnes	Western		Charlie MacArthur	Rocky Mountain
Bill Bowness	Western		Tom Marshall	Northern Rocky Mountain
Jeb Boyd	Eastern		Ross Matlock	Rocky Mountain
Matt Boyd	Eastern		Scott McGee	Intermountain
Lane Clegg	Intermountain		Tommy Morsch	Eastern
Gregg Davis	Rocky Mountain		Bobby Murphy	Rocky Mountain
Katie (Fry) Ertl	Rocky Mountain		David Oliver	Rocky Mountain
Mike Hafer	Western		Doug Pierini	Western
Nicholas Herrin	Rocky Mountain		Michael Rogan	Eastern
Geoff Krill	Eastern		Eric Rolls	Intermountain
David Lawrence	Northwest		Jim Schanzenbaker	Rocky Mountain
Eric Lipton	Eastern		Jennifer Simpson	Central
Dave Lundberg	Intermountain		Rob Sogard	Intermountain
Dave Lynch	Eastern		Josh Spoelstra	Western

PSIA-AASI TEAM ROSTER

2004–2008

Scott Anfang	Rocky Mountain		Megan Harvey	Rocky Mountain
Deb Armstrong	Rocky Mountain		Nicholas Herrin	Rocky Mountain
Bill Bowness	Western		Chris Kastner	Northwest
Jeb Boyd	Eastern		David Lyon	Northwest
Tor Brown	Western		Ross Matlock	Rocky Mountain
Dan Clausen	Central		Scott McGee	Intermountain
Andy Docken	Rocky Mountain		Bobby Murphy	Rocky Mountain
Mark "Spike" Eisenman	Rocky Mountain		Craig Panarisi	Intermountain
Kurt Fehrenbach	Rocky Mountain		Butch Peterson	Rocky Mountain
Chris Fellows	Western		Doug Pierini	Western
Mikey Franco	Intermountain		Randy Price	Rocky Mountain
Chad Frost	Northwest		Michael Rogan	Eastern
Katie Fry	Rocky Mountain		Rob Sogard	Intermountain
KC Gandee	Eastern		Nelson Wingard	Rocky Mountain

PSIA-AASI TEAM ROSTER

2000–2004

Rob Baker	Rocky Mountain		Scott McGee	Intermountain
Terry Barbour	Eastern		Dave Merriam	Eastern
Shaun Cattanach	Eastern		Kevin Mitchell	Western
Dan Clausen	Central		Craig Panarisi	Intermountain
Gregg Davis	Rocky Mountain		Doug Pierini	Western
Chris Fellows	Western		Randy Price	Rocky Mountain
Mikey Franco	Intermountain		Michael Rogan	Eastern
Urmas Franosch	Western		Earl Saline	Northwest
Chad Frost	Northwest		Jim Schanzenbaker	Rocky Mountain
Katie Fry	Rocky Mountain		Jill Sickels Matlock	Rocky Mountain
Megan Harvey	Rocky Mountain		Shawn Smith	Northwest
Steve Hindman	Northwest		Rob Sogard	Intermountain
Chris Kastner	Northwest		Carl Underkoffler	Western
James Ludlow	Intermountain		Sean Warman	Western
David Lyon	Northwest		Deb Willits	Rocky Mountain
Charlie MacArthur	Rocky Mountain			

PSIA-AASI TEAM ROSTER

1996–2000

Deb (Ackerman) Willits	Rocky Mountain		Scott Mathers	Intermountain
Terry Barbour	Eastern		Belenda Melschmidt	Alaska
Bob Barnes	Rocky Mountain		Dave Merriam	Eastern
Bill Batt	Intermountain		Jim Morocco	Western
Irv Bier	Northern Intermountain		Grant Nakamura	Central
Mermer Blakeslee	Eastern		Craig Panarisi	Intermountain
Rich Caballero	Northern Intermountain		Randy Price	Rocky Mountain
Dan Clausen	Central		Michael Rogan	Eastern
Alison Clayton	Eastern		Marie Russell-Shaw	Northern Rocky Mountain
Lane Clegg	Intermountain		Mike Shaw	Northern Rocky Mountain
Herb Davis	Northern Rocky Mountain		Eric Sheckleton	Northern Rocky Mountain
Jay Evans	Rocky Mountain		Shawn Smith	Rocky Mountain
Urmas Franosch	Western		Rob Sogard	Intermountain
Brad Gamblin	Alaska		Steve Sorensen	Alaska
Victor Gerdin	Rocky Mountain		Brian Spear	Eastern
Megan Harvey	Rocky Mountain		Mark Spieler	Western
Katie Harvey-Fry	Rocky Mountain		Mickey Stone	Eastern
Steve Hindman	Northwest		Travis Thelan	Northern Intermountain
David Holdcraft	Rocky Mountain		John Tickner	Northwest
Brian Maguire	Intermountain		Carl Underkoffler	Western
Dave Mannetter	Western		Amy Zahm	Northwest
Scottie Marion	Alaska		Mario Zlataric	Central

PSIA DEMONSTRATION TEAM ROSTER

1992–1996

Deb Ackerman	Rocky Mountain		Dave Mannetter	Western
John Alderson	Rocky Mountain		Scott Mathers	Intermountain
Bob Barnes	Rocky Mountain		Jane Mauser	Northwest
Bill Batt	Intermountain		Dave Merriam	Eastern
Dee Byrne	Rocky Mountain		Jim Middleton	Rocky Mountain
Rich Caballero	Northern Intermountain		Greg Moss	Northern Intermountain
David Chapman	Central		Paul Naschak	Rocky Mountain
Dan Clausen	Central		Nancy Oakes	Central
Alison Clayton	Eastern		Craig Panarisi	Intermountain
Herb Davis	Northern Rocky Mountain		Mark Pearson	Western
Scott Erickson	Northwest		Paul Peterson	Western
Jay Evans	Rocky Mountain		Mike Porter	Rocky Mountain
Mark Farmer	Eastern		Marie Russell-Shaw	Northern Rocky Mountain
Tony Forrest	Rocky Mountain		Bruce Sato	Northern Intermountain
Kerri Hannon	Rocky Mountain		Mike Shaw	Northern Rocky Mountain
Harald Harb	Rocky Mountain		Shawn Smith	Rocky Mountain
Lowell Hart	Rocky Mountain		Alexandra Smith Boucher	Western
Steve Hindman	Northwest		Mariam Sodergren	Western
David Holdcraft	Rocky Mountain		Steve Sorensen	Alaska
Chris Katzenberger	Intermountain		Mickey Stone	Eastern
Brian Maguire	Intermountain		Tom Tuttle	Western

PSIA DEMONSTRATION TEAM ROSTER

1988–1992

Dave Alden	Rocky Mountain	Dave Merriam	Eastern
Jerry Berg	Rocky Mountain	Kurt Meyer	Eastern
Dave Berman	Western	Paul Naschak	Rocky Mountain
JP Chevalier	Rocky Mountain	Craig Panarisi	Intermountain
Herb Davis	Northern Rocky Mountain	Mark Pearson	Western
Brian Dunfey	Rocky Mountain	Paul Peterson	Western
Jay Evans	Rocky Mountain	Mike Porter	Rocky Mountain
Jay Farmer	Eastern	Gary Posekian	Western
Tony Forrest	Rocky Mountain	Suzanne Rueck	Eastern
Victor Gerdin	Rocky Mountain	Chris Ryman	Rocky Mountain
Diana Golden	Independent	Jim Seachrist	Rocky Mountain
Jeff Grell	Western	Ray Sforzo	Rocky Mountain
Kerri Hannon	Rocky Mountain	Barry Smith	Rocky Mountain
Lowell Hart	Eastern	Shawn Smith	Rocky Mountain
Paul "PJ" Jones	Intermountain	Kent Stevens	Western
Dave Mannetter	Western	Whitney Thurlow	Northern Rocky Mountain
Scott Mathers	Intermountain	Tom Tuttle	Western
Jane Mauser	Intermountain	Jerry Warren	Intermountain
Dave McCormick	Intermountain		

PSIA DEMONSTRATION TEAM ROSTER

1984–1988

Dee Byrne	Northwest		Mark Pearson	Western
Walt Chauner	Northwest		Paul Peterson	Western
Ken Emerick	Rocky Mountain		Tim Petrick	Eastern
Nancy Fiddler	Western		Mike Porter	Rocky Mountain
Tony Forrest	Rocky Mountain		Don Portman	Northwest
Victor Gerdin	Rocky Mountain		Ellen Post Foster	Rocky Mountain
Bill Hall	Rocky Mountain		Chris Ryman	Rocky Mountain
Wayne Hansen	Northern Rocky Mountain		Shawn Smith	Eastern
Paul "PJ" Jones	Intermountain		Kent Stevens	Western
Carol Levine	Intermountain		John Tidd	Eastern
Dave Merriam	Eastern		Jerry Warren	Intermountain
Paul Parker	Rocky Mountain			

PSIA DEMONSTRATION TEAM ROSTER

1980–1984

John Boles	Rocky Mountain
Walt Chauner	Rocky Mountain
Amund Ekroll	Rocky Mountain
Ken Emerick	Rocky Mountain
Tony Forrest	Intermountain
Bill Hall	Rocky Mountain
Wayne Hansen	Northern Rocky Mountain
Jens Husted	Rocky Mountain
Dave Ingram	Rocky Mountain
Paul "PJ" Jones	Intermountain
Carol Levine	Northern Intermountain
Paul Parker	Rocky Mountain

Mark Pearson	Western
Tim Petrick	Eastern
Mike Porter	Rocky Mountain
Don Portman	Northwest
Ellen Post Foster	Rocky Mountain
Tim Ray	Northwest
Chris Ryman	Rocky Mountain
Shawn Smith	Eastern
John Tidd	Eastern
Joe Waggoner	Intermountain
Jerry Warren	Intermountain

PSIA DEMONSTRATION TEAM ROSTERS

1976–1980

Bruce Bowlin	Rocky Mountain
Michael Hickey	Eastern
Jens Husted	Rocky Mountain
Paul "PJ" Jones	Northern Rocky Mountain
Tim Petrick	Eastern

Mike Porter	Western
Chris Ryman	Rocky Mountain
Shawn Smith	Eastern
Jerry Warren	Intermountain

1975 Interski Team (Strbske Pleso, Czechoslovakia)

Bruce Bowlin	Rocky Mountain
Steve Bratt	Northwest
Gene Christiansen	Intermountain
Bill Duddy	Rocky Mountain
Jim Hinman	Eastern
Jens Husted	Rocky Mountain
Paul "PJ" Jones	Northern Rocky Mountain

David "Scooter" LaCouter	Rocky Mountain
Max Lundberg	Intermountain
Mike Porter	Western
Chris Ryman	Northwest
Jerry Warren	Intermountain
Weems Westfeldt*	Rocky Mountain

*selected – did not attend

PSIA DEMONSTRATION TEAM ROSTERS

1971 Interski Team (Garmisch-Partenkirchen, Germany)

Gene Christiansen	Intermountain	David "Scooter" LaCouter	Rocky Mountain
William Duddy	Rocky Mountain	Max Lundberg	Intermountain
Rene Farwig	Intermountain	Lyle Twedt	Northwest
Jim Hinman	Eastern		

1968 Interski Team (Aspen, Colorado)

Curt Chase	Rocky Mountain	Steve Morrow	Eastern
John Deschermeier		Ken Oakes	Rocky Mountain
William Duddy	Rocky Mountain	Bonnie Pond	Intermountain
Elizabeth Glenn		Dennie Raedeke	Central
Joan Hanna		Lavelle Saier	Rocky Mountain
George Ingham	Western	Steve Sherlock	
Craig Jacobie		William Sim	Western
Phil Jones	Intermountain	Carolyn Teeple	
David "Scooter" LaCouter	Rocky Mountain	Lyle Twedt	Northwest
Robert Locke		Al Voltz	Northwest
Max Lundberg	Intermountain	Elizabeth Voltz	Northwest
Robert MacDermott		Jean Weiss	Intermountain

PSIA DEMONSTRATION TEAM ROSTERS

1965 Interski Team (Bad Gastein, Austria)

Barry Bryant	Steve Marrow*
Curt Chase*	Toby von Euw
Phil Jones	Eric Windisch
Bill Lash	Glen Young

1962 Interski Team (Monte Bondone, Italy)

Rink Earl	Arthur Thorner
Sigge Engle	Paul Valar
Kerr Sparks	

*alternate

About the Author

Peter Kray is an award-winning writer, editor, and author who makes his home in Santa Fe, New Mexico. He is the special projects editor for *32 Degrees: The Journal of Professional Snowsports Instruction*, managing editor of the *SIA Snow Show Dailies*, and editor-at-large of the *Mountain Gazette*. Kray's feature writing has been honored by the Associated Press, while his editorial work has been recognized by Forbes.com and *Outside Magazine*. The Ski Channel named him one of the Most Influential People in the Snowbiz. He is also the founder of Shred White & Blue, a media and apparel company celebrating American boardsports.

Index

Performance Plants

Performance Plants

CREATING A GARDEN WITH YEAR-ROUND BEAUTY

Andrew Lawson

PENGUIN BOOKS

For Rosemary Verey, who opened my eyes to so many things

HALF TITLE PAGE
Allium christophii in summer

TITLE PAGE
An apple tree in midsummer has been brought to life by an under-planting of self-seeding blue *Campanula persicifolia* and by sprays of the rambler rose 'Paul's Himalayan Musk', trained into the tree.

LEFT
Lunaria annua 'Alba Variegata' earns its place in the spring with a show of flowers that coincides with late tulips. In autumn it extends armfuls of coin-shaped seedpods that glow silver in the low winter light, adding a touch of brilliance to the garden through the darkest months of the year.

PENGUIN BOOKS
Published by the Penguin Group
Viking Penguin, a division of Penguin Books USA Inc.,
375 Hudson Street, New York, New York 10014, U.S.A.
Penguin Books Ltd, 27 Wrights Lane, London W8 5TZ, England
Penguin Books Australia Ltd, Ringwood, Victoria, Australia
Penguin Books Canada Ltd, 10 Alcorn Avenue, Toronto, Ontario, Canada M4V 3B2
Penguin Books (N.Z.) Ltd, 182-190 Wairau Road, Auckland 10, New Zealand

Penguin Books Ltd, Registered Offices:
Harmondsworth, Middlesex, England

First published in Great Britain by Frances Lincoln Limited 1992
First published in the United States of America in simultaneous hardcover and paperback editions by Viking Penguin,
a division of Penguin Books USA Inc. 1993

1 3 5 7 9 10 8 6 4 2

Conceived, edited and designed by Frances Lincoln Limited, Apollo Works, 5 Charlton Kings Road, London NW5 2SB

ISBN 0-14-01.7375-7 CIP data available

Printed in Great Britain

Set in 11/13pt Perpetua

CONTENTS

CHOOSING PLANTS FOR A LASTING DISPLAY

Space is at a premium in most gardens. There are many gardeners who would like to grow more plants than their gardens can accommodate, and most of us would also like to extend the season in which our gardens look good. One of the best ways to get the most out of limited space is to grow plants that perform at least twice in the year. Among these will be a few that earn their keep year-round.

Unfortunately, some of the most spectacular garden plants have only a single season of display. A tree or shrub that produces blossom for just one glorious week in spring might give you intense pleasure for that short time – but you will be lucky if it does not rain that week, and of course you must not take a vacation or you will miss it altogether. For the rest of the year the plant will be a passenger in your garden. In this category of short-season plants I would put shrubs like forsythia and some – but not all – of the flowering cherries.

You will get better value from your garden if, for the majority of your plantings, you select plants that have a dual purpose and, better still, some that look attractive all through the year. You can find trees (including flowering cherries) that have magnificent fall color in addition to the more ephemeral show of blossom in the spring. Some produce eye-catching fruits that follow a good display of flowers. Others have colorful bark that is of interest all year but particularly in winter, when their principal attraction, the foliage, is absent.

Among the tens of thousands of shrubs and perennials available, some of the most valuable are those that flower more or less continuously across the seasons. They include the perennial wallflower *Erysimum* 'Bowles' Mauve', which is colorful for

Dominating a border in late spring, *Euphorbia characias* ssp. *wulfenii* makes a good companion for tulips, cowslips, forget-me-nots, and the golden young foliage of *Spiraea japonica* 'Goldflame'. A few weeks later, when this spring flush is over, the euphorbia flowers will still be in action to accompany the purple-flowered *Geranium* × *magnificum* growing around its base, and the blue *Geranium* 'Johnson's Blue' beside the spiraea. The euphorbia is useful not only on account of its long flowering season, but also for the unostentatious lime-green color of its flowers, which look good in association with almost any other color.

much of the year. Others can be found among the roses: 'Iceberg', for instance, has its first flush of bloom in midsummer and may still be in action in early winter.

Winter is a testing time for the gardener. Admittedly it may be a season when you do not often want to putter around outside, but even the view out of a window will be bleak indeed if there is nothing of interest in the garden. Many plants have second strings to their bow for winter color and form. Fruits and berries and colorful bark and stems are obvious examples, but you should also be aware of the possibilities of seed heads, dried flowers, and even the dead foliage of plants like grasses. If you have ever seen the lovely effect of frost on clumps of the tall grass *Miscanthus sinensis*, then you will resist the temptation to be overzealous when tidying up the garden in the fall. Plants that die gracefully are a great asset and will populate your winter garden with companionable ghosts. And there is always plenty of bounty to spare for the indoor winter flower arrangement, which can be a *compôte* of dried fruits and seed heads, leaves, and colored stems in addition to the traditional everlasting flowers.

RIGHT The tall grass *Miscanthus sinensis* 'Strictus' makes an effective backdrop for a clump of the fall-flowering daisy *Aster amellus* 'King George'. Within two months (OPPOSITE LEFT) winter has reduced both perennials to whispering skeletons. The plants are dead above ground level and could have been cleared in a late-fall purge of the borders, but it is a much better idea to let them decline in their own time. Dead foliage and seed heads give your borders an extra season of interest. In cold weather the plant skeletons provide a framework on which the frost builds a filigree of silver and white. There is also a practical reason for leaving the clearing of borders to the early spring: dead foliage acts as a blanket, and gives the growth some protection from the worst of the cold weather.

ABOVE A border ablaze in fall with *Cotinus* 'Flame'. This specimen has remained unpruned for several years, and has reached the size of a small tree. If it had been regularly pruned the fall color would be even more spectacular, as the young wood of cotinus bears larger leaves. However, there is a down side to pruning, as it prevents the plant from flowering. Unpruned, this cotinus flowers copiously in summer, with the fluffy flower heads that give the shrub its name of "smoke bush."

The evergreen background

Winter is a test too for the design of your garden. Walls, paths, steps, and other structural features such as pergolas and arbors take on a new prominence when stripped of their cosmetic decoration of flowers and foliage. This is where the evergreen plants come into their own. A few well-shaped evergreens at strategic points in the garden will keep the show going through the long, difficult months. A framework of sheared evergreen hedges and screens draws graphic patterns in the winter garden, especially when it is dusted with an overlay of snow and viewed from the comfort of the house.

As a rule, the evergreens tend to be slow-growing and long-lived and so they are ideal for providing the living backbone of the garden. Although many – mahonia and holly, for instance – have brittle leaves, giving a hard overall texture, there are a few, like *Kalmia latifolia*, that have soft and shapely foliage. The conifers are a natural choice to provide some evergreen interest in the garden, though as most of them change so little over the year they seem somewhat lifeless compared with the majority of garden plants, which respond so interestingly to the seasons. It is as well to mix them with foliage plants of a softer texture to relieve their rigid effect.

"Evergreen" is hardly the right word for plants with winter foliage that is colorful but far from green. I am thinking, for instance, of that invaluable plant for hedges, the beech, which has leaves that go russet in fall and remain on the hedge until they are pushed off by the fresh new growth of spring. And in some of the variegated "evergreens" – the hollies and ivies among them – patterns of white, cream, or yellow decorate the green background of the leaves and in some cases almost obliterate it altogether. Bright-toned foliage of this kind can be a welcome relief from the worthy but sometimes dull dark leaves of the true evergreens.

The evergreen framework of this garden ensures that it remains interesting year-round. The pair of stepped boxwood hedges will look much the same through the seasons, as will the yew structures – hedges topped with topiary and obelisks with square bases. Creating an evergreen structure of this quality demands up to ten years of hard work and patience, but the reward is a consistent effect that should last for many decades if the evergreens are properly maintained.

Plants that spread and seed themselves

Annuals and biennials will perform for you in a different way. Although they have a relatively short life – and certainly the individual flowers may be very short-lived – these plants will seed themselves with abandon, often appearing where you least expect them.

One of the sea hollies, *Eryngium giganteum*, is known charmingly as "Miss Willmott's ghost." The English gardener Ellen Ann Willmott (1858–1934) used to scatter seeds of this plant in every garden she visited. The plant soon established itself in these gardens by seeding itself in subsequent years. The descendants of Miss Willmott's seeds survive still in many a garden – her ghost lives on.

It is said that you can judge the age of a wild hedgerow by counting the number of species of tree that have taken root there. Rather the same sort of rule applies to gardens. You can judge the maturity of a garden by the number of plants that have arrived more or less by chance, and have been allowed to remain. Stray plants, seeding themselves in cracks in a stone terrace or in crevices in a wall, bring mellowness to a garden, softening the hard edges of the design, and filling out the bare areas that inevitably appear as the seasons draw on.

The distinction between uninvited weeds and welcome self-seeders is a fine one. A self-seeding plant in the wrong place becomes a weed and should be rooted out. None of them are difficult to remove, although many are so prolific that they have to be taken out in large numbers to prevent them from overrunning the garden. The virtue of these plants is that they are expendable. And their cultivation is the easiest form of gardening, because it is passive. You do nothing to encourage self-seeders to grow, but merely remove them when they are out of place.

Not many of the self-seeding plants will be stocked at your local nursery or garden center. Perennials like valerian and *Corydalis lutea* and biennials such as money plant and the Welsh poppy are often regarded as too common to be worth selling. They are not all available from seed catalogs either. Firms tend to specialize in plants that are difficult to grow, so that you have to keep coming back to them for more. Plants that go on for ever are, in marketing terms, like the everlasting light bulb – a product that is so successful it is bad for business. There is nothing else for it. You will have to cultivate a friendship with Ellen Willmott's descendants, and invite them to your garden.

LEFT The daisy *Erigeron karvinskianus* has found its way into this well-populated terrace by self-seeding among helianthemums and hellebores, artfully planted in gaps between the stones.

RIGHT A controlled plot of self-seeders. Spilling on to a gravel path, clumps of white and purple money plant (*Lunaria annua*) rise above a carpet of self-sown forget-me-nots (*Myosotis*), with the Welsh poppy (*Meconopsis cambrica*) providing a flash of contrasting yellow. Young wild daisy plants and self-seeded foxgloves (*Digitalis purpurea*) are poised to take over the scene a few weeks later.

Underplanting and ground cover

It can be helpful to think of a garden as composed of three distinct horizontal layers, although these layers are usually blurred by the intermingling of the plants. The top layer is composed of the trees. Most of them are perched on unbranched trunks, leaving room for the middle layer – of shrubs and perennials – to merge below. At the lowest level, creeping and ground-hugging plants can be used as ground cover to fill any remaining gaps between the plants – assuming, of course, that the gardener wants every scrap of the ground to be covered. Some gardeners like to look upon each plant as a specimen to be enjoyed in a degree of isolation from its neighbors. In this context ground-covering plants can be an interference. In my own garden, however, I regard any patch of bare ground as a failure on my part, at least in summer. Some gardeners, myself included, seem to be driven by a moral imperative to hide the ground and draw a skirt around the bases of shrubs, rather as our nineteenth-century ancestors covered the legs of pianos, which were otherwise considered naughty. In practice the selection of plants for this lowest layer can make a great contribution to the overall effect of the garden.

The feet of shrubs and trees are usually densely shaded and the best ground-cover plants need to be not only shade-lovers but also colored in such a way that they will shine out of the gloom. The variegated lamiums are ideal in this respect, with their silver-patterned foliage that sparkles with light. The variegated periwinkles are good for covering large areas under trees, but it is risky to use them among the

The horned violet, *Viola cornuta*, makes an effective underplanting for old-fashioned roses, such as the Portland rose 'Comte de Chambord' seen here. The viola flowers over a long period throughout the summer, and seeds itself to fill any areas of bare soil.

more delicate shrubs as they can become invasive and difficult to remove without disturbing the roots of the plants they surround.

Bulbs and corms make more ephemeral ground cover, but they can look wonderful in their season. *Cyclamen hederifolium* has a double performance, with a solo show of flowers in fall, followed by patterned leaves in winter and spring.

One way to enhance the performance of any plant is to place it in association with others that have complementary virtues. For instance, the lilac color of *Viola cornuta* harmonizes especially well with the pinks and mauves of old roses. And planting old-fashioned pinks under roses gives a rich cocktail of scents as well as a subtle harmony of color. Underplanting provides many opportunities for such associations. One of the highest achievements in the art of gardening is to plant a graduated border where the tallest plants, usually toward the back, are underplanted with slightly smaller plants, and so on toward the front, with each plant assisting to increase the impact of its neighbor. This art is perhaps at its most refined when the plants are selected to perform simultaneously in one single, harmonious chord. But it is equally valid when the arrangement is designed to extend the season, with the different plants reaching their peaks at different times.

Spring harmonies. The pink weeping cherry, *Prunus pendula* 'Pendula Rosea', is effectively underplanted with a mass of Dutch crocus in a range of colors from purple through lilac to white.

Making foliage flower

Another way to plant for performance, and to make the best use of limited space, is to mask one plant's weaknesses by putting it beside another with corresponding strengths. A perennial with striking flowers but dull leaves, for example, can be grown among foliage plants with modest flowers. The effect is of a single plant of double value. Hostas, for instance, are among the best of the foliage plants, but their striking flower spikes appear after the leaves have begun to look tired. You can achieve a virtuoso performance in spring by interplanting hostas with clumps of late tulips to give the illusion that the flowers are coming from the fresh green leaves of the hostas. Foxgloves interplanted with hostas or ferns give a similar effect later in the season. If you are really clever, you can achieve a progression of tulips first, then foxgloves, then the hosta flowers

ABOVE The orange flowers of *Crocosmia masoniorum* seem to suit *Hosta fortunei aureomarginata* better than its own lilac flowers.

LEFT Yellow lily-flowered tulips, planted among hostas, create the illusion that flowers and foliage belong to the same plant.

RIGHT The flame creeper, *Tropaeolum speciosum*, lights up the dark foliage of a topiary yew dome.

Clematis 'Rouge Cardinal' in *Rosa glauca*

A Viticella clematis, 'Venosa Violacea', in *Cornus alba* 'Elegantissima'

themselves – all appearing to emerge from the same clumps of foliage.

Many shrubs and trees that are grown for their spring or fall value can look dull at the height of summer. The flowering cherries, for instance, and the crab apples, may seem not to justify their space in the garden at the very time that the borders are at their glorious best. Growing climbing plants into such trees and shrubs cheats the passing of the months and brings interest to an otherwise dreary corner of the garden.

One group of flowering climbers is supreme above all others for adding a dash of color to a tree or shrub in its drabbest season of the year. This is, of course, clematis. There are different clematis available to flower in most months. And they come in an astonishing range of colors, shapes, and sizes. There are modest ground-hugging species that are best suited to the alpine trough or rockery. Others are so vigorous that they will cover the walls of a house within a few seasons. Clearly it is important to match your choice of clematis to the size and vigor of the host plant through which you plan to grow it. And the art of using clematis in this way is to match the flower with the foliage that it accompanies so that the two bring out the best in each other. The cleverest association of clematis that I have seen is the hybrid *C.* 'Rouge Cardinal' growing into the gray-leaved shrub *Rosa glauca*. This is a rose with modest flowers, but the clematis provides the flowers that the rose *ought* to have, of a color that perfectly echoes the pink-flushed foliage.

RIGHT Another purple-leaved shrub, *Prunus cerasifera* 'Pissardii', is almost invisible under a curtain of the vigorous climber *Clematis* 'Perle d'Azur'. Lavender and fuchsia fill the gap below the shrub, with a variegated apple mint adding sparkle and a touch of scent. Although it may appear that the clematis has swamped its host shrub, it is very unlikely that a clematis of this type will do any damage. *Clematis montana* could be a different matter, as it makes such a tangle of growth that it can cut out the light to its host.

LEFT A strong contrast. The white *Clematis* 'Miss Bateman' shines out brightly from its host plant, the dwarf maple *Acer palmatum* 'Dissectum Atropurpureum'. A clever feature of this planting is that the purple-brown stamens of the clematis match the color of the shrub's foliage.

The ornamental cabbage has earned a place in the flower border, where it offers color and form over a long season. Here, in a fall border, its purple tint combines well with hardy asters and annuals cosmos and echium. The annuals will be felled by the first hint of winter frosts, but the color of the cabbage will only intensify with colder weather. Ornamental cabbages can be used just as effectively in more formal arrangements. At the celebrated garden of the château of Villandry in France, cabbages are planted in formal rows so that they entirely fill shaped beds enclosed by low boxwood hedging. In this way they provide striking blocks that give the effect, at a distance, of a single color.

Ornamental herbs, fruits, and vegetables

Traditionally, fruits and vegetables have been relegated to a separate area, and, just as the kitchen was below stairs in the big house, so the kitchen garden was sometimes considered less important than the ornamental garden. Recently, however, more gardeners have discovered the ornamental value of herbs, fruits, and vegetables, often as a result of visits to the great *potagers* in gardens such as Villandry, in Touraine, and Barnsley House, in Gloucestershire. One of the attractions of the formal *potager* is the arrangement of plants in straight rows. Another feature is the construction of interesting supports for climbing fruits and vegetables – patterned arrangements of canes for beans, and trellis and pergolas for vines, gourds, and squash. But even when they are taken out of this formal structure, many vegetables are attractive plants in their own right. The ornamental cabbage, for instance, well deserves a place in the flower border.

Some of the common fruit trees are performance plants *par excellence*. An apple tree in blossom is one of the loveliest sights in springtime, and it performs again with a display of fruits that epitomizes fall. It would surely be grown as an ornamental tree even if the fruits were inedible. The decorative value of fruit trees can be enhanced by the shapes into which they are trained. Parallel rows of apples may be arched to make a tunnel. Trained as espaliers, apples and pears make effective divisions between one garden "room" and another. Espalier pears are suitable for growing against the walls of a house, where they make a feature that is every bit as attractive as the more conventional wisteria or Virginia creeper. You can extend the performance of apples and pears – as of other trees – by growing climbers into their branches, so that they are colorful with clematis or morning glory even at times when their own displays are subdued.

Performing in harmony

The pages that follow include a personal selection of plants that earn their place in the garden by their extended performance throughout the year. You may find that some of your favorites are absent. Everybody loves old-fashioned roses, for instance, and no garden, however small, would be complete without them, even though the majority flower only once in the year. A splash of spring color from tulips and narcissi is compulsory too. But these are not what I would call performance plants. They are more like prima donnas that take center stage for a spectacular but brief turn. Performance plants may be less ostentatious in their virtues, but a group of them will ensure a lasting display in the garden. Moreover – and this is the greatest test – you can arrange them so that they perform together in harmony, each one providing virtues complementary to those of its neighbors.

A pair of apple trees, trained on frameworks into goblet shapes in the *potager* of Barnsley House in Gloucestershire. Four main branches radiating from the stem have been trained vertically, with side shoots aligned horizontally to create a dense structure on which the blossoms, and ultimately the fruits, are closely spaced. The main branches are arched over to give a rounded top to these decorative trees.

TREES FOR ALL SEASONS

Trees are essential in any garden to raise foliage above ground level, giving a vertical element to the plant composition. Even the tiniest garden needs its complement of trees. They can even be grown in pots if necessary – it is surprising how well small trees will thrive in pots, provided that they are watered regularly.

The trees recommended here have been selected for features that they offer in addition to spring and summer foliage. Some have sensational blossom. Others have richly tinted leaves or colorful fruits in fall. Winter is the time when you come to appreciate not only the enduring contribution of the evergreens, but also the bare outlines of the deciduous trees. Where a tree's silhouette is enhanced by brilliant bark color, so much the better.

Trees are a sacred part of the landscape. Most gardeners love trees and will vigorously try to conserve them. This urge for conservation is right for the wild forests but it is not always appropriate in our gardens. So many gardens are ruined by trees that have grown too big for them. In my own garden it took me a year of vacillation before I could bring myself to remove an old yew tree which shaded the whole site and made gardening impossible. In the smallest gardens it may be necessary to replace trees quite often if it is not possible to keep them trimmed to size.

Gardening always involves a certain amount of artifice. Most plants, including trees, are amenable to a degree of manipulation. Topiary is the most extreme form, suitable for only a few trees, particularly yew. But many trees can be bent into shape to form arches or tunnels, trained as fans or espaliers against walls, or simply pruned to make mopheads. There are gardeners who regard such devices as an insult to nature. But if we wished to leave nature alone, we would not choose to make gardens.

A mature tree in its prime, this superb specimen of the dogwood *Cornus controversa* 'Variegata' is about twenty-five years old. Its early summer display of creamy white flowers coincides with the successful underplanting of *Gladiolus communis* ssp. *byzantinus*. Like many of the dogwoods, this cornus has reddish young branches and twigs that give added interest after leaf fall.

23

Acer griseum in winter

Acer griseum
PAPER-BARK MAPLE
Peeling red bark, good fall foliage

The maples are grown primarily for their brilliant fall foliage and this goes for the paper-bark maple too. But this tree has the additional virtue of spectacular bark, which ensures that it remains interesting year-round. The bark of *Acer griseum* is quite unlike that of any other maple. Curling strips of the cinnamon-red outer bark peel off to expose the slightly less highly colored young bark beneath. The bark peels continuously throughout the year, making the tree look rather like a red snake casting its skin.

Acer palmatum 'Osakazuki' in fall

Even without its special bark this tree would be worth growing for its foliage. The leaves are in three segments, with undulating margins. In spring the young leaves are a fresh pale green and they darken up as they mature. In fall they color to shades of fiery red.

The flowers and fruits of the maples are modest but attractive nonetheless. Loose panicles of reddish flowers hang down below the leaves in spring. They soon give rise to the double-winged seeds, commonly known as keys, which spin down in the wind when they mature.

• Height to 30ft/9m, spread to 25ft/7.5m. Full sun. Tolerant of any soil, but needs neutral to acidic soil for good fall color. Zones 5–8

OTHER ACERS TO GROW

Acer palmatum 'Osakazuki' This is one of the Japanese maples, and probably the best for fall color. Its leaves are broad, with up to seven pointed lobes, and they take on a vivid hue of pure red in fall, especially in neutral to acidic soil. Height and spread to 15ft/4.5m. Zones 6–8

Acer palmatum 'Senkaki' The coral-bark maple is another maple (also Japanese) with the double virtues of interesting bark and attractive foliage. The youngest twigs are a bright pinky red, which gives a stunning effect in winter. In fall the leaves turn to amber-yellow, which looks especially good with the red stems showing through. Again, neutral to acidic soil is needed for good fall color. Height and spread to 20ft/6m. Zones 6–8

Acer pensylvanicum The moosewood is a snakebark maple, with vertical stripes on its green bark that give the appearance of snakeskin. The bright green three-lobed leaves turn yellow in fall. Height

Acer palmatum 'Senkaki' in winter

20ft/6m, spread 12ft/3.5m. Other good snakebarks are *A. davidii* and *A. grosseri*, which grow to a height of 40ft/12m and a spread of 25ft/7.5m. Zones 3–7

Acer platanoides **'Drummondii'** Harlequin maple – a variety of the Norway maple – has midgreen leaves edged with white. From a distance they give a bright shimmering effect. Height to 50ft/15m, spread 35ft/10.5m. Zones 4–7

Acer pseudoplatanus **'Brilliantissimum'** A sycamore with shrimp-pink young growth in spring turning through lime-green to green in summer. Height and spread to 20ft/6m. Any soil, full sun. Zones 5–8

Acer pensylvanicum in fall

Acer griseum in fall

Amelanchier lamarckii
in spring

Amelanchier lamarckii

SNOWY MESPILUS

Abundant white spring blossom, brilliant red and
orange fall foliage

The quality of the blossom of any tree is decided as
much by the presence or absence of leaves as by the
flowers themselves. In the case of *Amelanchier
lamarckii* the blossom coincides with the first growth
of the young leaf shoots. These are the color of worn
copper and they impart metallic warmth to the
clouds of slender white flowers that cover the tree.

The spring blossom is followed in fall by small
black berries, but these are of little ornamental value
compared with the brilliance of the foliage, which
erupts into shades of bright red and orange.

● Height to 20ft/6m, spread 15ft/4.5m. Sun or part-
shade. Amelanchiers prefer a lime-free soil which,
for the best fall color, should be on the acidic side of
neutral. They may be grown either as shrubs or as
standard trees, according to the pruning regime.
Zones 4–8

OTHER AMELANCHIERS TO GROW

Amelanchier canadensis and **A. laevis** are also good amelanchiers, with attractive blossom and wonderful fall color. The different amelanchiers can be difficult to tell apart *A. canadensis* is best in zones 4–8, *A. laevis* in zones 5–7

Betula utilis jacquemontii

WEST HIMALAYAN BIRCH

Pure white bark, catkins in spring, yellow fall foliage

The birches are among the most graceful of trees. There are many striking species in the genus but *Betula utilis* var. *jacquemontii* is outstanding by virtue of its smooth and intensely white bark. This ensures that it is conspicuous in every season, but especially in winter. Then its whole framework is bare of leaves and it stands out like a sparkling white skeleton that has been picked clean by birds.

In common with all the birches, *B.u.* var. *jacquemontii* makes a graceful overall shape. It has delicate pointed oval leaves with serrated edges. These color attractively to yellow in fall, but the effect is very short-lived and for this reason the birches cannot be included among the most reliable trees for fall color. Their spring show, however, is more enduring, with the appearance of small catkins coinciding with the swelling and bursting open of the leaf buds.

• Height to 30ft/9m, spread 20ft/6m. Any soil. Tolerant of dry conditions. Although this birch makes a magnificent specimen tree, why not also consider planting several together in clumps? An odd number, say three or five trees, makes a natural-looking asymmetrical clump that might reasonably be considered three to five times more attractive than a single tree. Zones 5–7

OTHER BIRCHES TO GROW

Betula albosinensis A birch with pinky white stems. Height 30ft/9m, spread 20ft/6m. Zones 6–8

***Betula pendula* 'Laciniata'** (syn. 'Crispa') Sometimes wrongly called *B.p.* 'Dalecarlica'. An attractive form of the weeping birch, with finely cut leaves that enhance the drooping effect of the branches. Height 50ft/15m, spread 30ft/9m. Zones 3–7

***Betula pendula* 'Youngii'** An elegant weeping birch. Its branches make an arching dome over a stem of white, marked with vertical black cracks. Height only to 25ft/7.5m and spread to 30ft/9m at maturity. Zones 2–6

Betula albosinensis
catkins in spring

Betula utilis var. *jacquemontii*
bark in winter

A fall view of the *Cornus controversa* 'Variegata' that appears on page 22. The cream-variegated leaves have assumed a pinkish tinge. Soon they will fall and expose the red-barked younger branches which define the outlines of the distinctive tiered structure.

Cornus controversa 'Variegata'

Variegated leaves, dramatic summer flower display, red stems revealed in fall and winter

One of the most elegant trees available, *Cornus controversa* 'Variegata' has broadly sweeping horizontal branches that grow in tiers, tapering from a wide base near the ground to a point at the apex. The pyramidal shape alone would be enough to make this cornus a very special tree, but it has the additional attraction of cream-variegated leaves.

Furthermore, in summer the tiered branches are covered with a froth of white flowers, like creamy confections on a tablecloth. In fall the leaves turn slightly pink before dropping to reveal the red twigs that are characteristic of many of the dogwoods. The only thing that can be said against this marvelous tree is that it is extremely slow-growing.

With its horizontal thrust and bright foliage *C.c.* 'Variegata' looks especially good against a background of upright conifers which supply a contrast of both tone and shape.

Cornus kousa var. *chinensis* in summer

Cornus kousa var. *chinensis* in fall

Cornus mas flowers in winter

• This cornus eventually becomes a stately specimen 30ft/9m in height and spread. Does best in full sun and well-drained fertile soil, preferably neutral to acidic. Zones 5–8

OTHER CORNUS TO GROW

Cornus florida Flowering dogwood boasts white or pinkish white flower bracts and leaves that turn red in fall. There are several forms available, including *C. florida rubra*, which has flat midpink bracts. All do best in slightly acidic soils. Height to 18ft/5.5m, spread 20ft/6m. Zones 5–9

Cornus kousa* var. *chinensis Chinese or kousa dogwood in full flower in summer is a sensation. The branches are so densely crowded with pure white flower bracts that the effect is of broad white clouds filling the garden with light. The tree puts on a second performance in fall when the foliage colors up brilliantly and the flowers develop into hanging red fruits. The leaves are midgreen, turning to a flaming red before they fall. Height to 25ft/7.5m, spread to 20ft/6m. Zones 5–8

Cornus mas The cornelian cherry is an unostentatious tree, but attractive as one of the first harbingers of spring. It is covered with a haze of fragrant tiny yellow flowers on bare twigs while winter snows may still be on the ground. These develop into edible red fruits that look like cherries but are not so tasty. Height and spread to 20ft/6m. Zones 4–7

This beech hedge, here assuming its fall tints, makes a substantial boundary to a small enclosure within a much larger garden. When the hedge was planted, a space was left for a path to cross; as the adjacent trees grew, branches were trained across, tied together and pruned to make an arch. The beauty of a beech hedge is that it retains its leaves for most of the year – fresh lime-green in spring and brown in winter.

Fagus sylvatica

EUROPEAN BEECH

Soft lime-green young foliage, brown fall leaves remaining over winter

It is a curious phenomenon that the stately beech tree loses its leaves soon after they have colored up in fall, whereas the same plant, sheared and grown as a hedge, keeps its leaves throughout the winter. The beech tree becomes a winter skeleton but the beech hedge retains its splendid fall color of sienna brown until the dead leaves are finally pushed off by fresh new growth in spring. This retention of leaves is said to be a juvenile characteristic, but it can be induced in older trees by constant pruning.

Next to yew and boxwood, beech is perhaps the most useful hedging for creating screens and divisions and allées within the garden. Because of the relatively large size of its leaves, it is not suitable for low hedges, which would be better made from boxwood, *Buxus sempervirens.*

• To plant your hedge, place the young trees about 12in/30cm apart in a trench prepared with plenty of manure. Trim in fall, from the outset, to encourage bushy growth. Zones 5–7

ANOTHER BEECH TO GROW

Fagus sylvatica purpurea The copper beech is the favorite of many gardeners as a specimen tree, and it can equally well be the choice for a magnificent copper-colored hedge. It is even more effective to mix the two forms at random to produce a tapestry of overlapping colors. Zones 5–7

Liriodendron tulipifera

TULIP POPLAR

Unusual leaves, coloring well in fall; on mature trees,
bell-shaped flowers in summer

You will need plenty of space and a thought for the
next generation if your tulip poplar is to fulfill its
maximum potential. This stately tree eventually
reaches a height of 100ft/30m, and it will not flower
until it is at least 25ft/7.5m high and around fifteen
years old. So perhaps it is irresponsible of me to suggest that you could consider planting one in even the
smallest garden: it might be too frustrating to have
to take it out before it reached more than a tiny frac-
tion of its final size. But I have seen a tulip poplar
grown in a pot on a roof garden to great effect –
grown entirely for its lovely foliage.

The tulip poplar's leaves are unlike those of any
other tree, unless you can picture a maple leaf with
its pointed tip cut off square like a flour scoop. They
are midgreen and smooth to the touch and in fall
they color to a glorious butter-yellow. It would be
striking to underplant the tree with a mass of the
fall-flowering bulb *Colchicum speciosum*, which has
large, crocuslike, pale magenta flowers.

The tree, of course, is named for its flowers,
which have only a passing resemblance to tulips.
They are shaped like upright bells, the tips of the
petals curling over slightly to form a lip. The flower
is in an unusual combination of colors. The ribbon-
shaped stamens which fill the center of the bell are
pale orange, and the ground color of the petals is a
greeny cream, but they are marked from the base
with a spreading stain of orange. The flowers are
about 2½in/6cm across, quite small in relation to
the size of the mature tree on which they appear.

• Height to 100ft/30m, spread 50ft/15m. Prefers
fertile, well-drained, and slightly acidic soil. Propagate by seed. Zones 5–9

Liriodendron tulipifera
flower in summer

Liriodendron tulipifera 'Aureomarginatum'

OTHER LIRIODENDRONS TO GROW

***Liriodendron tulipifera* 'Aureomarginatum'** In
this superb variegated variety the leaves are edged
with a variable band of yellow. The overall effect of
the tree is a shimmering golden haze, and it will give
intense pleasure even as a small tree. Could be grown
in a tub. Zones 4–9

***Liriodendron tulipifera* 'Fastigiatum'** If you only
have a medium-sized garden but are determined to
grow a tulip poplar to flowering size, then you
should obtain this narrow-growing form, which
attains the same height as the standard tree but takes
up less lateral space. Zones 5–9

Trained as espaliers, dessert eating apples make an effective boundary hedge. Spring and fall are obviously the peak seasons for display, but even in winter the trained trees, bare of leaf, have a strikingly graphic structure, like a living fence. Apples and pears can also be trained to make a tunnel over a path. This involves training cordon trees over arched metal supports. Structures like this need constant maintenance – they can easily get out of hand if growth is allowed to go unchecked. But it is very rewarding to pick fruit from a hedge or tunnel that is part of the formal structure of your garden. If the idea takes your fancy you can have further fun by pruning bush fruits such as gooseberries and red-currants into standards or fans, and by training vegetables like marrows and gourds into arches.

Malus domestica

EATING APPLE

Spring blossom, fall fruits, amenable to
ornamental training

There are few sights more lovely in the garden than
an apple tree in full bloom, with the first bees of the
spring excitedly working their way through the
prodigality of blossom. Again in the fall, the apple
becomes the symbol of its season, weighed down
with fruits of green and golden red. Yet such is the
culinary value of the apple that its usefulness as an
ornamental tree is sometimes overlooked.

Over the centuries growers have selected a phenomenally wide range of apple varieties, according
to the flavor, texture, and color of the fruit, and to
their season of flowering and fruiting. The grafting,
pruning, and shaping of apples has been elevated to
the level of a fine art. All this accumulated wisdom
about apples can be intimidating, but growing
apples is simple, provided you bear three things in
mind. First, you need to be aware of rootstocks.
These are graded according to their vigor. If you
wish to grow apples decoratively, as fans and espaliers, you must buy plants with a dwarfing rootstock,
or else your trees will be too vigorous to control. The
most commonly used rootstock for this purpose is
M26. For cordons you need even less vigor: go for
M9 rootstock. If you have room for only tiny bushes
in your garden, choose the most dwarfing rootstock
of all, M27.

Second, apples are not self-pollinating. This
means that if you grow a single apple tree in isolation, out of bee-range of any other apple, the flowers
will not be fertilized, and you will have no fruit. So,
unless neighboring gardens are well endowed with
apple trees, it is best to grow two or more together:
if necessary they can be kept small, by choosing an
appropriate rootstock and by pruning. Choose varieties that come into blossom at the same time –

there can be a gap of several weeks between different
groups. The ornamental crab apples will function as
pollinators and they are sometimes grown in com-
mercial orchards for this purpose.

The third choice that you face is the more
personal one of fruit type. Do you want cooking
apples or eaters? Early or late fruiting? You will, of
course, have your own preferences for flavor, but
you might also think about color – green, yellow, or
red apples? If you have room for a selection, you
could consider some of the varieties listed in the
table below.

A well-trained apple fan or espalier is a lovely
thing. Trained against a wall or fence a tree will take
up minimum space but will produce a bounty of
flowers and fruits. Even more effective, to my mind,
are freestanding fans and espaliers, trained along
wires strung between posts. Planted in rows, these
can make the most attractive garden-dividers – open

Red and green apples
(TOP) and deep red apples
(ABOVE). If you plant
apple trees for their
decorative value, you
might like to consider the
color as well as the flavor
of the fruit.

Variety (type)	Fruit skin ground color	Flower season	Fruit season
Vista Bella (dessert)	yellow and green	early	very early
Paula Red (dessert)	yellow	mid	early
Empire (dessert)	green	mid	mid
Macintosh (dessert)	green	mid	mid
Spartan (dessert)	yellow	mid	mid
Gala (dessert)	greenish to golden yellow	mid	mid-late
Delicious (dessert)	solid red	late	mid-late
Jonagold (dessert)	green and yellow	late	mid-late
Cortland (cooking/dessert)	pale yellow	mid	mid
Idared (cooking/dessert)	yellow and green	mid	late
Crispin (Mutsu) (cooking/dessert)	greenish yellow	late	late
Golden Delicious (cooking/dessert)	greenish yellow	late	late

enough to allow glimpses through, but sufficiently dense to form a simple enclosure-hedge. Delightful from both sides in blossom and again in fruit, these look striking in winter too, when their filigree architecture becomes the main attraction.

Another way to create an apple hedge is to use cordons – individual plants pruned to a single stem with short side shoots along its length. You can use cordons trained parallel at a slant, at 36in/90cm intervals, but this can look a little regimental. It is more effective to train alternate cordons in opposite directions, so that they create a living trellis structure. This way, you might choose to construct an apple tunnel with cordon lattices on each side of a path, and further cordons at regular intervals trained around an arch to meet overhead. You can manipulate a freestanding bush too, to give it the shape you want: for example, by arching the branches upward and inward by tying them to a framework, you create a compact and elegant goblet-shaped bush. You might favor a flat-bottomed cone-shaped tree, which is created by anchoring the tips of the lowest branches to the ground, so that they grow out horizontally to the stem, and then trimming the upper branches to shape.

With one exception, there are no short cuts to all these special effects in fruit trees, and a strict pruning routine must be followed from the start. The exception is the new Ballerina apple, which is like a naturally growing cordon, requiring no pruning to preserve its columnar shape. This makes it especially useful for the small low-maintenance garden. However, to make the most of the apple's possibilities, there is no substitute for string, pruners and sweat.

• Height and spread to 30ft/9m, but dimensions can be controlled by choice of rootstock and by pruning. Any soil. Benefits from an annual top-dressing of manure. A dormant oil spray will keep many of the undesirable bugs at bay. Zones 4–8

LEFT In a tiny front garden that runs beside a terrace of cottages, the only place to grow fruit is against the wall. Here an ancient espalier pear gives a generous covering of blossom. This will be followed by a fall crop that should keep the household in fruit for several weeks.

RIGHT A ring of young crab apples creates a small garden enclosure. Trained as fans and espaliers, the trees will make an informal hedge with dual seasons of interest. Here the rose-pink blossoms of *Malus* 'Profusion' complement the pink tulips beyond. The white-flowered *Malus* 'Golden Hornet' will produce a spectacular display of small yellow apples in fall.

OTHER FRUIT TREES TO GROW ORNAMENTALLY

Pears are as amenable as apples to pruning and training to decorative shapes. As with apples, two plants are required for pollination.

Plums and cherries are suitable for training into ornamental fans. Many plums, including the popular 'Victoria', are self-fertile. The cooking cherry, the bing, is self-fertile and may also be used as a pollinator of sweet cherries. Among the sweet cherries themselves there is one variety, 'Stella', that is self-fertile.

Malus 'Golden Hornet'

GOLDEN HORNET CRAB APPLE
Prolific spring blossom, fall fruits
that last into winter

Some of the crab apples, like their cousins the domestic apples, are star performers that put on a double act of equal value in spring and fall. Some are also reliable and easy to grow. They are small trees that will not get out of hand, and if you need to restrict their growth for a very small garden, they can be kept compact by pruning. There is a wide choice of varieties that have been selected for their blossom,

Spring and fall effects. Crab apples and flowering cherries alternate in this avenue that leads to a pretty stone summerhouse. The two crab apples in the foreground are *Malus* 'Golden Hornet'.

and color and size of fruit. Among the best is *Malus* 'Golden Hornet'.

In spring, 'Golden Hornet' is covered with clusters of clear white flowers, about 1in/2.5cm across, along the length of its branches. The only quibble that you might have about this spring display is that it is not very long-lasting – a week or so at the most. The fragile blossom is easily scattered by a strong wind. The fall fruits more than compensate for the short life of the blossom – they survive on the tree for several months, well into winter and long

after the leaves have been shed. These fruits are miniature apples, about 1in/2.5cm long, golden yellow in color and hanging in bunches along the branches. Crab apples are bitter-tasting, but they can be cooked to make a delicious jelly. However, though using windfalls for cooking is permissible, picking crab apples is sacrilege in my book. The whole point of growing the tree is for ornament. In a good season a mature tree will be weighed down under its burden of fruits, glowing golden in the fall sun.

Unlike some of the domestic apples, crabs like 'Golden Hornet' are self-fertile. This means that a single tree will produce fruit. However, it is said that fertilization is improved if several crabs are grown together, and, provided you have the space, this is in any case an effective way to use them. The crabs are usually grown as standard trees but there is no reason why they should not be pruned to make fans, espaliers, or goblets, just like domestic apples (see pages 33–4). I admit that I have never seen this done, but I cannot think why not. I have started to train two 'Golden Hornets' as espaliers in my own garden, but it is still too early to report on the results.

It is a test for a gardener to provide effective associations for trees like these that perform at both ends of the season. Of course the spring display coincides with the peak season for bulbs, and a carpet of cream or white flowering bulbs makes a stunning underplanting to *M.* 'Golden Hornet'. You might try *Narcissus* 'Thalia', with its multiheaded white flowers, or cream *N.* 'Mount Hood' and the white *Tulipa* 'Purissima' – but you will need to be

Malus 'Golden Hornet' blossom

Malus 'Golden Hornet' fruits

Malus 'Red Sentinel' fruits

Malus 'Evereste' fruits

very clever, or very lucky, for their flowering to coincide precisely with that of the crab. These bulbs can be interplanted with shrubs chosen to combine with the second performance of the tree. Here you might pick plants with fiery fall colors, such as cotinus, fothergilla or deciduous azaleas, though some of these will thrive only on an acidic soil. Among these fall treasures the yellow crab apples will shine like amber jewels.

• Height to 20ft/6m, spread to 15ft/4.5m. Any well-drained soil, in sun or part-shade. *M.* 'Golden Hornet' will benefit from an annual topdressing of well-rotted manure. If necessary, prune to keep compact; otherwise, just cut out any dead wood and trim to keep the canopy in good shape. Zones 4–8

OTHER CRAB APPLES TO GROW

Malus floribunda The Japanese crab is probably the loveliest in flower, with dark pink buds opening to pale pink flowers which completely cover the tree. Height and spread to 15ft/4.5m. Zones 4–8

Malus hupehensis The tea crab apple is larger than the average crab. The white flowers, pink in bud, are large too, up to 1½in/3cm across, and fragrant. Small red fruits. For orange-red fruits buy *M.* 'Red Sentinel', for scarlet fruits *M.* 'Evereste'. Height to 30ft/9m, spread to 20ft/6m. Zones 4–8

***Malus* 'Profusion'** A more upright variety, with purple leaves in spring, maturing to dark green. The flowers have a deep rose tint; the tiny fruits are red. Height to 20ft/6m, spread to 12ft/3.5m. Zones 4–8

Malus sargentii Sargent crab apple is a dwarf species. The leaves are unusual, with three lobes. Small white flowers are followed by tiny red fruits. Height and spread to 8ft/2.5m. Zones 4–8

Ostrya virginiana fruits

Ostrya virginiana

HOPHORNBEAM OR IRONWOOD

Spring catkins, hoplike fruits in fall

A deciduous tree from the eastern United States, the hophornbeam is an asset in the garden throughout the year, but it has two special seasons of glory. In spring the branches are hung with the delicate tassels of the male catkins. These are green-yellow and appear before the hornbeamlike leaves open, making a striking sight when seen against the spring sky. In fall the curious leafy fruits hang from the tree. They look like hops and they are greeny white when they first appear. They turn brown later, as the tree's foliage turns to gold.

• Height to 50ft/15m, spread 40ft/12m. Any soil. Zones 3–8

Ostrya virginiana catkins

LEFT TO RIGHT *Prunus × subhirtella* 'Autumnalis' in fall, in early winter, in midwinter and in spring

Prunus × subhirtella 'Autumnalis'

FALL-FLOWERING CHERRY

Pinkish white flowers through most of winter, fall foliage color

Any tree that blossoms through most of the winter is a boon in the garden; one that also provides fall color is a double treasure. For a week or two in midfall, the leaves of *Prunus × subhirtella* 'Autumnalis' turn a brilliant hue of rusty orange. The flower buds are already swelling, and by the time the last leaves have fallen, the first of the pinkish white flowers have opened. If the weather is mild, the tree may soon be covered with blossom, giving the happy illusion that winter has passed by unnoticed and spring is already here.

I have seen the blossom of this tree covered with a rime of frost and surviving, but a spell of cold weather depresses further flowering for a time. However, this prunus may go on giving a few flowers throughout the winter, especially in warm spells. Bare branches picked in midwinter can usually be coaxed into flower in a vase beside the fire. Then, in early spring, after almost six months of intermittent activity, the tree will often have a final burst of flower as the leaves begin to open.

During the summer this tree, like many flowering cherries, looks relatively undistinguished. Be sure to buy a shapely specimen at the start – its shape is all it has to offer when the rest of your garden is at its peak. One way to get it to contribute to the garden's summer activity is to grow a climber through it. Choose a vigorous clematis, like Viticella clematis 'Abundance', as the tree has a dense canopy. Plant it at least 4ft/1.2m away from the trunk, as the prunus has dense and shallow roots, and provide a cane for the clematis to climb up into the tree.

The tree is suitable for the smallest garden, and should flower in the first season that you buy it. The equally attractive variety *P.* × *s.* 'Autumnalis Rosea' has pink flowers.

If I had room for only one tree in the garden, this would be it. The gift of spring in winter is as precious as a whole bed of summer flowers.

● Height and spread to 20ft/6m. Prefers full sun. All prunus species are rather shallow-rooted and this can be detrimental to shrubs and other plants growing nearby. *Prunus* × *subhirtella* 'Autumnalis' is usually grafted onto the rootstock of another species: check that the graft is near ground level, as this produces the best-shaped tree. Zones 5–8

A line of *Prunus serrula* brings color into the garden in winter as well as summer. This summer view shows *Echinops bannaticus* in the foreground, and behind it the purple foliage of another useful cherry, *Prunus cerasifera* 'Pissardii', planted as a hedge at the back of the border.

OTHER PRUNUS TO GROW

***Prunus cerasifera* 'Pissardii'** The purple-leaved plum is covered in small white blossoms in early spring. The red-purple leaves follow. Makes a good hedge. Height and spread to 30ft/9m. Zones 5–9

***Prunus pendula* 'Pendula Rosea'** (syn. *P. × subhirtella* 'Pendula') A weeping tree with pink spring flowers. Height and spread to 20ft/6m. Zones 6–8

Prunus serrula Modest in flower but treasured for its bark, which is shiny fox-red. This makes it one of the most striking trees in winter. Height and spread to 30ft/9m. Zones 5–6

***Prunus* 'Shōgetsu'** (syn. *P. serrulata longipes*) One of the best of the Japanese cherries, making a broad spreading shape, covered with pure white flowers in spring. The leaves color magnificently in fall. Height to 20ft/6m, spread 25ft/7.5m. Zones 5–8

Salix alba 'Britzensis'

SCARLET WILLOW

Spring catkins, orange-brown stems for winter color

The willows range from the stately weeping willow, familiar as a specimen tree in many large gardens, to tiny, prostrate forms that belong in the alpine garden. Many have fluffy catkins appearing before the foliage in spring. The varieties with colored stems also look sensational in winter. Among the best of these is *Salix alba* 'Britzensis' (syn. 'Chermesina').

With this willow it is only the young stems that have bark of a fiery orange-brown color: after the first year the old wood becomes relatively dull. So you have to be merciless with the pruners each year to ensure plenty of young growth and to get the best decorative value from the plant. If grown as a shrub, this willow should be pruned on the coppicing principle by cutting right back to the woody framework at ground level in spring, just before the leaf buds open. Then it has the whole summer to put out twiggy new growth for next winter's display. If it is grown as a standard tree, the principle is the same except that pruning is done on the pollarding basis, by cutting back the young branches to within a few inches of the main trunk of the tree.

Unfortunately, with this plant you cannot have the best of both worlds. If it is pruned as vigorously as I propose for the maximum winter effect, you will miss out on the decorative spring catkins. The ideal solution, if you have space, is to grow several willows together, choosing some species for their colorful catkins, others primarily for their bark.

• Left to its own devices, *S.a.* 'Britzensis' will make a tree with a height of 80ft/25m and spread of 50ft/15m. However, coppiced annually as described, it can be kept to a rounded shrub with a height and spread of 6ft/1.8m. Full sun, any soil, but needs plenty of moisture for best results. Zones 2–8

OTHER WILLOWS TO GROW

All will flourish in any soil, provided they have sufficient moisture.

Salix alba* var. *vitellina The golden willow has butter-yellow stems that stand out prominently in winter, especially against a dark background. For best stem effect, prune vigorously in spring, as above. Unpruned, it will make an attractive tree, growing to about 50ft/15m. Zones 2–8

***Salix caprea* 'Kilmarnock'** A compact tree for a small garden, the weeping pussy willow produces curtains of branches from a central trunk, arching down to ground level. In spring these are covered

ABOVE *Salix gracilistyla* 'Melanostachys' is grown primarily for its spring catkins.

LEFT *Salix alba* 'Britzensis' in late fall. Pruned regularly to give colorful young stems, this willow makes a graceful and compact shrub.

with powder-puff catkins with bright yellow anthers which are a favorite destination for early flights of bees. For a good overall effect, underplant with spring flowers that will not mind being shaded when the tree is later covered with leaves – narcissi or polyanthus primroses, for example. Height and spread 6ft/1.8m. Zones 5–8

Salix daphnoides The violet willow has purple shoots, overlaid with a white bloom that gives them a misty violet color. For the best stem effects hard pruning is necessary. Zones 5–8

Salix gracilistyla One of the best shrubs for catkins. The immature male catkins are silvery gray and silky in texture, opening into an upright, elongated shape with bright yellow anthers. Height 10ft/3m, spread 12ft/3.5m. The variety 'Melanostachys' has very dark catkins, with yellow anthers. Zones 6–8

Salix lanata A dwarf species, up to 4ft/1.2m in height and spread, grown for its lovely gray foliage. The leaves are broad and woolly and they open in spring in the company of the yellow-anthered catkins. Suitable for the rock garden or beside a small pond. Zones 2–5

Salix* × *sepulcralis* var. *chrysocoma The weeping willow is seen at its best as a specimen plant with plenty of space around it, or growing beside a lake or river, where its long, pendulous branches will lap the water. Narrow, lance-shaped leaves are bright green in spring, yellow in fall and midgreen between these seasons. It is a fabulous sight in midwinter with its long, hanging twigs a brilliant golden yellow. Needs sun and plenty of moisture in any soil. Height and spread to 60ft/18m. Zones 4–9

Salix caprea 'Kilmarnock' in spring

Sorbus aria 'Lutescens'

WHITEBEAM
White spring foliage, fall fruit
and foliage color

The whitebeam's maximum impact is in the spring, when the buds unfurl to give young leaves that are slightly woolly to the touch and silvery white to the eye. The tree seems to glow with this new growth and, for me at least, it is one of the most potent symbols of spring.

There are several forms of whitebeam and most of them lose their ethereal haze of white after the first flush of spring. *Sorbus aria* 'Lutescens' is the best variety because it retains at least a vestige of whiteness in the mature leaves. This quality comes from a white bloom, or "tomentum," that covers the leaves, like the bloom on the skin of a newly picked plum.

The tree's white flowers, borne in late spring, tend to merge into the general whiteness of the foliage. The fall fruits, however, are conspicuous red berries, a vivid touch of pure color against the brownish background of the turning leaves.

- Height to 40ft/12m, spread 25ft/7.5m. Any soil, including over limestone. Suitable for urban and seaside planting as it is tolerant of pollution and salty air. Zones 5–7

An unusual and effective arch of *Sorbus aria* 'Lutescens' at Kiftsgate Court in Gloucestershire, England. The arch was created by planting young trees at each side and training them onto a metal support. Regular trimming encourages dense and bushy growth.

Sorbus hupehensis 'Rosea' berries in fall

mountain ash, as almost all of them flower in late spring, with white flowers held in flat heads above the leaves. There is some diversity in foliage though. They all have ashlike leaves with many leaflets fanning out from a central midriff but some species have fine filigree leaflets and others have coarser foliage. In some species, but not all, the leaves give fiery fall colors. There are erect varieties among them and there are weeping ones. But the main basis of choice is in the color of the berries. According to your preference you can go for red berries or yellow, or for shades of orange in between. Or you might venture to the slightly less common species which have white or pink berries.

On balance, if I could choose only one, I believe

Sorbus cashmiriana flowers in spring

Sorbus hupehensis

HUPEH MOUNTAIN ASH

Spring flowers, delicate foliage that colors red in fall, and white or pink fruits that last into winter

The mountain ashes belong to a large, highly desirable group of trees, almost all of which are performance plants *par excellence*, attractive in all their parts and at all seasons of the year – many a gardener's dream tree. In the floral department there is very little to choose between the different species of

that it would have to be a form of mountain ash of Chinese origin, *Sorbus hupehensis*. In *S. hupehensis* itself the berries are white with just a hint of pink around their tips. The stalks that hold the berries are vivid scarlet, and the leaves provide a delicate gray-green tracery all around, so that from a distance the tree in early fall has a pale and enchantingly ghostly appearance. Later in the season the leaves turn red.

The pink-berried variety, 'Rosea', is perhaps even more beautiful. As the berries begin to color up in fall to a warm peachskin pink, the gray-green leaves pick up a pinkish tinge as if in sympathy. Later the leaves turn reddish brown before falling, to leave the clusters of berries still hanging gracefully from the bare branches.

Sorbus commixta berries in fall

• Height eventually 50ft/15m and spread 25ft/7.5m, but it will take a long time to reach that scale. In a small garden it will give many years of pleasure before it grows too big for its site. Any well-drained soil. Zones 6–8

OTHER SORBUS TO GROW

Sorbus aucuparia In this, the European mountain ash, the leaflets have toothed edges like a saw. The foliage turns a golden orange in fall, making a fiery combination with the vivid orange-red berries of the species. Height up to 35ft/10.5m, spread 25ft/7.5m. There is also a variety, *S.a.* 'Fructu Luteo' (syn. 'Xanthocarpa'), which has amber-yellow berries. Other mountain ashes with red berries and good fall foliage are *S. commixta* and its variety 'Embley'. Both have an erect habit with feathered branches. Zones 3–6

Sorbus cashmiriana A handsome mountain ash with bunches of white berries in fall, accompanied by golden-brown leaves. Height to 30ft/9m, spread 25ft/7.5m. Another good choice for white berries is *S. prattii*. In a good fall, it looks like a snowstorm. Zones 4–7

Sorbus 'Joseph Rock' berries in fall

***Sorbus* 'Joseph Rock'** A tree of upright habit with golden-yellow fruits which make a lovely combination with the fall tints of its leaves. These turn through shades of orange, yellow, and purplish green. Height to 35ft/10.5m, spread 20ft/6m. Zones 4–8

Sorbus vilmorinii One of the most petite-looking mountain ashes, with very fine dark gray-green leaflets and gracefully arching branches. The leaves turn to bronze-red in fall to accompany the loose clusters of pink berries. Height and spread to 15ft/4.5m. Zones 6–7

Sorbus cashmiriana berries in fall

Immaculate topiary in yew. The hedge has been sheared as flat as a tabletop but at regular intervals the leaders of some of the constituent plants have been allowed to grow upward and shaped to make simplified mushrooms and birds.

Taxus baccata

ENGLISH YEW

A versatile evergreen for hedges and topiary

The English yew can be a lugubrious tree. Grown as a freestanding specimen it casts such dense shade that nothing will grow happily beneath it. Its evergreen foliage is such a dark green that it may appear black in comparison with its garden neighbors. This tree looks most at home in a graveyard, where its somber presence lends an appropriately funereal air and its evergreen foliage can be taken as a symbol for everlasting life.

It may seem surprising to commend the yew, with its morbid associations, as a key plant to supply the background structure to any garden, however large or small. But it has a quality that makes it outstanding: its almost infinite capacity for regeneration. The more punishment it receives from trimming and shaping, the more densely it sprouts new

growth. This makes it one of the best plants for hedging or for topiary. A yew hedge makes a perfect boundary or partition within a garden. As a background to a border its somber tone sets off the brighter plants. It can be effective too when shaped into buttresses to divide a border into compartments. Yew looks good as an arch over a gateway or as an isolated topiary shape, whether of a rigidly geometric form like a pyramid, cylinder, or cone, or else as a more whimsical creation such as a dove or a peacock.

Because of the great age of some venerable yew trees, people tend to assume that yew is very slow-growing. This is not strictly true, and it is possible to establish a good yew hedge or a shapely piece of topiary within, say, eight years of putting in young plants. What is true, however, is that a yew structure can be "frozen" in a desired shape, once it is established, by judicious pruning of new growth. Some topiary gardens have remained virtually unchanged for decades, with only an annual "haircut" needed to keep them in shape.

If you follow my advice and restrict the yews in your garden to hedging and topiary, I admit that you will probably miss two attractive features of the plant. First the trunk, seen best in a mature tree, is full of character, bumpy and twisted, and covered with scaly mahogany-red bark. And the fruits, borne most freely on an unpruned tree, are unexpected on a conifer and an attractive bonus. Ripening in fall and persisting into winter, they are like oblong red buttons, of the consistency of jelly beans – but do not let your children or pets eat them. The single seed inside is highly poisonous.

• An unpruned mature yew tree will reach a height of 40ft/12m and a spread of 30ft/9m. As a hedge, yew can be maintained at a height of, say, 8ft/2.5m by regular trimming. In the wild, *T. baccata* grows on dry limestone. In cultivation too it thrives in alkaline conditions, but it is perfectly tolerant of acidic soils, provided that there is good drainage. When planting a yew hedge, allow 24in/60cm between plants and give them a good start by mixing a generous handful of bonemeal with the earth around their roots. As with any plant, the rate of growth is dependent on regular watering and feeding in the growing period. For hedging or topiary, trim the side shoots in late summer to encourage bushy growth, but keep the main leader until it has reached the required height. When growing a yew hedge behind a border, it is a good idea to construct an underground barrier of metal edging or thick plastic to deflect the hedge roots from the border. Otherwise, a mature hedge can seriously deplete the soil of moisture and nutriments needed by the border plants. Zones 7–8

Taxus baccata 'Fastigiata' berries

OTHER YEWS TO GROW

***Taxus baccata* 'Elegantissima'** The new growth of this yew is yellow, later fading to green. It is slower-growing than English yew, but much less gloomy. Ideal if you are looking for a yellow hedging or topiary plant. Zones 7–8

***Taxus baccata* 'Fastigiata'** The Irish yew is a good architectural tree, with upward-pointing branches giving a tapering, columnar shape. It forms a slim column when young, but in a mature tree – which may be up to 15ft/4.5m high – the branches tend to spread a little and may need to be tied in with hoops of string or wire. This tree is particularly useful if you want a formal effect combined with easy maintenance. Planted at regular intervals along a drive or allée, Irish yews make neat and repetitive columns – but with rough edges. Zones 6–8

Taxus baccata 'Standishii'

***Taxus baccata* 'Standishii'** Another columnar form, even more tightly erect than the Irish yew, but very slow-growing. Golden-green foliage. Zones 6–8

DOUBLE-VALUE SHRUBS AND CLIMBERS

A garden is much more than a collection of plants. The way in which you group and associate your plants will determine the character of your garden, making it particular to you alone. Gone are the days when shrubs were to be grown in "shrubberies," away from other plants. The modern garden tends to be a medley of trees, shrubs, perennials, and annuals all mixed in together. Shrubs provide the foundations of the mixed border, because they form the largest and least mobile elements in it. Perennials and annuals can be juggled around each year with impunity, but shrubs make deeper roots and resent being moved.

Many shrubs, such as berberis, cornus, and cotinus, are selected primarily for their foliage. Flowers, fruits, or colored stems come as a bonus. With the roses, the ultimate in flower power, the bonus comes in the form of hips, fall foliage color, or decorative thorns.

Most shrubs (like most trees) are amenable to pruning and training. You can make hedges by multiple plantings of boxwood and berberis, for instance. More tender shrubs, like choisya, will often benefit from being trained against a wall. This gives them protection against cold and also provides a flat base against which they can produce a perfect foliage background.

Climbers, generally, are the most useful of plants, not only for clothing walls and screening unsightly structures but also for associating with trees and shrubs. Plants that are in action in different seasons can be particularly effective when they are grown together. Growing climbers like clematis or wisteria through earlier-flowering shrubs or trees is one way to cheat the passing of the months.

A small city garden, superbly planted with a framework of shrubs, and decorated with swathes of climbers. The plants are graduated by height, with trees around the perimeter. These include a golden elm (top left), the yellow-leaved *Robinia pseudoacacia* 'Frisia' and the purple-leaved *Prunus cerasifera* 'Pissardii' (top right). Occupying the middle ground are conifers and shrubs including *Lonicera nitida* 'Baggesen's Gold' (with small yellow leaves), draped with purple-blue *Clematis* × *durandii*. Plants in the center of the scheme include *Lavatera trimestris* 'Silver Cup', *Campanula persicifolia,* astilbes and (in the foreground) *Lychnis coronaria* 'Oculata'. In this masterpiece of planting the smallest plants, low-growing polygonums, grasses and pulmonaria, are grouped at the front alongside the path.

Aronia arbutifolia

RED CHOKEBERRY

White spring flowers, red leaves and berries in fall

The aronia's period of glory is in fall when its foliage turns a fiery red and matches the shiny red berries that mature at the same time. It is one of the better medium-sized shrubs for fall color, but it is not sufficiently distinguished for the rest of the year to stand on its own as a specimen shrub. It looks well in a mixed planting with other plants grown for their foliage, such as maples. Here it will contribute its own special flame to the general fire that sweeps the border in fall. It would be a good neighbor to *Cotinus coggygria* 'Royal Purple', because the leaf shapes of the two shrubs make a pleasing contrast. The aronia has a narrow, pointed leaf in comparison to the broad, rounded leaf of the cotinus. What is more, the two plants color to different shades of red, the aronia to scarlet, the cotinus to a dusky velvet crimson.

The pretty little flowers of *Aronia arbutifolia* are typical of the rose family, to which the shrub belongs. About 1in/2.5cm across, they are white and single, with five petals each, reminiscent of the blossom of an apple or crab apple tree but not usually so abundant.

● Height and spread to 8ft/2.5m. Sun or part-shade. Like many shrubs grown for fall color, aronias produce the best effects when grown on neutral to acidic soils. Propagate by cuttings. Zones 4–9

Matching pictures of *Aronia arbutifolia* show its spring performance of a mass of small white flowers, rather like apple blossom, followed by vivid red foliage in fall. The brilliant leaves tend to eclipse the small red berries that ripen at the same time.

LEFT Centerpiece among a spring display of tulips, *Berberis thunbergii atropurpurea* associates well with plants in the warm color range, from reds through crimson to purple. The shrub retains its browny purple leaf color through the summer, but becomes more ruddy in fall.

ABOVE *Berberis thunbergii* 'Red Chief ' flowers in spring

Berberis thunbergii atropurpurea

BARBERRY

Purple foliage, yellow spring flowers,
bright red berries in fall

There are over a hundred varieties of berberis, many of them outstanding shrubs of all-round interest. Some are deciduous, some evergreen, but all are thorny and all carry flowers within a color range of cream through yellow to orange.

A single species, *Berberis thunbergii*, has a variety of forms to satisfy the most discerning gardener. The purple-leaved form, *B.t. atropurpurea*, is one of the best purple shrubs. It reaches 6ft/1.8m in height and spread, and looks good in back of a mixed border, especially one planted with harmonizing hot colors in the range of crimson, red, and orange. A dwarf purple variety, *B.t.* 'Atropurpurea Nana', which reaches a height of 24in/60cm, is useful for small gardens. In spring both produce numerous small pendulous yellow flowers which contrast with the developing purple foliage. Small bright red berries ripen in fall, to coincide with a deepening intensity of color in the leaves before they drop. The rich purple foliage takes on a reddish tinge, which complements the berries hanging below the leaves.

For the most showy flowers, choose the purple-leaved *B.t.* 'Red Chief'. This has larger flowers than

Berberis thunbergii atropurpurea berries in fall

B.t. atropurpurea, and the outer bracts are suffused with red. Disappointingly, though, it is not a reliable producer of berries. Another striking purple-leaved berberis is *B.t.* 'Rose Glow'. In this variety the young leaves are mottled with pink and creamy white patterns, later darkening to purple. Aptly named, the plant appears to glow with a halo of pink from its young shoots. The variegated forms tend to be smaller and less vigorous than the type. 'Rose Glow' grows to 5ft/1.5m.

With their vicious battery of thorns, *B. thunbergii* and its varieties make impenetrable hedging plants. The larger varieties, such as *B.t. atropurpurea*, should be spaced 24in/60cm apart. For a dwarf hedge of *B.t.* 'Atropurpurea Nana', place plants 12in/30cm apart.

• Any soil, provided it is not waterlogged. Sun or part-shade. Propagate by cuttings. Zones 4–7

ANOTHER BERBERIS TO GROW

Berberis darwinii A good evergreen barberry for a mild climate, *B. darwinii* grows to 8ft/2.5m and is covered in spring with bright orange flowers. The fall display, of purple berries, is less reliable. Zones 7–9

Many berberis species are generous producers of berries in fall. They remain on the shrub well into winter when, as here, they look sensational with a sprinkling of hoar frost. The berries are not always red. There are species with blue berries, others with purple, and some that have a bloom on their surface that makes them appear white.

Buxus sempervirens

COMMON BOXWOOD

Aromatic evergreen for hedges and punctuation marks

There is a place for boxwood in every garden. It is a most adaptable plant and has been used for hedging and topiary for centuries. In some historic gardens the boxwood infrastructure has survived long after the more ephemeral plants have vanished.

Left to its own devices over many years, boxwood makes a small evergreen tree. Its greenish gray trunk is usually fairly bent and twisted – an indication of its age – and it bears modest but sweet-scented flowers. These are rarely seen on boxwood when it is pruned to shape, which is the way that it is usually grown.

With its small leaves growing densely together to give good coverage year-round, boxwood is the perfect plant for shaping. It is easily propagated by cuttings, and perhaps its only disadvantage is that it is so slow-growing. If you fancy a boxwood edging to your borders, you will do best to plant rooted cuttings about 6in/15cm high and 6in/15cm apart, but you will have to wait four or five years before they grow together to give any effect, and much longer for any height. Meanwhile you will need to restrain the more vigorous border plants from swamping the baby boxwood.

Boxwood shapes such as cones, cubes, balls and spirals make delightful architectural punctuation marks at strategic points such as the corners of borders, or beside entrances or steps. They can also be grown in pots to be moved around as the mood takes you. Unless you have the patience of Job it would be wise to buy your boxwood shapes ready-made from the nursery. They may be expensive, but the price will be a fair reflection of the years it has taken to create them.

• Any soil. After planting boxwood plants for hedging, trim the top shoots to stimulate further growth

from the base. Prune hard as the hedge develops; it may be discouraging for the gardener to cut back a plant that grows so painfully slowly, but this is vital to encourage compact growth. Do not neglect to feed the plants – preferably with a topdressing of well-rotted manure – to stimulate growth. Zones 6–9

OTHER BOXWOODS TO GROW

***Buxus sempervirens* varieties** There are numerous forms of *Buxus sempervirens* with slight distinctions in leaf shape or color, or in overall habit. *B.s.* 'Suffruticosa' is a dwarf form of common boxwood, with brighter green leaves, and is ideal as an edging plant or for small topiary shapes; *B.s.* 'Aureovariegata' has leaves mottled with yellow; *B.s.* 'Bullata' (syn. 'Latifolia') is a more loosely spreading shrub with larger leaves; and *B.s.* 'Angustifolia' (syn. 'Longifolia') has larger, oblong leaves. Zones 6–9

Buxus microphylla This boxwood is good in colder climates, and has the additional advantage that it grows naturally into a compact dome shape. So, provided this is the shape you want, there is no need to prune it. The variety *B.m.* 'Compacta' is a dwarf version, ideal for the rock garden. *B.m.* 'Green Pillow' is another good compact form, with brighter green leaves. Zones 5–8

Simple but effective. Boxwood topiary shapes grown in containers provide punctuation marks in a tiny urban garden. Untrimmed ivy makes a clever contrast around two of the boxwood structures. Both boxwood and ivy will look much the same in winter, but both need regular trimming – the box to keep its shape and the ivy to ensure that it remains in its juvenile state. Ivies become bulky and the leaves less shapely in their adult phase.

Choisya ternata

MEXICAN ORANGE BLOSSOM

Aromatic evergreen foliage, perfumed white flowers
over a long season

Many evergreen shrubs have thick and waxy leaves,
to give them some protection from extremes of tem-
perature. Choisya, the Mexican orange blossom, is
an exception, with leaves that are thin and sen-
suously soft. Admittedly, it is not the hardiest of
evergreens, but in a temperate area it should come
happily through most winters.

In a colder climate choisya can be grown as a wall
shrub, and, if you want to take the process a stage
further, you can train it flat against the wall. It is
content to be trained and sheared to shape and it is a
pleasure to prune, as the leaves release a strong but
pleasant scent, reminiscent of oil of eucalyptus,
when bruised or cut.

The flowers of choisya are scented too, but their
perfume is quite sweet. They are white and look
rather like orange blossom – which is why the plant
was given its popular name. The main flush of
flowers is in late spring but the shrub sometimes
blooms again in fall.

• Height and spread to 8ft/2.5m. Full sun for maximum flowering, but it will flower in shade. Any
well-drained soil. Protect from frosts in cold areas.
Propagate by cuttings. Zones 7–9

Choisya ternata flowers

Choisya ternata in flower in
an untypical woodland
setting. Choisya is not
generally regarded as a
woodland shrub, but it
will thrive in conditions
of shade or part-shade.
One advantage of this
situation is that the
surrounding trees will
give it protection from
frosts.

Clematis species and varieties

An invaluable group of climbers that, between them, produce flowers year-round

Clematis are the most versatile of climbers. While no individual clematis has a particularly long flowering season, between them they may provide flowers year-round. They are invaluable for extending the season of interest of the trees and shrubs through which they are trained. If you select your clematis carefully you can create the illusion that a tree or shrub is coming into flower again long after its own season has ended.

Some of the most useful clematis are those that are relatively late-flowering, coming to a peak toward the end of the summer when many of the star acts in the garden, such as roses, are past their best. The **Viticella group** is especially valuable, offering a range of colors to suit most tastes and garden situations. The Viticellas are characterized by small flowers, many of them bell-shaped. There are also some wonderful eccentrics among them, like 'Purpurea Plena Elegans', with its double flowers like opulently embroidered mauve buttons.

Most subtle among the Viticellas is 'Alba Luxurians', with its wavy white sepals tipped with green. It is too modest in color to decorate a green-leaved shrub, but it can look magical growing among the purple foliage of the barberry, *Berberis thunbergii atropurpurea*, or a purple form of the smoke bush, *Cotinus coggygria*. Another good white Viticella is the variety 'Huldine'. The flowers are slightly in-turned and have a beautiful silvery pink sheen.

Try one of the red Viticellas as a contrast to a plain green or white-variegated host plant. 'Abundance' is among the best. It is as freeflowering as its name suggests, with flattish flowers of a slightly dusty mid-pink. 'Madame Julia Correvon' is another good one, with cupped flowers of a richer pink, and pointed sepals.

Shrubs with yellow or yellow-variegated foliage are well suited as hosts for the darker colors among the Viticellas, particularly those within the purple range, like 'Etoile Violette' or 'Venosa Violacea', which has violet flowers streaked with white. Perhaps the most splendid in color of all the Viticellas is 'Royal Velours', which has the texture and hue of deep burgundy velvet. It makes a regal complement to any tree or shrub.

The hybrid ***Clematis* × *durandii*** is another useful plant that flowers in late summer. This clematis has flowers of deep blue, many of them with only four sepals, each slightly twisted and with surface corrugations along its length. One of its parents is a herbaceous clematis and so, although it makes sturdy and vigorous growth, it is a weak climber, only reaching a height of about 5ft/1.5m. Its blue flowers make an effective decoration for a yellow-leaved shrub such as *Lonicera nitida* 'Baggesen's Gold'.

The delightful ***Clematis rehderiana*** also comes into flower toward the end of summer, producing masses of diminutive nodding flowers, colored pale primrose-yellow. This climber will reach 20ft/6m, and if you can get your nose to the flowers you will enjoy their subtle but deliciously sweet scent.

Clematis **'Bill Mackenzie'**, a vigorous clematis reaching 25ft/7.5m, has an impressive double act – a spectacular late summer display of medium-small flowers, followed by a mass of fluffy seed heads or "old man's beard" carried well into winter. The flowers are bright yellow bells with brownish stamens, and

A white clematis weaves together the separate elements in a white and silver planting. The clematis is a Viticella, 'Alba Luxurians', which looks good in the silver-leaved sea buckthorn (*Hippophaë rhamnoides*), planted beside a white-flowered *Buddleja davidii*, with double white leucanthemums and feverfew at their feet.

A well-matched partnership between *Clematis* 'Prince Charles' and the dwarf *Berberis thunbergii* 'Atropurpurea Nana'. This clematis is similar to 'Perle d'Azur', but it is less vigorous and has smaller flowers.

the sepals are often upturned at the tip. **C. tangutica** is a slightly less vigorous climber with smaller yellow flowers but seed heads that are just as enduring.

Clematis cirrhosa actually begins to produce its small bell-shaped creamy yellow flowers (usually mottled with maroon) around midwinter. It then remains in bloom for two or three months. It has attractive feathered foliage, but this is apt to form a dense mat, so *C. cirrhosa* is not suitable for growing through the more delicate shrubs. It is better used to cover the bare trunk of a tree, or the side of an unsightly building.

With any luck, *C. cirrhosa* will still be flowering when **Clematis armandii** comes into bloom, in very early spring. If you judge by its foliage *C. armandii* looks very unlike any other clematis, with evergreen leaves like dark green leather straps. But when the flowers open they are unmistakably typical of clematis, with four to six petallike sepals surrounding a crown of anthers. The flowers grow in clusters from buds which develop over the winter at points where the leaves meet the main stem. Typically they are creamy white, waxy in texture, and scented sweetly of almonds. But my favorite cultivar is the pale pink one called 'Apple Blossom'. The leaves offer a broad surface area to be attacked by frost, so it is advisable to cover the plant during hard winter weather.

Coinciding with the spring bulbs, **Clematis alpina** has small, nodding flowers, normally blue, but with a pink form called 'Ruby' and a double white called 'White Moth'. One of the best forms is *C.a.* 'Frances Rivis', which has long blue sepals and a prominent white center. *C. alpina* is another clematis that produces fluffy seed heads. They last throughout the summer and make an attractive association with later climbers such as roses, sweet peas, or later-flowering clematis.

Clematis montana, which blossoms in late spring, has lovely small flowers, from white to dark pink according to the variety. Among the most perfect are *C.m.* 'Tetrarose', which has deep pink flowers with creamy yellow stamens, and *C.m.* var. *rubens*, which has pink flowers and bronzy red foliage. If you need a climber to clothe an eyesore in the garden, this is the one for you, because it is extremely vigorous and freeflowering. I offer a note of caution, however, having made a bad mistake in siting a *C. montana* in my own garden. I decided to grow one into the old apple tree which is the centerpiece of the garden. Within five years there were bare stems as thick as my wrist, reaching up into the canopy of the tree, and the apple had stopped bearing flowers and fruit. Bruised by this experience, I would only recommend *C. montana* to clothe a building or a really sturdy tree. It would look effective, for instance, draped through the dense foliage of a conifer such as Leyland cypress.

The clematis with the most spectacular blooms are the **large-flowered hybrids**, most of which flower in mid- to late summer. Among them there is a wide diversity of forms and colors ranging from white through pink and mauve to blue and deepest purple. Apart from a few less vigorous varieties, they all climb to about 15ft/4.5m. Collectively they give great opportunities for clever associations with other plants of harmonious or contrasting foliage and flower color.

The best of the large single white hybrids is *C.* 'Marie Boisselot' (syn. 'Madame le Coultre'). A double variety with flowers like big white pom-poms is *C.* 'Duchess of Edinburgh'. If it blooms a second time in fall the flowers are single, which is also

Clematis cirrhosa in winter

Clematis 'Bill Mackenzie' in early fall

the case with other double clematis. C. 'Miss Bateman' is another good white clematis, with contrasting brown stamens.

Among the best of the pinks, C. 'Comtesse de Bouchaud' has abundant medium-sized flowers. I have seen it growing into an apple tree to great effect. For a cooler pink and more star-shaped flowers, C. 'Hagley Hybrid' is a good choice: it associates well with *Rosa glauca*. C. 'Bees' Jubilee' is an improvement on the familiar 'Nelly Moser', offering a generally more richly colored version of Nelly's rather insipid combination of pale pink with darker pink bars.

Clematis 'Lady Northcliffe' is a good lavender-blue clematis, and ideal for the smaller garden, as it reaches only 8ft/2.5m. C. 'Prince Charles' is another good smaller variety, with exquisite pale blue flowers. It is rather like a miniature version of the magnificent 'Perle d'Azur', everybody's favorite for a vigorous pale blue climber. C. 'H.F. Young' and C. 'Lasurstern' are among the best of the darker blues. I have seen 'Lasurstern' planted in daring combination with the orange-flowered honeysuckle *Lonicera × tellmanniana*. The two climbers flower simultaneously in a startling dazzle of orange and blue.

For a clematis of deep velvety purple, a color that has overtones of royal occasions and solemn state funerals, choose C. 'Jackmanii Superba'. It is a glorious tone of purple, subtly marked with bars of purple-magenta. There is also a variety called C. 'Jackmanii Rubra', in tones of magenta and pink.

• All clematis do best in alkaline conditions, where there is lime in the soil. There are several points to bear in mind when growing clematis in association with trees and shrubs. Clematis thrive best with their roots shaded from sun, and (in common with most plants), they grow up toward the light. It is best therefore to plant any clematis on the shaded side of the host plant, so that it will grow up and through the host toward the sun. It is also important that the roots of the climber should not have to compete with its host for water and nourishment, so clematis need to be planted outside the sphere of influence of tree roots. As a rough guide, you might estimate the edge of the host's canopy in five years' time and plant the climber there. A cane support, angled into the host plant, will direct its early growth, and you will need to tie the shoots to this cane as they progress upward. Regular watering, and feeding at weekly intervals in the summer, will give a strong plant that ought to flower in its first year.

There is something of a mystique about the pruning of clematis, but in fact the principles are fairly simple. The main reason for pruning is to encourage growth from the base and to keep the plant within bounds. If left to its own devices it will start growing from the point at which it left off the previous season, and so the most vigorous species can quickly get out of hand. As a rule all clematis will flower on the growth they have made the preceding summer. In the case of late-flowering types the preceding summer is usually the current one. So these are species that may be cut back boldly in late winter; they will flower on the growth they make in the subsequent months. The spring-flowering species also flower on the growth of the preceding summer, but in their case, of course, this is the summer of the previous year. So these species need to be pruned after their spring flowering, to give them the summer to make new growth for next year's flowering. Propagate clematis by cuttings or layering.

The clematis of the Viticella group, C. × durandii, C. rehderiana, C. 'Bill Mackenzie', C. tangutica, and all the large-flowered hybrids mentioned, are best in zones 6–9; C. cirrhosa in zones 8–9; C. armandii in zones 7–9; the species C. alpina, 'Ruby', and 'Frances Rivis' in zones 4–8; 'White Moth' in zones 3–9; and C. montana and its varieties in zones 4–9.

A medley of clematis. This is only a small selection from over 300 varieties that are available, but they have been chosen to illustrate the range of colors and flower forms that clematis have to offer. The blue-flowered *Clematis × durandii* looks good growing in a yellow-leaved shrub such as *Lonicera nitida* 'Baggesen's Gold', but it is not a vigorous climber and will not reach the upper branches of a tall shrub. *Clematis* 'Huldine', on the other hand, is extremely vigorous and is effective planted with old-fashioned roses. When the rose flowers are finished, the clematis replaces them for several weeks with its own silvery flowers.

C. × *durandii* in *Lonicera nitida* 'Baggesen's Gold'

C. 'Jackmanii Superba'

C. 'Huldine'

C. 'Comtesse de Bouchaud'

C. 'Lady Northcliffe'

C. 'Perle d'Azur'

C. *alpina* 'Frances Rivis'

C. 'Bees' Jubilee'

C. 'Hagley Hybrid'

C. *montana* 'Tetrarose'

C. *armandii* 'Apple Blossom'

Cornus alba 'Elegantissima'
VARIEGATED REDTWIG DOGWOOD
Patterned foliage, creamy white summer flowers, and
wine-red young stems for winter color

The genus *Cornus* comes in a wide range of shapes
and sizes, from medium-sized trees (pages 28-9) to
lowly ground-cover plants (page 110). The shrubby
species probably have the greatest general appeal and
among them there is a wide diversity of forms. Even
within the species *Cornus alba* there are at least three
varieties very different from each other but of equal
value. I would place *C.a.* 'Elegantissima' very high on
my list of top plants, with *C.a.* 'Sibirica' and *C.a.*
'Spaethii' jostling for space on the pedestal.

'Elegantissima' is an appropriate name tag for a
plant with such exquisitely decorated leaves. Oval,
with sharply pointed tips, they are midgreen and
patterned with margins of pure white. There is considerable variety among the leaves in width and outline of variegation. As with a fine painting you can
enjoy this foliage at any distance. In close-up it is the
intricate patterns of variegation that appeal. From
further away the patterns merge and the overall
effect is of a bright and slightly shimmering silvery
shrub. As such it is invaluable in the mixed border
and will bring a touch of light to a planting design,
especially in contrast with darker shrubs and hedges.

In early summer the shrub bears heads of small
creamy white flowers. These are attractive enough
in themselves but they tend to merge visually with
the white edging of the leaves and so they are not a
conspicuous feature. Likewise the fruits – this
variety is very shy to produce fruits but when it does
they are white and almost invisible against the
foliage. The white berries are a more prominent
feature on the unvariegated forms of *C. alba*. Not
only do they appear more consistently but they also
contrast effectively with the coppery red of the fall
leaves in the plain variety.

Cornus alba 'Elegantissima' makes a good host for the more colorful flowers of climbers such as clematis or nasturtiums. I would propose the Viticella clematis 'Venosa Violacea', with its subtle purple and white flowers, as a perfect foil to the white-variegated leaves of the cornus. The deep purple *C. × jackmanii* would look good too, twined through the cornus foliage.

A star feature of all varieties of *C. alba* is the colored bark of the young stems. These are revealed when the leaves drop in fall and they make an outstanding contribution to the garden in winter. In *C.a.* 'Elegantissima' they are a deep wine-red.

• Unrestrained, *C. alba* and its varieties (see below) will reach a height of 8ft/2.5m and a spread of 12ft/3.5m, but you can keep plants within bounds by boldly cutting back in spring. A severe pruning regime is crucial if you want to get the best effects of winter color from the bark. Remember that it is only the new shoots that color up. The plant will survive if you cut all new growth back to base wood in spring, but it is prudent to leave one-third of the shoots each year so that it can make a good start when the sap rises. An advantage of severe pruning is that the foliage grows more vigorously on young shoots and you will get larger and more brightly decorated leaves. This shrub is impartial between sun and part-shade, and thrives in any soil. You will often see it planted near water, not only because it enjoys plenty of moisture, but also because its winter color gives double effect when reflected in water. Propagate by cuttings. Zones 2–7

OPPOSITE *Cornus alba* 'Elegantissima' makes a fine background to a handsome terracotta urn. The shrub is amenable to pruning and it can be trained flat against a wall.

RIGHT *Cornus alba* 'Sibirica', the Westonbirt dogwood, is the variety with the brightest red stems.

OTHER DOGWOODS TO GROW

Cornus alba 'Kesselringii' A dogwood with stems that are such a dark purple-brown that they appear almost black in the thin winter sun. It looks good as part of a mixed planting of cornus and willows with their different stem colors for winter effect. Prune annually in spring, as with other dogwoods grown for stem color. Zones 2–7

Cornus alba 'Sibirica' The Westonbirt dogwood is the best of the group for winter color. The young stems are brilliant scarlet and the leaves color up well before they drop in fall. For outstanding winter effect prune severely in spring. Zones 2–7

Cornus alba 'Spaethii' A variety with glorious yellow and green variegated foliage. It looks fine in the mixed border, particularly with hot-colored flowers in the red to yellow range. Pruned down to the ground in spring it will put up young growth with much larger leaves than normal. Zones 2–7

Cornus alternifolia 'Argentea' A beautiful shrub with silvery variegation, its branches distinctively arranged in tiers. In this respect it resembles the tree *C. controversa* 'Variegata', but the shrub is more compact and the foliage more dense. Height and spread to 20ft/6m. Its slowly developing shape is its virtue, so do not prune, unless you need to remove dead wood. Zones 3–7

Cornus stolonifera 'Flaviramea' (syn. *C. sericea* 'Flaviramea') Grown for its young stems of golden yellow which give superb winter color, especially when grown beside varieties of *C. alba* with red stems to give contrast. If left to its own devices it will grow to the same dimensions as *C. alba*, but like its cousin it will perform best if severely cut back in spring. Zones 2–7

Corylus avellana 'Contorta'

HARRY LAUDER'S WALKING STICK

Twisted corkscrew branches, catkins in early spring

This is an eccentric shrub, but there is room for one or two eccentrics in most gardens. Its twigs and branches twist into shapes that imply great age. In fact Harry Lauder's walking stick is not necessarily old; it is merely a freak variety of the common hazel. It was first spotted in an English hedgerow in the 1860s, which only goes to show that observation is sometimes all that is needed to discover a new plant. Its twisted stems are seen to best effect in winter when they are bare of leaves. They look especially striking with a stubble of hoar frost, which increases the illusion of wizened old age.

In early spring the branches are hung with tassels of pale khaki-colored catkins that contrast with the stems. Later the leaves appear, obscuring the twisted branches. They are attractive leaves, rounded and typical of the hazels, and coloring up yellow in fall. Since the shrub is relatively dull in summer it is a good candidate to decorate with a clematis.

• Height and spread to 15ft/4.5m, which is a little shorter than the common hazelnut or filbert, *C. avellana*, of which it is a variety. Any soil, sun or part-shade. It may be propagated by cuttings. Zones 4–8

OTHER HAZELS TO GROW

Corylus maxima 'Purpurea' The purple-leaved filbert is one of the best shrubs for purple foliage, with generously broad leaves of deep purple-brown. The leaves grow larger if you keep the shrub low by coppicing, but then you will miss the purple-tinted catkins, which appear in spring on bare branches, and also the fall bounty of hazelnuts. Height to 20ft/6m, spread 15ft/4.5m. Zones 4–8

A heavy hoar frost inscribes a white outline to the crazy twisted stems of *Corylus avellana* 'Contorta'. Although it is midwinter the catkins are beginning to form, and within a few weeks the shrub will be decked out in its spring display.

Cotinus coggygria 'Royal Purple'

PURPLE SMOKE BUSH

Purple summer foliage with red fall tints, fluffy flower heads in summer, lasting into fall

The summer foliage of this shrub is a deep velvety purple, which makes it an excellent choice for the back of a mixed border. Against this dark backdrop the inevitably brighter flowers of the border will shine out. In fall the leaves turn to fiery red.

The flowers from which this cotinus earns its name of "smoke bush" are produced by mature plants. Individually tiny, the flowers grow together in a diaphanous plume. In the case of 'Royal Purple' they are reddish brown. The candyflosslike structure of the inflorescences lasts into fall, while the flowers turn into tiny fruits. Unfortunately, if you are to get full value from the foliage, you have to dispense with the flowers. The leaves are fresher and larger on young wood, and for the best foliage you should prune the shrub close to the base each spring. But in doing so you sacrifice its ability to flower.

• Height and spread to 10ft/3m. Sun or part-shade. Any soil; for best fall color, should not be richly manured. Propagate by cuttings. Zones 5–8

OTHER COTINUS TO GROW

Cotinus 'Flame' and **C. 'Grace'** are both larger than *C. coggygria*, with bigger, bolder leaves. *C.* 'Flame' has green foliage that colors in fall to a bright orange-red. 'Grace' has purplish red leaves that turn orange-red. Zones 5–8

So dark that it appears black in contrast with the yellow golden rod (*Solidago*) planted beside it, this *Cotinus coggygria* 'Royal Purple' has been cut back to ground level each spring. Pruning ensures that the plant does not grow too big. It also stimulates it to produce larger leaves.

Cotoneaster horizontalis
Scarlet fall foliage and red berries that
last into winter

The branches of this shrub radiate from the main stems like the bones of a fish. Collectively the stems spread out flat from the center like a fan – a very colorful fan in fall when the leaves color up to a bright scarlet to match the red berries that hug the outline of the "fishbone." In a warm climate this cotoneaster is evergreen. Where it is colder the leaves fall in winter, but the berries remain on the leafless skeleton.

Its growth pattern makes this cotoneaster an excellent plant for growing against a wall. It will form naturally a fan of up to 6ft/1.8m in height and spread. Its radiating habit makes it useful for ground cover too and it is ideal for masking an eyesore like a drain cover. Again, very little maintenance is needed, short of the occasional tidying up with pruners to remove any branches that refuse to lie flat.

In the floral department this cotoneaster is a bit of a disappointment. You would be forgiven for not noticing the tiny pink cups produced in midsummer; they are, however, irresistible to bees.

• A very forgiving plant that will survive in any soil, however poor. Sun or part-shade. Fallen berries will produce seedlings which may be transplanted. Otherwise propagate by cuttings. Zones 5–7

OTHER COTONEASTERS TO GROW

Cotoneaster is a large genus, having over fifty species and many more varieties with widely different uses in the garden. The main feature that they have in common is a fecund production of berries – usually red, but there are some yellow-berried varieties available. They range in habit from prostrate species to small trees.

Cotoneaster horizontalis in fall

Cotoneaster **'Cornubia'** A small tree, up to 20ft/6m in height, with arching branches which are loaded in early summer with clusters of white flowers. In fall the branches sag under their harvest of red berries. The leaves, larger than many others of the genus, are semievergreen. Zones 7–8

Cotoneaster dammeri A prostrate species that spreads out to 6ft/1.8m at a height of only 18in/45cm. Its deciduous leaves color scarlet in fall. Inconspicuous white flowers are followed by waxy red berries. Zones 5–8

Repeat performances by *Fothergilla major*. In spring the modest-looking flowers are powerhouses of scent. In this shaded situation the leaves turn yellow in fall, not red as they might have done in full sun.

Fothergilla major
Cream-colored scented flowers in spring, colorful foliage in fall

Fothergillas produce small flowers, rather like powder puffs, in spring. Cream-colored, they consist of a mass of stamens without petals and produce a strong scent. They appear on bare stems before the leaves open. Fothergillas make good companions for other acid-loving and spring-flowering shrubs, such as the smaller rhododendron species and camellias. After the flowers have passed, *Fothergilla major* (syn. *F. monticola*) makes an inconspicuous, spreading shrub with rounded leaves not unlike those of the related witch hazel *(Hamamelis)*. In fall the foliage comes into its own, coloring brightly before it drops. The fall tints appear to be influenced by the amount of sun that reaches the leaves. Parts of the fothergilla that

are in full shade tend to color to pure yellow. In sun the leaves may assume patches of scarlet, so the overall effect of the plant in fall is of a burning bush, glowing with red and gold.

• Height to 8ft/2.5m, spread 6ft/1.8m. Requires limefree, acidic soil with plenty of humus. Suited to open woodland conditions of part-shade. Propagate by cuttings. Zones 5–8

ANOTHER FOTHERGILLA TO GROW

Fothergilla gardenii The witch alder is the fothergilla to buy if you have a small garden, as it will not exceed 36in/90cm in height or spread. Like its larger relation it requires acidic soil and part-shade. Despite its small size, the plant has flowers and leaves that are almost identical to those of *F. major*. Zones 6–9

An informal area of woodland. The trunk of an oak would normally be quite dark in summer, shaded by its dense canopy of leaves. But this one has been lightened by the bright-leaved ivy *Hedera helix* 'Goldheart' planted at its base. Given free rein, this ivy will shin up into the lower branches of the tree and the heart-shaped immature leaves, seen here, will give way to the mature phase. At this stage the climber becomes more bushy in its upper reaches and gives rise to flowers and fruit. Ivy does not normally damage a healthy tree, unless its foliage cuts out light from the leaves of the host, in which case it should be cut back.

Hedera helix 'Goldheart'

GOLDHEART IVY

Evergreen foliage with a bright yellow
and green pattern

The whole point of gardening, it seems to me, is to tame nature. However much we wish to cultivate the "wild" look in our gardens, this involves a degree of selection of desirable plants and the suppression of the less desirable ones. Here, in the ivies, is a genus of plants that is the epitome of wildness. Think of ivy and you think of neglect: overgrown gardens choked by rampant ivy, ivy-clad ruins, trees strangled by a straitjacket of dense ivy. And yet if you take care with the selection of plants and with pruning and training, ivy can be tamed to work for you. With imaginative treatment, it becomes a most sophisticated and adaptable plant, while still retaining something of an air of wildness.

For a start, ivy is almost infinitely variable. Countless strains have been selected and named, according to their distinctive leaf color or shape, or to their pattern of variegation. *Hedera helix* 'Goldheart' (more properly called 'Oro di Bogliasco') is an attractive variety, with its central pattern of bright yellow, framed with green, but I might equally well recommend others, such as 'Buttercup' (overall yellow), or 'Glacier' (gray-green, with frosted white margins). One curious feature of the ivies is that they remain variable, even when a desirable strain has been selected. The chances are that your *H.h.* 'Goldheart' will have slightly different patterns of variegation from your neighbor's. Even as it grows it may change so that you have different leaf patterns on the same plant. Also, the plant changes character when it enters its adult phase. The adult ivy is more bushy and less clinging, and its leaves become less "ivy-shaped" and more rounded. Only the adult ivy carries flowers and fruit. Growing ivies is an mysterious adventure.

The simplest way to use ivy is to grow it up a wall or fence. It will grow tightly against the surface, with no loose growth to sway around in wind, and make a valuable contribution to the vertical garden. You can regard it as a background against which to grow an outer layer of climbers such as clematis or even roses. *H.h.* 'Goldheart' makes a wonderful background for blue or purple clematis such as *Clematis alpina* (spring-flowering), *C.* 'Lasurstern' (summer-flowering), and Viticella clematis such as 'Etoile Violette' or 'Royal Velours' (flowering in late summer). It is perfectly easy to grow such climbers together, provided that their roots are well separated so that they do not compete for nourishment. Simply plant the ivy to fan out radially from the base and place the clematis at least 36in/90cm to the side away from

Some ivies, while remaining "evergreen," give fall color. *Hedera helix* 'Gracilis', shown here, is one of them.

the sun. This way the clematis will grow across the ivy toward the light; unlike the ivy, it needs wires to support it and the occasional tying in to ensure that it grows in the desired direction.

Ivy is equally happy grown as ground cover, but as such it may be so successful that nothing much can be grown with it. Bulbs are an exception, and snowdrops and daffodils may survive happily under a carpet of ivy, with their flowers and foliage reaching up in the appropriate season. Ivy's tolerance of dry shade makes it a very useful ground cover under most trees. Here, however, it has one limitation: the variegated forms, of which *H.h.* 'Goldheart' is one, need sunlight to make them color up well. In deep shade it would be better to select pure green forms with interesting leaf shapes: a good example is *H.h.* 'Merion Beauty', which has leaves shaped like those of a maple.

Hedera helix 'Marginata Major'

Hedera helix 'Conglomerata'

For lovers of the eccentric, there is a variety of English ivy that is neither climbing nor ground-covering, but which stands independently as a small shrub. This is *H.h.* 'Conglomerata'. It is an admirable curiosity, will puzzle your visitors, and makes an appealing evergreen mound. If you like the idea of ivy in three dimensions, you can make a solid shape by growing a climbing ivy on a wire frame.

You might also consider tinkering with ivy in two dimensions. I was so taken with the idea in a magazine photograph that I took my pruners and went straight into the garden and cut out the shape of a hand in a fan of ivy growing against the wall. This light-hearted joke took no more than half an hour. Within a few weeks the ivy had regenerated and filled the gaps. So you can use a wall of ivy as a drawing slate, the beauty of it being that nature eventually wipes the slate clean – as it always does.

• *Hedera helix* varieties will reach a height and spread of 30ft/9m on suitable supports. Any soil, sun or shade. Zones 5–9

OTHER IVIES TO GROW

Hedera algeriensis 'Gloire de Marengo' (sometimes called *H. canariensis* 'Gloire de Marengo') An outstanding large-leaved variegated ivy, which is not reliably hardy and so is often grown as a houseplant. It has red stems and the leaves are dark green, broken with patterns of gray-green and with margins of white. Makes good ground cover in a mild climate. Grows to 12ft/3.5m. Zones 9–10

Hedera colchica The Persian ivy has much larger leaves than *H. helix*, with several variegated forms. *Hedera colchica* 'Sulphur Heart' has patterning similar to that of *H. helix* 'Goldheart' on leaves up to 10in/25cm long. This ivy grows rapidly, to a maximum height of around 30ft/9m. Zones 6–9

Hedera helix 'Glacier'

The crude shape of a hand has been cut into a broad-leaved ivy, *Hedera algeriensis* 'Gloire de Marengo', growing on a stone wall. Finer effects can be achieved with small-leaved ivies.

Hedera colchica 'Sulphur Heart'

Hydrangea quercifolia in summer

Hydrangea quercifolia

OAK-LEAVED HYDRANGEA

Late summer flowers, interesting foliage that colors
to deep red and purple in fall

All the hydrangeas give great value with their generous heads of flowers, usually carried in late summer,
a season when relatively few flowering shrubs are in
action. This one has the additional merit of outstanding foliage. The lobed leaves are, as the name
suggests, reminiscent of oak leaves. In fall they color
to deep shades of red and purple. Some of them remain on the shrub through the winter, bringing a
little much-wanted color to the garden. These old
leaves are pushed off by the fresh bright green
growth in spring.

The flowers of *Hydrangea quercifolia* are more
oblong than the globular heads of the familiar
mopheaded hydrangeas. The individual florets are
pure white, but the unopened buds give the flower
heads a hint of green. The flower heads tend to flop
under their own weight, more so when they are
weighed down by rain. In fact the habit of the whole
plant is a little droopy, and it may need support. I
have seen *H. quercifolia* trained against a wall, to great
effect. One of the best varieties is the double-
flowered *H.q.* 'Snowflake'.

Hydrangea macrophylla
in fall

• Height and spread to 7ft/2m. Like other hydrangeas *H. quercifolia* thrives in part-shade and hates its roots to become dry. Any soil. Zones 5–9

OTHER HYDRANGEAS TO GROW

Hydrangea arborescens 'Grandiflora' A lovely mopheaded shrub with huge greeny white flowers. Zones 4–9

Hydrangea macrophylla The colors of the popular Hortensia mopheads vary according to the acidity of the soil. Good blues only occur naturally on acidic soils. On alkaline soils, if you are desperate for blue flowers, you can treat the plants regularly with an iron sulfate. Good varieties include sky-blue 'Gentian Dome' ('Enziandom'), 'Générale Vicomtesse de Vibraye', which ranges from rose-red to bright blue, and 'Maréchal Foch', which can vary from deep pink to dark blue. One of the best features of these hydrangeas is that the flowers die gracefully. They fade on the plant, without withering, and in the process assume a progression of rich tints. If you cut the flower heads during this fading process and dry them off, these colors are often preserved. Zones 6–9

Hydrangea sargentiana The special merit of this species lies in the foliage, which is like dark green velvet. The flower heads are pale blue. Zones 7–9

Complementary colors. The sky-blue flowers of *Hydrangea macrophylla* 'Gentian Dome' make a strong contrast against the orange fall foliage of *Acer japonicum* 'Vitifolium'. The maple will soon shed its leaves, but the hydrangea flowers will die slowly and gracefully. First the blue tint will discolor slightly and fade to purple. Gradually the flowers will brown off and become brittle, but they will never look unsightly, and it is not necessary to remove them until new growth begins in spring.

Mahonia × media

Evergreen foliage, scented yellow winter flowers, purple fruit bunches in summer

The multiple flower spikes of *Mahonia × media* light up the garden in midwinter like bright yellow candelabra. They cast a delicate scent on the air, giving a happy illusion that spring is not far behind.

Even without its lovely winter flowers, *Mahonia × media* would be well worth growing as an architectural shrub, and for its handsome evergreen foliage. The leaves are arranged in rosettes, each leaf divided into numerous leaflets which are brittle and prickly and reminiscent of holly leaves. The plant has a

Mahonia aquifolium flowers in spring

Mahonia × media 'Lionel Fortescue' flowers in winter

Mahonia aquifolium berries in summer

somewhat stiff, erect habit and the flowers grow from the center of the leaf rosettes. In addition to the flowers and foliage, the mahonias have a third string to their bow, the purple-blue bunches of fruit that follow the flowers and decorate the shrub throughout the summer.

There are several excellent named varieties of *Mahonia* × *media*, including 'Charity', which grows to a height of 10ft/3m and spread of 8ft/2.5m; its leaves are up to 18in/45cm long, with long prickly leaflets. *M.* × *m.* 'Lionel Fortescue' has broader leaflets with upright flowers. These and other mahonias may be pruned after flowering to contain their size for the smaller garden.

• Any well-drained soil, sun or shade. Zones 8–9

OTHER MAHONIAS TO GROW

Mahonia aquifolium The Oregon grape is a less striking shrub than *M.* × *media*, growing only to a height of 5ft/1.5m. Its yellow flowers appear in dense clusters in spring – later than the other mahonias – and they are followed by generous bunches of the purple fruits that earn the plant its popular name. Most seed-raised plants sold as *M. aquifolium* are hybrids, which tend to send up numerous suckers from their roots, and may colonize a shady corner of the garden within a few years. Zones 5–8

Mahonia japonica One of the parents of the hybrid *M.* × *media*, with many of its attractive features. However, it is more bushy in habit and less upright, with drooping flower spikes and more spindly leaves. It comes into flower a few weeks later than *M.* × *media* and so you can extend the flowering season by planting the two together. The hybrid inherits its more rigid characteristics from its other parent, *M. lomariifolia*, which is a magnificent tall and erect shrub, but not reliably hardy. Zones 6–8

The passion flower produces flowers over such a long period that by the end of the season the fruits derived from earlier flowers coincide with the latest blooms. Winter frosts put an end to this production line. This climber will benefit from the protection offered by a house wall.

Passiflora caerulea
PASSION FLOWER
Decorative foliage, exotic summer flowers, colorful fall fruits

The passion flower is so called because the parts of its wide-open flowers can be taken to represent the Passion of Christ. The frill of striped filaments around the center, for instance, can be read as a symbol for the crown of thorns. Whatever the interpretation, *Passiflora caerulea* is a most dramatic flower, exotic in all parts, with leaves divided into five fingerlike leaflets, and bright orange fruits ripening in fall and hanging heavy on the climber as it begins to die back in winter. Flowers are produced over a long season, and continue to appear while the fruits are ripening.

• Height and spread up to 20ft/6m on a sunny wall or trellis. Originating in South America, *P. caerulea* is not hardy in an area that has cold winters. To be on the safe side you may elect to grow it in a sun porch, but it is so vigorous that it may become matted unless you cut it back hard every winter. Any soil. Propagate by seed or cuttings. Zones 9–10

Phlomis fruticosa

JERUSALEM SAGE

Evergreen foliage, yellow flowers over a long period in summer, winter seed heads

Jerusalem sage grows wild in the rocky limestone scrub of the Mediterranean, where it is hot and dry in summer. The more closely you can match these conditions in the garden, the better it will perform for you. In a sunny spot it will put out heads of yellow flowers throughout the early summer. Hooded, like those of the true sages, the flowers are arranged in loosely circular flower heads and their yellow hue picks up a hint of the same color as the

Phlomis fruticosa in early summer

Phlomis fruticosa in winter

pale gray-green tint of the foliage. The leaves are narrow, soft, and slightly hairy, and remain on the plant throughout the winter.

The individual flower heads drop off in time, but the rounded seed heads remain. Leave these on the plant and they will be rewarding in the winter. By then they will have dried into brittle, brownish pepperpots which look attractive with a seasoning of hoar frost. You might pick a few for the everlasting flower display.

Like other yellow-flowered shrubs, this phlomis looks good associated with flowers in the blue to lilac range. It is wonderful underplanted with the clear blue *Geranium* 'Johnson's Blue'.

• Height up to 5ft/1.5m, spread to 6ft/1.8m, but it can be pruned in spring to make a smaller shrub. Requires full sun. Any soil, including poorly nourished ground. Propagate by cuttings. Zones 7–10

ANOTHER PHLOMIS TO GROW

Phlomis russeliana A herbaceous perennial, reaching a height and spread of 36in/90cm before dying back in winter. The individual flowers are similar in form and color to those of *P. fruticosa*, but the rounded flower heads are spaced along the stem in tiers, with gaps of about 3in/8cm between them. These make dramatic seed heads in winter. Propagate by division in spring or fall. Zones 5–8

Pieris 'Forest Flame'

JAPANESE ANDROMEDA

Evergreen with scented flowers in spring and colorful young foliage through the summer

There is a time in late spring when the two star features of pieris coincide. Before the hanging bunches of creamy pearllike flowers have passed over, the stems are beginning to glow red with new leafy growth. The bright young scarlet leaves sprout from the tips of the shoots and the shrub remains ablaze with color for much of the summer.

Pieris 'Forest Flame' is one of several hybrids related to *P. japonica,* all of which perform this double act with flowers and foliage. *P.* 'Firecrest' is a hybrid with similar flame-red young shoots. In *P.* 'Bert Chandler' the young foliage is salmon-pink, fading to cream before assuming its mature green coloration. There is also an attractive variegated form of *P. japonica* which has leaves edged with white.

• Height to 12ft/3.5m, spread 8ft/2.5m. A shrub for the open woodland, requiring acidic soil and rich humus. Propagate by cuttings. Zones 6–8

Pieris 'Forest Flame' in late spring

A double act by *Pyracantha coccinea*. In summer (ABOVE LEFT) the cream flowers harmonize with the amber rose 'Climbing Lady Hillingdon'. By fall (ABOVE RIGHT) the rose is bare but the pyracantha is still ablaze with berries.

Pyracantha coccinea

FIRETHORN

Evergreen with red fall berries following creamy white summer flowers

As a shrub that has something to show for itself in most months of the year, *Pyracantha coccinea* takes a lot of beating, although it is deciduous in the northern part of its hardiness range or during particularly harsh winters. Its greatest glory is the blaze of bright red berries that sets the garden alight in fall. The berries last well into winter, although they make a tempting larder for migrating robins and waxwings.

The prolific flowers appear in midsummer and we would pay more attention to them if they did not coincide with the more conspicuous performers in the border such as roses, delphiniums, clematis, and poppies. The flowers are cream-colored and tiny

but they grow in dense swathes that cover the plant. A clever association that I have seen is the rambler rose 'Wedding Day' climbing through a mature wall-trained pyracantha. The creamy white flowers of the rose open at the same time as those of the shrub, and again in the fall the rose hips coincide with the pyracantha's berries. In both seasons, the two plants display similar features that are just different enough to create interest.

Although perfectly satisfactory as freestanding shrubs, pyracanthas are often trained flat to cover a wall. The evergreen foliage of small, finely toothed leaves makes an attractive background year-round and it provides a good contrast when the flowers and berries hold sway.

To train a pyracantha as an espalier, you will need to fix horizontal wires against the wall or fence, some 12in/30cm apart. Start with a young pot-grown plant with a straight stem, and plant it at least 12in/30cm away from the wall to give the roots a chance to find moisture. Wear gloves and handle the plant with respect, as it has long, sharp thorns along the stems. Keep the leader vertical and tie in the laterals horizontally, cutting out any that cannot be made to lie flat. As it grows, tie in new laterals and maintain the leader until it reaches the required height. At that point, trim the tip to arrest further vertical growth.

Pyracantha can be grown as a hedge too, and here its thorns can be considered an advantage as they help to make it an impenetrable barrier. However, the display of flowers and berries is bound to be reduced in proportion to the amount of trimming that is needed to keep the hedge tidy.

• As a freestanding shrub, height and spread to 20ft/6m. A spread of up to 30ft/9m can be achieved on a wall-trained espalier. Pyracanthas are tolerant of any soil and will flourish in sun or part-shade. Propagate by cuttings of the current year's shoots in late summer. Trim trained plants, including hedges, in summer. Zones 6–9

OTHER PYRACANTHAS TO GROW

Pyracantha coccinea 'Lalandei' This is the variety of *P. coccinea* that is most commonly available. It is more vigorous and larger in leaf and berry than the species. The berries are light red, verging on orange. Zones 5–9

Pyracantha 'Mohave' A disease-resistant hybrid with red berries. Zones 6–9

Pyracantha 'Orange Glow' If you aspire to bright orange berries, this is the hybrid for you. The berries are so bright that you could use it to bring a little fall cheer to a part-shaded corner. Zones 6–9

Rosa glauca

Gray foliage, single pink flowers in summer,
red fall hips

A rose grown for its dark gray foliage suffused with pink, *Rosa glauca* (syn. *R. rubrifolia*) has the added bonus of a magnificent display of deep red hips in fall. It originated as a wild rose in Central Europe, and like many wild roses it has flowers that are modest but delightful. They are single, of a shade of pink that echoes the traces of pink in the leaves, with yellow stamens. Compared to the concentration of hips in fall, the flowers are sparsely scattered over the shrub at any one time, but they do appear over a relatively long period in summer.

I have seen this rose grown very effectively in a red fall border, with great sprays of red hips arching over penstemons and the deep red *Dahlia* 'Bishop

Rosa glauca flower

Rosa glauca hips in fall

Rosa moyesii flowers in summer

Rosa moyesii hips in winter

of Llandaff'. But in this red color combination, the earlier pink flowers would look unsightly; it is a challenge to a gardener's ingenuity to arrange the planting so that the pink flowers associate well with a pink or blue partner in summer, only to be replaced by a bright red partner to accompany the fall hips. The leaves alone, however, make an attractive foil for almost any plant.

If it is allowed a free rein, *R. glauca* will grow into a bushy shrub. But it is a forgiving plant and in a small garden it can be pruned right back so that fresh young growth begins again from the base in spring.

• Height and spread 7ft/2m. Leaf color is better in sun; any soil. Propagate by cuttings. Zones 2–7

Rosa moyesii

Single scarlet flowers in summer, followed by bright red fall hips

Grown for its magnificent hips, *Rosa moyesii* is a large shrub with a height and spread of up to 15ft/4.5m. This species rose is clearly unsuitable for the small garden, but its hybrid *R*. 'Geranium' is more containable at about 8ft/2.5m.

The species *R. moyesii* itself is a magnificent sight in fall, with long branches arching under the weight of its bright red hips, which grow in clusters down each branch. *R. moyesii* has elongated hips, swollen at the base, while those of *R*. 'Geranium' are more rounded. Both are a vivid red, and last well on the shrub provided that the local birds do not develop an appetite for them; this seems to vary with the area.

There can be no fruit, of course, without flowers, but in this rose the flowers are sometimes regarded as a poor relation. This is unfair, as the single flowers are handsome, if small in proportion to the plant, and short-lived. In the species and in *R.* 'Geranium' they are a rich blood-red, but in the hybrid *R.* 'Highdownensis' they are pink.

• Will grow on any soil, though shallow limestone needs good preparation, with ample compost dug in to sustain the deep roots. Sun or part-shade. Propagate by cuttings. Zones 5–7

Rosa rugosa
Crinkled foliage, scented flowers throughout the summer, large red fall hips

The majority of roses, of course, are grown for their flowers. There are others in which the hips are the strong suit. Others again are chosen for their foliage. In the Rugosa roses all three features, flowers, hips, and foliage, are of value in the garden.

The Latin word *rugosa* means wrinkled, and refers to the slightly rough texture of the leaves that characterizes the group. This roughness is due to the slight depression of the veins below the surface. The leaves are resistant to diseases to which many roses are prone, such as black spot and mildew. In my experience they never need spraying, unless against aphids. A further feature of the foliage, unusual in a rose, is the good (albeit short-lived) fall color. For a short time the leaves turn yellow.

It is the color and form of the flowers that distinguish the different members of the group. The species *Rosa rugosa* itself has flowers of a clear magenta-pink. If you find this hue a little harsh you might prefer to go for the white form, 'Alba'. For a

Rosa rugosa hips in winter

Toward the end of the summer, late flowers on Rugosa roses often coincide with hips derived from earlier flowers. This example is 'Fru Dagmar Hastrup'. The earliest hips endure and the late ones catch up with them so that by late fall the hip-bearing Rugosas are a mass of color.

Rosa rugosa 'Alba' in summer

double white, choose the deliciously scented 'Blanc Double de Coubert'. 'Roseraie de l'Haÿ' is a double mauve, the color of a bishop's cassock, and is also beautifully scented. 'Fru Dagmar Hastrup' has exquisite single flowers of a pale shell-pink. All the Rugosas are repeat-flowering.

With some, but by no means all, of the Rugosas, the flowers give rise to fat and succulent red hips. The best plants for hips are *R. rugosa* itself, and *RR. rugosa* 'Alba', 'Scabrosa', and 'Fru Dagmar Hastrup'.

• Height and spread 7ft/2m, though these roses can be kept pruned to a more compact size. Sun or light shade, any soil. Suitable to be grown as a loose hedge. Salt-resistant, so suitable for seaside gardens. Propagate by cuttings. *R. rugosa* is best in zones 2–8; 'Alba' and 'Fru Dagmar Hastrup' in 3–8; and 'Blanc Double de Coubert' and 'Roseraie de l'Haÿ' in 4–8.

Rosa Floribunda Group

Multiple blooms over a long period

The Floribundas are some of the most useful roses, not only because they flower so generously, with several blooms on a single stem, but also because they often remain in flower over such a long period.

Rosa 'Iceberg' is one of the most popular of the Floribunda roses, and deservedly so, because of its exceptionally long flowering season. Its first flush of pure white flowers coincides with the peak rose season of midsummer. Provided that you keep it deadheaded, it continues to flower abundantly into fall and may even produce buds intermittently until midwinter. It will reach a height of 5ft/1.5m and spread of 36in/90cm. There is also a climbing variety, which reaches a height of 10ft/3m, but it is not as hardy as the bush variety.

Rosa 'Iceberg'

If your taste runs to a rose of an outrageously vivid red, then *R.* 'Eye Paint' may be the one for you. The single flowers are scarlet, with a pure white center that makes the color all the more intense. Although this rose does not flower over such an extended season, it offers a second performance in fall when it is covered with a mass of small vermilion hips. It is a vigorous rose, making a dense shrub of 5ft/1.5m in height and spread.

Another outstanding white Floribunda is 'Margaret Merril'. Like 'Iceberg' it produces trusses of well-formed pure white flowers, which can be identified by their pinkish stamens. As an additional attraction it has a lovely scent. On the down side, though, its flowering season is not so long, and it does not stand up very well to wet weather. If you have space, you might consider growing 'Iceberg' and 'Margaret Merril' together, so you can enjoy the longevity of the one and the fragrance of the other.

• Best in full sun and rich soil. Zones 7–10

RIGHT An eyeful of pure color. *Rosa* 'Eye Paint' is one of the most powerful scarlet roses – not one for the faint-hearted. It has a second innings (ABOVE) with vermilion hips in fall. It looks especially good when planted in quantity in a larger garden.

Rosmarinus officinalis

ROSEMARY

Aromatic evergreen leaves, blue spring flowers

There is no need to confine rosemary to the herb garden. It will hold its own in the mixed border in association with more obviously glamorous shrubs and perennials. It is best placed beside a path where you will catch the fragrance as you brush past. The small, pointed, aromatic leaves are held year-round. They are grayish green, paler on the underside, and release their scent when you run them through your hand.

In a mild season the flowers begin to appear in winter and extend well into the spring. They are modest in size but appear in profusion. In the common form of rosemary they are insipid in color, a pale blue that tends to merge into the foliage. It is worth seeking out the variety 'Benenden Blue', which is sometimes also listed as 'Collingwood Ingram'. This has flowers of a more full-blooded blue, and darker foliage. It looks good with a spring-flowering variety of ceanothus behind it, and an underplanting of blue spring bulbs such as Siberian squill. There is also a variety, *R. officinalis* var. *albiflorus*, with white flowers.

• Height and spread 6ft/1.8m. Being a plant of Mediterranean origin, it demands full sun and a mild climate, though in colder areas it can be grown in a pot and moved into shelter for the winter. It needs well-drained soil. Rosemary has a tendency to become leggy, and it is good practice to prune shoots back to half their length in spring. In mild areas it is possible to grow rosemary as a hedge, but it is hard to keep it tidy. Propagate by cuttings. Zones 8–9

A well-placed pair of *Rosmarinus officinalis*, beside a flight of steps. You can hardly avoid brushing against them, so releasing the scent.

Rubus phoenicolasius

JAPANESE WINEBERRY

Decorative flowers and fruits in early and late summer, arching red stems for winter color

This rubus arrived in my garden as a chance seedling, hitching a ride with another plant that I had bought at a nursery. Now I would not be without it. It has something interesting to offer year-round. Its star performance is in winter when it reveals its long, arching stems, bare of leaves but covered along their length by a stubble of fine thorns, rather like a moss rose. These stems are reddish brown in color, glowing orange when they catch the light of the low winter sun.

In spring and summer the stems are masked with leaves and it is the clusters of developing flower buds that demand our attention. Red and bristly like the stems, the buds are slightly sticky to the touch. They open briefly to reveal the small star-shaped white

LEFT The curious little flower of *Rubus phoenicolasius*. The buds, which have sticky bristles, open for a day or two to allow the flowers to be fertilized. Then they close again to protect the developing fruit (ABOVE).

flowers. Bees go about their work of fertilization and then, curiously, the buds close up again to cover the developing fruits. At this point it is prudent to drape the plant with netting, because when the buds re-open to reveal the fruits they are irresistible to birds. The fruits are shaped like blackberries, their near relations, but they are bright scarlet. They are delicious to eat but if, like the Japanese, you grow them for the table, you need to have a modest appetite. A bush will only feed a family for a single dessert.

• Height to 8ft/2.5m, spread to 10ft/3m. Sun or part-shade, any soil. Left to its own devices the plant will make an untidy bush. It is better to train it flat against a wall, tying the stems against wires to make a loose fan; cut out from the base those stems that grow away from the wall. Each spring cut out about one-third of the stems to encourage new growth. Propagate by layering, cuttings, or seed. Look out for self-seeded plants, spread by birds. Zones 6–8

OTHER RUBUS TO GROW

Rubus biflorus Another winter performer, grown for its stems. However, in this rubus the stems are a silvery white, the color coming from a white bloom overlaying stems of a pale greenish pink. The stems are upright, with branches coming off them at right angles. The general effect is of a tangled white bird-cage. Zones 5–8

Rubus cockburnianus Similar to *R. biflorus*, with white stems conspicuous in winter, but the stems are arching, like those of *R. phoenicolasius*, and the white bloom overlays a reddish brown base color. In summer the plant produces gray-green ferny foliage, but flowers and fruit are insignificant. Height and spread to 15ft/4.5m. Zones 5–9

Rubus phoenicolasius in winter, with *Mahonia japonica*

Tropaeolum speciosum

FLAME CREEPER

Brilliant red summer flowers followed by
colorful fruits in fall

There are gardeners who baulk at bright red flowers but make an exception for this vivid red nasturtium. Given the delicate scale of the flowers and leaves it is surprising how far it can shin up a host plant. It makes drooping curtains of scarlet up to 15ft/4.5m above the ground. It needs a supporting plant where the stems or leaves are close together, and nothing is better for this purpose than topiary yew or boxwood. The intense red flowers of the tropaeolum look sensational against this dark green background. And the informality of the creeper makes a pleasing contrast with the stiff regularity of the topiary.

In fall the flame creeper produces blue berries, this color made all the more intense by the fringe of faded red flower bracts that surround them. The first frosts wipe out all vestiges of the plant above the ground, but its underground rhizome survives over winter.

• Any soil, full sun. Propagate by division of roots in spring. Zones 8–10

The scarlet flowers of *Tropaeolum speciosum* (RIGHT) give rise to brilliant blue berries (ABOVE).

Viburnum opulus flowers in late spring

wonderful in late spring growing next to plants with flowers of contrasting form. The best juxtaposition I have seen is with another good viburnum, *V. plicatum* 'Mariesii'.

● Any soil, sun or part-shade. Propagate by cuttings. Zones 3–8

OTHER VIBURNUMS TO GROW

The viburnums are a large and useful genus of shrubs. Some of the best give good value in winter.

Viburnum × bodnantense 'Dawn' This slightly ungainly and lanky deciduous shrub produces its first flowers in late summer, when they are hardly noticeable in comparison with all the summer splendors that are still around. But when in mild areas it is still

Viburnum opulus

EUROPEAN CRANBERRY BUSH
Attractive foliage, white spring flowers, bright red fall berries

A classic dual-purpose shrub, *Viburnum opulus* has large white flower heads, rather like hydrangea flowers, in late spring, followed by brilliant red berries in fall. In between times the deciduous foliage is a good feature, the leaves being lobed rather like those of field maple (*Acer campestre*).

The shrub makes a height of 15ft/4.5m, and if space is tight you should consider *V.o.* 'Compactum', which is identical in all other respects but only reaches a height of 6ft/1.8m. For yellow berries, choose *V.o.* 'Xanthocarpum'.

Another very different variety of the same plant is *V.o.* 'Roseum' (syn. 'Sterile'). This has spherical flower heads like creamy white bobbles. Being sterile, it has the disadvantage of not bearing berries; it is also very aphid prone. However, it looks

Viburnum opulus berries in fall

Viburnum × *bodnantense* 'Dawn' in winter

flowering in midwinter, after all its leaves have fallen, it is another matter. The flowers are pale pink and gloriously scented. Zones 6–9

***Viburnum plicatum* 'Mariesii'** An outstanding shrub, with gracefully tiered branches which are dressed in summer with large white flower heads. In fall the leaves turn a coppery red and there is sometimes a crop of small scarlet berries. In *V.p.* 'Pink Beauty' the flowers are tinged with pink. Height 8ft/2.5m, spread 15ft/4.5m. Zones 5–8

Viburnum tinus An evergreen, with glossy dark green leaves. It flowers throughout the winter with clusters of small white flowers with pink buds. 'Eve Price' is a good variety, more compact, with smaller leaves and flowers tinged with pink. Zones 9–10

Viburnum plicatum 'Pink Beauty' in summer

ESSENTIAL PERENNIALS, BIENNIALS, AND ANNUALS

This group offers a huge range of plants, and the performance plants among them make a diverse collection. Some have been selected for their double action of flowers and seed heads. This category includes allium, iris, lunaria, and pulsatilla. Others qualify because, in addition to their flowers, they have especially worthwhile foliage. Among these are acanthus, alchemilla, hosta, and silybum. Others again have been included because their display is so long-lived: among them are the hellebores and *Viola cornuta*. Substantial coverage is given to the ornamental grasses and sedges, a family of plants that is sometimes underrated in gardens. The grasses have a subtle beauty that makes them irresistible to the discerning gardener. Moreover, as with most plants grown predominantly for their foliage, their peak season lasts much longer than the majority of floral displays. The same goes for ferns, for instance.

Most of the annuals and biennials featured here come under the heading of "self-seeders." Once established they will spring up all over the place, and will often produce more than one generation in a season. With self-seeders it is difficult to draw the line between asset and pest, but the best of them will bring distinction to your garden. Walls, steps, and paths look all the better when clothed with an improvised display of plants that have arrived under their own steam. The effect is to soften the hard structural lines. By definition, of course, self-seeders can be left to their own devices. But they do not always appear in the right place. Gardening with these plants is not the usual active concern of growing seeds and planting out, but rather the passive business of rooting up self-sown seedlings that have sprung up where you do not want them.

The first mists of fall have appeared, but still the annual *Cosmos* 'Sensation' is flowering at full strength. Young plants were put into the ground to replace tulips in early summer. The wispy fern-like foliage of the cosmos makes an unobtrusive companion to a sequence of border perennials. The cosmos comes into its own at midsummer and flowers continuously until midfall, when the nights become too cold and the days too short for its buds to open. Then it is time to heave the plants out of the border and to replace them with bulbs, so that the cycle begins again for next year.

Acanthus spinosus seed heads

Acanthus spinosus

BEAR'S BREECHES

Architectural foliage, tall flower spikes
in late summer

Wherever it is placed in the garden, acanthus will create a powerful effect for much of the season, first by its dense and graceful foliage of shiny intense green, later by the sensational bicolored flower spikes. Placed on its own in a prominent position it makes an attractive eye-catcher, but, by virtue of the subdued colors of its flowers, it is also a polite partner for other plants. It grows large, with arching leaves reaching a spread of 5ft/1.5m and the flowers towering to 6ft/1.8m. At this size you might assume that it only has a place in a large garden, but I would disagree. Even a garden that is little bigger than a pocket handkerchief does not have to be limited to miniature plants. Contrasts of scale are important in any planting, and in a small garden striking architectural perennials like acanthus can play a role equivalent to that of shrubs in a larger one. They are useful too if you want a labor-saving garden with fewer, larger plants.

Among the best of the acanthus is *Acanthus spinosus*. Its leaves are deeply divided and pointed, but though they look prickly they are perfectly soft and harmless. In shade the plant will produce only leaves, no flowers, but you would be perfectly justified in growing it solely for its foliage. It looks splendid in the company of hostas and ferns in a shady foliage garden.

A position in full sun will encourage the plant to flower. Held aloft on long, stiff stems, the flower spikes are as bold and prickly as the foliage is soft. The individual flowers are white, but they are hooded by an outer structure, the calyx, shaped like a mussel shell, of a distinctive silvery green color, tinged with purple. The base of each flower is fringed with stiff, thistlelike bracts, which make the flower head extremely prickly to handle. After the flowers have dropped, the spike, with its decorative calyces and bracts, survives well into the fall while the seed containers swell to the size of marbles. Cut down at this stage, the spikes can be dried to join the vase of "everlasting" flowers which extends the pleasure of your garden through the winter.

• Grow acanthus in full sun, in any well-drained soil. Split the plants after several years, when they become overcrowded. Propagate by seed or by cuttings. Zones 6–9

ANOTHER ACANTHUS TO GROW

Acanthus mollis The leaves of *A. mollis* are not so deeply divided as those of *A. spinosus*. Otherwise it is very similar in appearance, and the harmless-looking flower heads have the same prickly bracts. It is a slightly less hardy plant, however. Zones 8–10

An appropriate setting, in front of a classical column, for a clump of *Acanthus mollis*. The Ancient Greeks used acanthus leaves as a *motif* in their architecture. Companion plants here include the thistle *Onopordum acanthium,* with acanthuslike leaves.

Agapanthus Headbourne Hybrids in late summer, with *Geranium psilostemon*

worth waiting for. And when it is finally time to cut down the seed heads they can easily be dried for the everlasting flower arrangement.

Agapanthus Headbourne Hybrids belong to the lily family and their flowers are not unlike those of another genus within the same family, the alliums or onions. The flower head is a globe of azure blue, made up of a mass of trumpet-shaped flowers on slender stalks radiating from the central stem.

Agapanthus is a native of South Africa, and even *A.* Headbourne Hybrids, hardiest of the clan, are only fully hardy in a warm climate. The need to protect the plants is one reason for growing agapanthus in pots, which you can put under cover for the winter. The plants also benefit from a relatively dry soil while they are dormant.

If you choose to grow agapanthus in the border, its blue flowers look well in association with yellow companions, especially the pale yellow of *Achillea* 'Moonshine' or *Anthemis tinctoria* 'E.C. Buxton'. For a

Agapanthus Headbourne Hybrids

AFRICAN BLUE LILY

Globes of sky-blue flowers in late summer, fall seed heads

It is possible to be *too* tidy in the garden. When the glorious blue flower heads of agapanthus begin to fade after several weeks of late summer display, it is tempting to cut them to the ground for the sake of tidiness. If you can resist this urge the plants will reward you with an fall show of seed heads; more modest, I admit, than the summer flowers but still

Agapanthus Headbourne Hybrids in fall

cool effect, a background of silver foliage is striking; any of the artemisias will do. If your garden palette runs to bold color relationships, then you might consider underplanting agapanthus with the lovely Californian fuchsia, *Zauschneria californica*. This produces a mass of pale red trumpets on silver-green foliage which will, with any luck, coincide with the flowers of your agapanthus.

• Height to 30in/75cm. Full sun, any soil. The strap-like leaves form clumps up to 24in/60cm wide, which die back in winter. Propagate by division of the roots in spring or fall. Repot container-grown agapanthus every two or three years, splitting the plant each time so it can expand. Agapanthus can be grown from seed, but will not reach flowering size for four years. Zones 8–10

OTHER AGAPANTHUS TO GROW

There are numerous varieties available, selected for size and for hue, and names are constantly changing. The hardiest types are those with narrow leaves that die back in winter. Plants with broad evergreen leaves are the least hardy, and need winter protection, but are among the most spectacular if you can protect them over winter.

Agapanthus campanulatus The ancestor of *A.* Headbourne Hybrids, similar in habit and size, with variable blue flowers ranging from powder-blue to ultramarine. There is an excellent white form, *A. campanulatus* var. *albidus*. Height 30in/75cm, spread 60cm/24in. Zones 8–10

Agapanthus 'Loch Hope' One of the best, but not commonly available. It is tall and sturdy, growing to a height of 4ft/1.2m with deep blue flowers that come late enough to coincide with early fall performers such as sedums. Zones 8–10

Agrostemma githago
CORN COCKLE
Pink flowers throughout the summer

Agrostemma githago 'Milas' in summer, with phalaris

Agrostemma githago, the corn cockle, may originally have been brought into the United States accidentally in a sack of grain, or deliberately as an ornamental flower. A native of grainfields, it thrived in its new environment – so much so that in some farming states it is now considered a noxious weed. Kept under control, however, it makes an excellent, low-maintenance garden plant.

One of the virtues of the corn cockle is that it takes up very little space. The plant is adapted to surviving side by side with a tall-growing crop and so it should fit in with your existing planting without your having to make space for it.

The flowers, which are upward facing and held on the tips of the plant, are wide open to the sun. The rims of the petals are dark pink, lightening to white toward the center tube, and there are rays of dotted lines radiating inward. They are pretty flowers, and look especially good in association with other flowers in the pink range, for instance the magenta *Geranium psilostemon* and old-fashioned roses, or else against a background of silver foliage, such as that of *Artemisia arborescens*.

The flowers last for several weeks but when they do begin to die off you are faced with a quandary. You will want to save seed for next year, and so the sensible course of action is to leave the seed heads to mature until the seeds are ready (after about six weeks). On the other hand, if you elect to deadhead the plants after flowering, you will have a second burst of flowers – but by the time they appear, up to two months later, it may be well into fall, when it will be too late for seeds to mature. The best thing – as so often in gardening – is to compromise. Deadhead just half the plants within every clump for a second flowering and leave the remaining seed heads to mature.

• Grows to 36in/90cm high. Any soil, full sun or part-shade. Plant seeds in places where you wish the plants to flower, staggering sowings over several weeks to make sure that germination takes place and also to extend the flowering season. If the plants are not supported by their neighbors they will need a few twigs to hold them up. One useful seed cultivar is *Agrostemma githago* 'Milas', which is almost identical to the wild form but a little more vigorous. Grow as an annual.

Alchemilla mollis

LADY'S MANTLE

Long-lived lime-green flower sprays above soft scalloped foliage

Alchemilla is the perfect foil. Almost any other plant looks good against its sprays of lime-green flowers and soft, velvety leaves. Used at the edge of a border it makes a gentle frame to the garden picture. It tumbles attractively from raised beds and across paths and steps, softening the hard lines of the garden wherever it falls.

And few plants are so easy to use. It is adaptable to any soil and any prospect, sun or shade. In short, it is a near-perfect gardener's friend and its only disadvantage could be that it is so widely recommended that it may become something of a cliché. My philosophy, however, is totally to ignore fashion in one's choice of plants. If you like a plant, whether it is common or not, use it.

The young clumps of tiny flowers stand above the leaves but they soon begin to slump and sprawl. Nobody would accuse this of being a tidy plant. Its relaxed habit makes it a useful element in the romantic garden, where it looks good as an underplanting to heavy swags of old-fashioned roses.

Although the flowers look presentable for at least a month in summer, they do begin to turn brown sooner or later. At this stage – provided you have moist soil – you can cut back the whole plant down to the base. This encourages it to put on new growth. Fresh young leaves soon appear and occasionally the plant will even flower again in early fall. The cut flowers can be dried for the winter.

The leaves make a dense and attractive ground cover. Scallop-shaped, they are as soft to the touch as blotting paper, yet totally unabsorbent. It is one of this plant's most endearing properties that drops of rainwater or dew collect in hollows in the leaves and remain there until the sun dries them off.

RIGHT The lime-green flowers of *Alchemilla mollis* provide a good foil for almost any other color.

FAR RIGHT Despite being so soft, the leaves of *Alchemilla mollis* are impervious to water. Rainwater collects on the surface in drops like beads of mercury.

• Height 18in/45cm, spread 24in/60cm. Propagate by division of the dense root clump in fall or spring. The plant will also seed itself, often finding its way to cracks between stones on paths and terraces. Zones 3–7

ANOTHER ALCHEMILLA TO GROW

Alchemilla conjuncta A more compact and tidier version of *A. mollis*. Again the flowers are lime-green, but they are held in smaller, tighter inflorescences. The leaves are more brittle-looking, star-shaped in outline, with their edges defined by a line of tiny white hairs. A useful plant for the rock garden, to accompany miniature bulbs and alpines. Height 8in/20cm, spread 12in/30cm. Zones 4–7

Allium christophii in summer

Allium christophii

STARS OF PERSIA

Lilac-colored flowers in early summer,
everlasting seed heads

No garden, however small, is complete without
bulbs. Every gardener loves tulips, narcissi, and lilies,
and will find space for them. Sadly, though, most
bulbs are unquestionably single-season plants. Their
performance has only one act – sensational perhaps
in its time but usually of brief duration. When their
flowers are finished there is not much supporting
show from the leaves. But there is an exception
among bulbous plants, one that produces spectacular flower heads that can be dried and kept for ever.

Allium christophii in fall

This is *Allium christophii* (syn. *A. albopilosum*), a member of the onion family, as you will recognize from the smell if you accidentally cut into its bulb. The flower heads of *A. christophii* are among the most exotic in the summer garden. Each head is made up of star-shaped, lilac-colored flowers arranged around the circumference of a globe and supported by stalks radiating like spokes from the center. They might remind you of one of those fireworks that shatters into trails of light, each line terminating in its own starlike burst.

Unlike a firework, however, this allium flower goes on and on. For up to a month the flower head keeps its color, and when it fades it retains its lovely structure. It dries on the stem so that its intricate skeleton remains in place, with round black seeds developing in threes in the eye of each flower. These dried seed heads look striking in the border, but sadly they are very brittle and easily damaged by wind and rain. I think that you would do best to pick them from the base and keep them inside, where they will last for ever. I admit, however, that I love them so much that when in late summer I come to show a guest around the garden, I go beforehand and gently push a few of the stems back into the ground to make a temporary clump.

When deliberating where to plant this allium, you might bear in mind that its structure, rather than its color, is its most striking feature. Regard it as an architectural plant and use it in clumps as an eye-catcher at the corners of beds and similar strategic points. It looks good in silhouette against the dark background of yew or boxwood. If you can associate it with plants whose color complements that of the allium flower, so much the better. I think that its rather subdued lilac color could do with a lift and would suggest placing it with colors from the opposite side of the spectrum, the yellows for example. It would look attractive growing through the yellow-leaved ground-covering creeping jenny, *Lysimachia nummularia* 'Aurea', and backed by a golden shrub such as *Philadelphus coronarius* 'Aureus' or the yellow privet, *Ligustrum ovalifolium* 'Aureum'. A clever idea would be to underplant it with yellow-flowered *Allium moly*, which grows to a height of 10in/25cm and flowers at the same time.

● Height 24in/60cm, spread minimal, but allow 12in/30cm for the foliage. The flower heads are up to 9in/23cm in diameter. Plant the bulbs in fall. For growing in clumps, place them 8–10in/20–25cm apart, and 3in/8cm below the surface. Full sun is preferable but they are tolerant of any soil. Early in the season feed the leaves with foliar feed so that the bulbs flower the following year. Zones 4–8

OTHER ALLIUMS TO GROW

Once you have grown one type of allium you are likely to become addicted and will want to grow more. There is a wide range available, with a huge diversity of flower color, form, height, and season. They are among the most rewarding of plants.

Allium aflatunense Spheres of pinky lilac star-shaped flowers 4in/10cm across are held high above the foliage on stems of 36in/90cm. It flowers in late spring, and looks sensational in mass plantings, as at Barnsley House in Gloucestershire where it is used as an underplanting along the laburnum walk. The flower heads keep well when dry. Zones 4–8

Allium cernuum In summer the deep rose-pink flowers hang gracefully from loose flower heads about 15in/40cm above the ground. Full sun and dry conditions. Zones 4–10

Allium sphaerocephalon Flowers in late summer, with compact burgundy flower heads about 24in/60cm high. Zones 6–10

Allium sphaerocephalon

Allium cernuum

Allium moly

Arum italicum pictum

LORDS AND LADIES

Striking foliage, creamy yellow spring flowers,
red berries in fall and winter

The hardy arums are among the earliest foliage plants to show themselves in spring. The first young leaves, furled up in tight cylinders like umbrellas, may appear above the last of the winter snows and in spite of their delicate appearance they survive all but the hardest frosts. There are about sixteen species of arum, not all of them hardy, and they all have beautiful arrow-shaped leaves. In several varieties this foliage is enhanced by patterns of variegation and perhaps the best among these is *Arum italicum pictum* (syn. *A. italicum* ssp. *italicum*). This form has narrow dark green leaves with a network of veins picked out in white. These striking leaves make a bold accompaniment to the earliest spring bulbs such as snowdrops, crocus, and scillas, some of which have modest foliage of their own. The arum leaves look good, too, with the young growth of many of the smaller grasses, such as *Milium effusum* 'Aureum'.

If you are lucky, your arums will flower for you in spring. The flowers are creamy yellow spathes, hooded like a monk's cowl, but they are unostentatious and you may need to stoop down and grope among the foliage to see them. In summer, as the leaves die back, the seed spike is left standing with shiny green berries developing along its length. By fall the berries have colored to vivid scarlet and soon they are joined by the first of the new leaves. So here is a plant of almost continuous interest, with something to offer in every season.

• Height to 15in/40cm, with clumps spreading to 24in/60cm. Any soil but prefers plenty of moisture, provided that drainage is good. Part-shade or full sun. Arums survive underground as tubers: propagate by splitting congested clumps. Zones 7–9

OTHER ARUMS TO GROW

Zantedeschia aethiopica The arum lilies are a separate genus from the arums, but they belong together in the same family, the Araceae or aroids. Grown for their wonderful funnel-shaped white flowers, the arum lilies have dark green leaves, arrow-shaped like those of the arums, but on a much larger scale. Clumps of *Zantedeschia aethiopica* reach 4ft/1.2m height and 36in/90cm spread. They are not hardy in any but the mildest sites and in most areas it is best to consider them as greenhouse plants. They like full sun and plenty of moisture – they can be grown as aquatics with their feet in water. Among the best varieties are *Z. aethiopica* 'Crowborough' with pure white spathes, and *Z. aethiopica* 'Green Goddess', in which the spathes have broad green lips and margins. Zones 8–9

Arum italicum pictum in late winter

Beta vulgaris
RUBY CHARD

Long-lasting red stems below dense green foliage

Here is a vegetable that deserves promotion from the kitchen garden to the ornamental border. Closely related to perpetual spinach and Swiss chard, it has stems like those of rhubarb, but more intensely red.

Ruby chard will contribute an exciting flash of scarlet to a mixed border, and is an obvious choice as an ingredient of an all-red border. Here it can be associated with perennials and annuals with red flowers to give an illusion that flowers and stems are part of the same plant.

• Stems up to 18in/45cm long. Ruby chard is simple to grow from seed sown directly in the ground in spring. Any soil, sun or part-shade. Grow as an annual.

Beta vulgaris in summer, with red *Nicotiana alata*

Brassica oleracea
ORNAMENTAL CABBAGE

Colorful foliage, maintained over a long season

A plant that invites a lot of interest in my garden in the late season is only a cabbage – a selected form of the common cabbage, grown as an annual for its attractive variegated foliage. I like to grow it in clumps of two or three in the herbaceous border, where it is so unexpected that many visitors ask what it can be.

There are two color forms of this plant, purple and cream. Evidently they cannot be separated by breeding as they appear in more or less equal numbers from each packet of seeds. Fortunately the color bias is already evident in young plants even before the pattern of variegation has developed. You can discern a tinge of pink in the leaf bases of plants that are going to be purple; those of the cream plants are clear green. It is useful to know which is which when you place the young plants in the border, so that they will associate well with their neighbors.

The cream version looks effective in a white border, with white companions such as Shasta daisies, annual sweet peas, and *Dimorphotheca pluvialis* 'Glistening White'. I like to place the purple form in the border among blue penstemons and *Aster × frikartii*, whose purple-blue flowers pick up an echo in the intense, shiny purple of the cabbage. Unlike most plants in the border, the ornamental cabbage improves with the onset of winter. The first frosts intensify the coloration of the plant. With a sparkling layer of frost the cabbage looks like some deep-frozen delicacy of *nouvelle cuisine*. It can survive a hard winter, but when it begins to look tatty in early spring it is doomed, I am afraid, for the compost pile. Then it is time to grow new plants from seed.

• Height and spread 15in/40cm. Any soil, sun or part-shade. Grow as an annual.

Brassica oleracea 'White Peacock' in summer, in a white and cream planting

Brassica oleracea in winter

Campanula portenschlagiana
Profuse blue flowers in summer

If you can establish *Campanula portenschlagiana* (syn. *C. muralis*) in a crack between the stones of a terrace, with any luck it will spread by runners between the stones so that eventually you have a network of low-growing blue flowers for midsummer. Provided that it has full sun, this campanula is a great colonizer of inhospitable corners.

The violet-blue flowers are bell-shaped, which is typical of the genus. They grow so densely on the plant that you can scarcely see the leaves when it is in bloom. For the rest of the summer the leaves, which are small and scallop-shaped, make a mound of some 15in/40cm height and spread.

A closely related species is *C. poscharskyana*. This has flowers with narrower petals, so that they look star-shaped; they are a more subtle, washed-out lilac. It is another colonizer of gaps in stone paths and it will take root in a dry-stone wall and climb some way up. This makes it a useful underplanting for wall shrubs, provided that the sun can reach it.

For ground cover on a larger scale, you might also consider the tall perennial *C. persicifolia*, which reaches a height of 36in/90cm, comes in blue, lilac, or white varieties and spreads itself by seed.

• *C. portenschlagiana* and *C. poscharskyana* thrive on benign neglect. *C. persicifolia* is happy in sun or part-shade, any soil. *C. portenschlagiana* and *C. persicifolia* are best in zones 4–8; *C. poscharskyana* in zones 3–7.

Campanula poscharskyana in summer

Filling in the cracks. *Campanula portenschlagiana* colonizes a stone path where few other plants would survive. The path bakes in the sun, but the campanula's roots reach under the stones to find moisture.

Centranthus ruber

VALERIAN

Flowers from summer to fall

Valerian is a survivor. You will see it on wasteland and in derelict gardens where it competes successfully with encroaching weeds, unlike the more refined garden plants which disappear as soon as they have to fend for themselves. Valerian will seed itself in the most unlikely places, and you will see it growing high above the ground from cracks in the mortar on buildings and on garden walls. Don't dismiss it as a weed, though, just because it behaves like one. Valerian is a beautiful and useful garden plant, with an exceptionally long flowering period. Butterflies and other insects find the deep pink flower heads irresistible.

Valerian looks good when grown in clumps in the herbaceous border. The pure white form is even more useful in this context, as it may be easier to associate with the other occupants of the border. Another way to grow this perennial is to encourage it to seed in the cracks between stones on a terrace or wall. Here, like other colonizers, it will soften the hard lines of the garden architecture, and give your garden a lived-in look.

• Height and spread 36in/90cm. Any soil, even poor ground, limestone, or rubble, where few other garden plants will survive. Does best in full sun. Propagate by seed. Zones 5–8

Pink, red, and white seedlings of valerian *(Centranthus ruber)* have taken root under the iron railings of a small cottage garden, contributing to a cheerful riot of color. Beyond, a smoke bush, *Cotinus coggygria* 'Royal Purple', is just coming into flower. Its dark and somber tone provides a good foil for the brilliant colors around it. Behind it against the wall is the climbing version of the curious bicolored rose 'Masquerade'.

Cornus canadensis flowers

Cornus canadensis

CREEPING DOGWOOD

Foliage for ground cover, white flowers in summer,
followed by red berries

It comes as something of a surprise to find that this useful ground-cover perennial is a relation of the dogwood trees and shrubs (pages 28–9, 64–6), but if you look carefully at its flowers and leaves you will see that they are similar in structure to those of the more familiar dogwoods. The flowers, which appear in midsummer, are pure white and about 1in/2.5cm across. They consist of broad, flat white bracts surrounding small flower parts of green and purple. In fall the plant bears clusters of red berries. The leaves are midgreen and oval and grow in whorls at the tips of the spreading shoots.

• Height 6in/15cm, spread 24in/60cm. Requires acidic soil and is suited to peat beds and acidic woodland conditions in shade or part-shade. Zones 2–6

Corydalis lutea

Ferny foliage, yellow flowers from spring
right through the summer

Once you have *Corydalis lutea* (syn. *Pseudofumaria lutea*) in the garden you are unlikely ever to be without it again. Some would call this a mixed blessing but, as with most other self-seeders, if you keep this plant under control it will be a tremendous asset. It will appear and survive in the most unlikely places, where few other plants will find a hold. In particular, it will colonize old walls and paths and establish lush growth in the smallest gaps between the stones, somehow finding moisture in places where you would have thought there was none. Its effect is to soften the hard edges of a garden, like a curtain softening the line of a window.

The foliage is blue-green and frilly, like that of one of the more delicate ferns. The flowers appear from spring right through the summer. They are little yellow down-turned tubes, growing together in short inflorescences just above the foliage.

Corydalis ochroleuca (syn. *Pseudofumaria alba*) has cream-colored flowers but is identical to *C. lutea* in all other respects. Many gardeners find it even more desirable, as the cream flowers are perhaps easier to associate with other plants.

• Corydalis makes a gently rounded mound up to 15in/40cm in height and spread. A plant that thrives on neglect, it will make its own way around your garden, seeding as it goes and surviving in dry, poor soil and sun or shade. The only cultivation necessary is to pull it up by the roots in places where it is unwelcome. Zones 5–8

Corydalis lutea, self-seeded in a wall

Cosmos 'Sensation'

Feathery foliage, flowers from midsummer
through to fall

The majority of annuals selected for this book are self-seeders that, once established, will appear every year without any effort on the part of the gardener. Cosmos and other tender annuals only self-seed in frost-free climates; elsewhere, they are used as bedding plants. Cosmos is the only bedding plant that I have included here, selecting it for its exceptionally long flowering period and the additional attraction of its fine feathery foliage. It is a controversial choice, I have to admit, because there are so many worthy bedding plants that deserve a space in every garden and might claim one in this book. What about the tobacco plant, *Nicotiana alata* (syn. *N. affinis*), with an equally long flowering period and a divine scent, or the annual rudbeckias that light up the summer and fall border? I am also tempted by the exotic *Cleome hassleriana* (syn. *C. spinosa*) and the magnificent foliage plant *Ricinus communis*. But this cosmos will have to stand for all of them.

Cosmos 'Sensation' is a robust plant, but not at all bulky, as its delicate fernlike foliage permits you to see through to the plants beyond. This attractive framework is covered with flowers from midsummer right through to the first frosts of fall. The flowers are like broad-petaled daisies in shape, in shades of dark pink, magenta, and white, with golden-yellow centers. As with other annuals, it is important to deadhead the plant to encourage it to continue flowering. The flowering stems of cosmos have a branching structure that makes deadheading easy. Each mature flower has two budding stems which branch off at the base of its stalk. To remove the dead head, you simply cut the stalk at the branching point and one flower is replaced by two. When these two are over, you cut their joint stem lower down, at the point at which two further

branches rise. Aided by deadheading, multiplication of flowers continues through the summer.

The magenta and pink tones of the cosmos flowers harmonize well in the summer-to-fall border with verbenas, penstemons, and perennial asters selected within the range of pink through purple. I find that the cosmos also makes a striking contrast with yellow foliage; it looks marvelous as an underplanting to a yellow-leaved tree such as *Robinia pseudoacacia* 'Frisia'.

• Height 4ft/1.2m, spread 30in/75cm. Sow seed under glass in spring, and prick out into larger pots, as with other tender annuals. Harden the plants off gradually. Do not plant out until all risk of late frosts has passed. This time usually coincides with periods at which it is safe to remove the foliage of spring bulbs and, whether or not you lift the bulbs, the cosmos and other annuals may be planted out to take their place. Cosmos will thrive in any soil but it needs full sun. Grow as an annual.

Cosmos 'Sensation' in
summer

Crambe maritima in summer

Crambe maritima

SEA KALE

Young growth used as a vegetable, silvery gray
foliage, white flowers in summer

Sea kale is equally at home in the border or the
vegetable lot, but you have to decide at the outset
whether to grow it to eat or for its ornamental effect.
If you pick the young growth for the pot you will
have a delicious vegetable, but the summer display
will be much reduced. I favor planting it in the
border, where it makes a mound of curly leaves, not
unlike true kale but silvery in color. In midsummer
the plant is crowned by dense sprays of small white
flowers.

• A perennial 24in/60cm in height, 4ft/1.2m in
spread. Happy in any soil, prefers full sun. Propagate
by seed or by division. Zones 6–9

ANOTHER CRAMBE TO GROW

Crambe cordifolia One of the most dramatic of all
architectural plants, C. cordifolia produces a haze of
sweet-scented white flowers on stems up to 7ft/2m
tall at midsummer. The plant makes a romantic
accompaniment to old-fashioned roses and delphiniums. However, it has a long lead-up time to its
brief moment of glory, and it produces large dark
green leaves which take up a lot of space in the
border and are irresistible to slugs. Zones 6–8

Cyclamen hederifolium

Fall flowers, decorative winter and spring foliage

There can be few more cheering sights in the wood-land garden than that of the first flowers of *Cyclamen hederifolium* (formerly known as *C. neapolitanum*) peeping bareheaded from the dark soil in early fall. These woodland beauties are far smaller and more delicate in proportion than the cyclamen hybrids that we give and receive as houseplants. Their little shuttlecock heads are only about ½in/1cm long and stand a mere 3in/8cm above the ground. But what they lack in stature they make up – once established – in quantity. A mature colony in ideal conditions can cover a large area, within which the ground will be overlaid for several weeks in fall with a carpet

Cyclamen hederifolium in fall

Cyclamen hederifolium in winter

of flowers. But there is no need to aspire to this scale of display. You can enjoy this plant in the smallest garden, provided that you can reproduce the conditions that it favors. It will need an undisturbed site, in shade, and an annual topdressing of leaf mold, corresponding to the natural covering of leaves that it would receive in its woodland habitat.

One of the charms of this species is the variability of both flowers and leaves. At the two extremes the flowers may be pure white or dark mauve, but they are most commonly somewhere between the two, in a shade of pale pink. This cyclamen is appropriately named *hederifolium*, which means "ivy-leaved." The leaf is reminiscent of the ivy not only in its shape, but also in its extraordinary variability of pattern. No two plants seem to have the same leaves. Some are dark green, marked with patterns of a paler tone. Others are overlaid with bold dashes of silver like the brush strokes of an expressionist painter. Others again are silver all over. The underside, however, is always a deep red. It is a lovely feature of this plant that the leaves usually emerge after the flowers have appeared but before they have died down, so both are present together for some of the time. The foliage survives through the winter and well into spring, to give an attractive ground cover at a time when there is not much other greenery on the woodland floor.

The cyclamen survives from year to year as a corm, just below the surface of the soil. The corm is flattish and grows up to the diameter of a saucer: a corm of mature size will give up to fifty flowers at a time, growing from little knobs on the top surface. A curiosity of the plant is that the roots appear from the top surface of the corm, so it is easy to make the mistake of planting the cyclamen upside down. The safest thing is to buy the plants in flower, in pots, and transplant them gently into your garden. Then you can be certain that they are the right way up.

• Requires a shady site, as described above, and a shallow mulch in summer of compost or leaf mold to cover the corm. The plant will spread by seeding itself, but you can help it along by distributing the seed. The seed heads mature in late spring, at the tip of the coiled stalks. When they are ripe, plant them directly into the soil. Zones 5–9

ANOTHER CYCLAMEN TO GROW

Cyclamen coum An early spring beauty on the same scale as *C. hederifolium*, and in a similar range of coloring. Typically the flowers are fuchsia-pink, on a relatively short stem, and the leaves are variably patterned with silver on the upper surface, and crimson on the underside. Zones 7–9

Cynara cardunculus

CARDOON

Silver foliage from spring to fall, blue summer flowers that can be dried for winter display

A close relation to the globe artichoke, the cardoon is one of the best silver foliage plants, if you have space in the borders to accommodate its bulky spread of 6ft/1.8m. Its young growth, in spring, looks wonderful underplanted with black tulips, such as *Tulipa* 'Queen of Night', or *T.* 'Black Parrot'. It also combines effectively with silver-leaved *Artemisia* 'Powis Castle' and purple-leaved sage. Its long leaves, coming from the center, soft and deeply cut, are enough for it to qualify as an outstanding plant, but as a bonus it offers summer flowers like huge deep blue thistle heads, perched some 8ft/2.5m above the ground. The flowers can be picked and dried for winter.

• Any soil, full sun. Propagate by seed or by division in the spring. Not fully hardy in cold, damp areas, where it is prudent to cover it in winter. Zones 7–10

Centerpiece of a silver garden, a superb specimen of the cardoon, *Cynara cardunculus.* At its feet are the silver grass, *Festuca glauca,* and lamb's ears, *Stachys byzantina.* Behind is one of the best silver-leaved shrubs, *Elaeagnus angustifolia* 'Caspica'. White-flowered phlox and blue delphiniums add an appropriate touch of cool color to the silver harmonies of this border. It makes sense to grow silver-foliage plants together as, with a few exceptions, they tend to flourish in similar conditions. All the plants in this picture prefer full sun in summer and resent becoming waterlogged in cold winter weather.

Dicentra formosa 'Stuart Boothman' in late spring

Dicentra spectabilis in early summer, with forget-me-nots

Dicentra formosa 'Stuart Boothman'
Gray-green foliage, pink flowers in late spring
and early summer

The dicentras are invaluable foliage plants with the additional virtue of attractive flowers. One of the very best of them is *Dicentra formosa* 'Stuart Boothman', in which the subdued midpink flowers provide a perfect complement to the finely cut gray-green leaves. This fernlike foliage looks particularly good in shady corners with ferns and hostas. The long-lasting heart-shaped flowers hang on short arching stems just above the leaves.

• Makes a mound of height and spread 18in/45cm in any humus-rich soil. Thrives in shade or part-shade. Zones 5–8

ANOTHER DICENTRA TO GROW

Dicentra spectabilis The ever-popular "bleeding heart" grows considerably taller, to a height and spread of 30in/75cm, with rather coarse foliage but with intriguing heart-shaped pink flowers, tipped with white. The flowers last over many weeks in early summer. There is also a beautiful pure white form, *D. spectabilis alba*. Zones 3–8

Erigeron karvinskianus
White and pale pink flowers from spring to fall

With flowers shaped like a child's drawing of the sun, daisies are among the most popular groups of perennial and annual garden plants. Known collectively as the Compositae, they span the seasons, from the spring-flowering doronicums to the autumn-flowering asters, known as Michaelmas daisies. Mid-summer is the season for the majority of asterlike erigerons, but there is one species among them that is especially useful for its long flowering season. This is a low-growing perennial daisy from Mexico called *Erigeron karvinskianus* (syn. *E. mucronatus*).

The flowers of this daisy are relatively modest in size, but they are borne in prolific numbers. About 1/2in/1cm across, they are white with a golden eye and, as they age, they take on a pale pink tinge. This gives the plant a special two-tone attraction when there are young and old flowers together. The flowers keep coming the whole summer long. The lance-shaped leaves are also highly attractive.

The erigeron is equally at home in a rock garden or tumbling down between the stones of a dry-stone wall, and it looks marvelous growing in the cracks between the stones on a patio or terrace. It seeds itself prodigiously, but it is so pretty that you will probably be delighted when it pops up in unexpected places. If it arrives in the wrong place you can simply pull it up by the roots (it will not survive in a lawn).

● Height 9in/23cm, spread 15in/40cm. Prefers sun, but is happy in any soil. Propagate by division or allow it to seed itself. Best in zones 9–10; grow as an annual elsewhere.

Cascading down a low wall, a mound of *Erigeron karvinskianus* makes a fluid outline at the edge of a flight of steps. In this position, in full sun, the daisy ought to flower for most of the summer and will seed itself further in cracks between the stones of the wall.

Eryngium alpinum in summer, with erigerons

Eryngium alpinum

ALPINE SEA HOLLY

Blue-green foliage, long-lasting blue summer flowers

If you scrutinize a single flower of *Eryngium alpinum* it might remind you of one of those seventeenth-century Dutch portraits of a solemn burgher of Amsterdam, his oval head rising from the most monumental ruff, and the whole effect tinted overall with a blue haze. Add together the dozen or more heads produced by a single plant and you have an astonishing picture.

Eryngium alpinum is probably the most striking member of a dramatic genus, the sea hollies. It is thistlelike in its upright habit and in the dry prickliness of its parts. As the flowers mature, the whole of the upper part of the plant becomes suffused with blue. This blue tinge extends throughout the stems to the knobbly cones of the flower heads and to the surrounding fringe or "ruff" of bracts. It is these bracts that give this plant its distinction. They are smooth and metallic in texture, with cut, spiny edges like the finest filigree silverwork. Lower down on the plant the leaves are similarly patterned but less emphatically. They are dark blue-green veined with white, deeply divided and quite prickly along the edges.

In the border the drama of this plant would be heightened by partnering it with plants of contrasting textures and colors. I would venture to try it with one of the verbascums with woolly gray leaves, such as *Verbascum olympicum*. Not only would

Eryngium × *oliverianum* in summer

the leaves provide an effective contrast, but the pale yellow flower spikes of the verbascum would complement the blue of the eryngium. Another idea would be to back the eryngium with a mound of yellow grass: *Hakonechloa macra* 'Aureola' or *Carex elata* 'Aurea'.

Alive in the border the plant already looks like a dried flower, with a seemingly artificial spray-coat of blue. Removed, it dries readily to join the arrangement of everlasting flowers in the vase on the mantelshelf for winter.

• Height 36in/90cm, spread 24in/60cm. Needs full sun but will survive in any soil, including poor, stony soils, and even on gravel paths. *E. alpinum* is a perennial that can be propagated by division, from root cuttings, or from seed. Zones 4–8

OTHER ERYNGIUMS TO GROW

Eryngium bourgatii A relatively delicate plant with numerous small globular flower heads fringed with spiky bracts. The flower heads take on a lilac-blue tinge as they mature. For attractive flower color it is important to choose a good form, such as *E. bourgatii* 'Oxford Blue'. Reaches a height of 24in/60cm, spread of 18in/45cm. Zones 5–9

Eryngium giganteum Known as "Miss Willmott's ghost" (see page 12), this biennial dies after flowering but will readily seed itself. Growing to a height of 4ft/1.2m and spread of 30in/75cm, it has striking flower heads with broad, silvery bracts. Zones 4–8

Eryngium × oliverianum Another blue-headed sea holly, not unlike *E. alpinum*, which may well be one of its ancestors. It grows to a height of 36in/90cm and spread of 24in/60cm and the flowers, stems, and bracts are a steely lilac-blue. The bracts are less intricately cut than in *E. alpinum*. Zones 4–8

Eryngium giganteum, with evening primrose and pink phlox

Erysimum 'Bowles' Mauve'

Evergreen foliage, mauve flowers year-round

The perennial wallflower *Erysimum* 'Bowles' Mauve' is included here by virtue of its almost constant performance year-round. The more familiar biennial wallflowers, in any color between sulfur-yellow and deep crimson, flower for up to six weeks in early summer. 'Bowles' Mauve', however, can be almost guaranteed to flower in most months of the year, unless the winter is especially harsh (in which case the plant may be wiped out, as it is not reliably hardy). It is evergreen and its dark gray-blue leaves make an attractive combination with its flower heads, which are a delicate shade of mauve.

Its very vigor is its undoing. Within a year it makes a mound up to 39in/1m high, covered in flower spikes. But it is woody and brittle and tends to look leggy. It is best to take a few cuttings and grow fresh plants at least every other year.

There are other perennial wallflowers available, in a range of colors. One of the best is *E.* 'Moonlight', a hybrid of height 12in/30cm, with yellow flowers.

• Height and spread up to 39in/1m. Full sun, any soil (like other wallflowers it thrives in poor soil). Propagate by cuttings. Zones 8–9

Erysimum 'Bowles' Mauve'

Euphorbia characias wulfenii
Blue-green foliage, lime-green flower heads
from late spring into summer

I have found that the more obsessed you become with gardening, the more you begin to appreciate the relatively modest-looking plants that would not earn a second glance from a nongardener. Here is a case in point. When a friend gave me a seedling of *Euphorbia characias* ssp. *wulfenii* some years ago I grudgingly allowed it space in the border to avoid hurting his feelings. Now, several years on, I would say that this single plant has given me more continuing pleasure than any other in the garden.

It is a plant that never looks unsightly. It matures elegantly through the fall and winter, and then flowers for a lengthy period from late spring into summer. It is graceful even in decline. And yet, in color at least, it is a discreet plant; never dominant, but a well-mannered foil for the more colorful flowers around it.

In full flower it is a symphony of greens. The leaf fronds are gray-green. Fanning out from a narrow base, they are surmounted by moplike flower heads, which are lime-green. The flowers themselves are tiny and are enclosed within rounded bracts rather as a candle sits within a wall sconce. It is these bracts that give the flower head its overall lime-green color. They are also the secret of the flower head's long life. As each little flower passes through its life cycle – from bud, through the fertile stage when it

Two phases in the long-lasting performance of *Euphorbia characias* ssp. *wulfenii*. In this border the euphorbia is already in action when narcissi come into flower in early spring, but it is at its peak to coincide with tulips a few weeks later. Later still, in midsummer, when *Geranium × magnificum* and white marguerites are in flower around its base, the euphorbia flowers are still presentable, though the seeds are now forming.

Euphorbia myrsinites in spring, with *Muscari armeniacum*

sports bright yellow stamens, to its final globular seeds – all this time the surrounding bract hardly changes. Between twelve and sixteen weeks the bracts hold out, only becoming a little more brittle and coloring to bronze as time wears on. Picked, the flower head dries well. Even without their flower heads, the remaining leaf fronds look attractive. And beneath their skirts next year's growth has already begun. Miniature fronds are growing up from the base, to take the place of the spent stems.

• Being a plant of Mediterranean origin, this euphorbia requires full sun but is content with poor soil, even growing from gaps between stones in a path. Zones 8–10

OTHER EUPHORBIAS TO GROW

Euphorbia characias Identical to *E. characias* ssp. *wulfenii* in size and shape, but has a tiny black eye to the individual flowers. Zones 8–10

Euphorbia amygdaloides 'Purpurea' A euphorbia for shade, but rather susceptible to mildew in dry conditions. The pointed leaves are a lovely tint of green tinged with purple. It has khaki-colored flower heads in early summer. Height to 24in/60cm. *E. amygdaloides* var. *robbiae* is a more vigorous plant, with dark green leaves in rosettes and loose heads of lime-green flowers. Zones 8–9

Euphorbia cyparissias An attractive but invasive low-growing euphorbia, up to 12in/30cm in height. It has wispy gray-green foliage and small lime-green flower heads in late spring. It spreads by runners under the soil and can be difficult to eliminate if it gets out of hand. Zones 3–8

Euphorbia myrsinites A lovely sprawling spurge, suitable for the rock garden or raised bed, where its stems can hang over the side. They are covered with stiff blue-green leaves and tipped with long-lasting lime-green flower heads. Looks especially good with blue bulbs such as scilla or muscari. Zones 5–9

Euphorbia polychroma A marvelous accompaniment to spring bulbs, this euphorbia makes a mound 18in/45cm high and 24in/60cm in diameter, covered with bright yellow flower heads. Zones 4–8

Euphorbia polychroma in spring, with forget-me-nots

Geranium psilostemon

Long-lived magenta flowers in summer, finely cut
leaves, coloring in fall

No garden would be complete without its quota of
hardy geraniums (or cranesbills). Most of them will
contribute to a plant combination without becoming dominant or overbearing. Their flowers are re-
freshingly simple in shape and come in a range of
clear colors, from whites through pinks and blues to
mauves, magentas, and purples. Most flower over
quite a long season, and when they are over they die
gracefully. When the flower petals have dropped the
deeply cut foliage provides further interest for the
rest of the season, and in some cases the leaves color
up well in fall.

Another advantage of geraniums is that they
come in sizes to suit any garden, from tiny alpine
species to the magnificent *Geranium psilostemon*,
which reaches a height of 5ft/1.5m and spread of
7ft/2m. This geranium has flowers of the most
exotic color – a vivid magenta veined with black and
with a black center. The leaves are exotic too, fan-
shaped and deeply cut. They turn to shades of red
and yellow in fall. Some gardeners find it difficult to
place this geranium as its color is so intense. But it
harmonizes well with old-fashioned roses in the
deep pink to purple range, such as *Rosa* 'Madame
Isaac Pereire' or *R.* 'Cardinal de Richelieu'. It also
makes a striking contrast with gray-leaved plants
such as artemisias, and looks good with blues. With
reds and yellows, however, the contrasts are just too
strong for comfort.

• Flourishes in any soil. Sun or part-shade. In an
open border it will need staking, but if it is beside
roses or other shrubs it will find its own support by
sprawling among them. Propagate by division or by
seed – you will often find self-sown seedlings around
the base of the plant. Zones 4–9

OTHER GERANIUMS TO GROW

Geranium endressii An evergreen geranium, with a
very long flowering season. The silvery pink flowers
appear throughout the summer and there are
usually a few to be seen during mild spells through
the winter. It seeds itself readily and makes good
ground cover, especially under roses. The variety
'Wargrave Pink' has prolific salmon-pink flowers.
Height 18in/45cm, spread 30in/75cm. Zones 4–8

Geranium 'Johnson's Blue' A deservedly popular
blue geranium. Clumps reach a height of 18in/45cm
and a spread of 24in/60cm. I have seen it planted im-
pressively *en masse* along a winding gravel path. All
traces of the leaves disappear in winter. Zones 4–8

Geranium × *magnificum* One of the larger geraniums, making a clump of height 24in/60cm and
spread 4ft/1.2m. The flowers are deep violet, with

An effective partnership
between *Geranium
psilostemon* and an old-
fashioned rose. Not only
do their colors
harmonize, but also the
geranium can use the
rose as a support.

OPPOSITE Old-fashioned roses underplanted with *Geranium endressii.* The geranium has spread to fill all the available ground space, suppressing weeds and covering the bare stems of the roses. The rose in front supports a tall *Geranium psilostemon.*

BELOW A border containing plants in the blue to purple range, contrasting with yellows and creams. Central at the front, *Geranium* 'Johnson's Blue' is framed by the yellow flower heads of *Allium moly* and variegated astrantia.

darker veins, and the leaves are rounded and deeply cut. It looks good with yellow or lime-green partners, such as *Achillea* 'Moonshine', or any of the euphorbias. Unfortunately, the flowering period of *G. × magnificum* is relatively short – just a few weeks – and its bulk may put off some gardeners. There is another dark violet geranium which would be an excellent substitute. This is *G. clarkei* 'Kashmir Purple', which reaches a height of 20in/50cm and spread of 30in/75cm, and flowers over a long period in summer. There is also a good white variety, *G. clarkei* 'Kashmir White'. Zones 5–8

Geranium × riversleaianum A low-growing geranium for the front of the border or the rock garden, this hybrid has gray-green foliage and flowers ranging from pink to deep magenta on different plants. It has a trailing habit and will scramble about among other plants, covering the ground between them.

Geranium × magnificum in summer

Among the best varieties are *G. × r.* 'Mavis Simpson', with flowers of a silvery shell-pink, and *G. × r.* 'Russell Prichard', with deep magenta flowers. Height 12in/30cm, spread 36in/90cm. Zones 6–8

Geranium sanguineum The bloody cranesbill has flowers of an intense magenta that contrast well with the smooth, finely divided dark green leaves. The foliage goes red in fall. *G.s.* var. *striatum* (syn. *G.s.* var. *lancastrense*) is a form with pale pink flowers. Height 10in/25cm, spread 18in/45cm. Another good plant of similar size and habit is *G. cinereum* var. *sub-caulescens,* which has magenta flowers with black centers, and soft silvery green leaves. Zones 4–8

***Geranium wallichianum* 'Buxton's Variety'** Flowering over a long period in late summer, this geranium has a trailing habit and will scramble through shrubs and over low walls. The flowers are a gorgeous pale blue with white centers. Zones 4–8

Another extended performance, this one lasting the whole year. The blue oat grass, *Helictotrichon sempervirens,* makes a good cornerstone to a herbaceous border in which all the other perennials wax and wane at different intervals, many of them dying off above ground in winter. The grass loses some of its leaves, but enough survive over winter for it to be regarded as an evergreen. It is a good idea to comb through the tufts in spring to clear out the dead leaves.

Helictotrichon sempervirens

BLUE OAT GRASS

Evergreen tufts of blue-green foliage,
graceful summer flower heads

The ornamental grasses and the grasslike sedges tend to be the great workhorses of the border, whose virtues are unsung. They may not display the obvious glamour of some neighboring plants, but they have a grace and charm that are a source of lasting pleasure in the garden. All are grown principally for their handsome foliage, and between them they offer an astonishing diversity of leaf color, texture, size, and form. According to your taste and the size of your lot you have a choice ranging in color from yellow to silvery blue, plain or variegated, and in all sizes from towering giants to tiny dwarf forms. Some of them have splendid architectural presence and these are ideal for use as punctuation marks at key points in the garden.

One of the most useful "punctuation" grasses is the blue oat grass, *Helictotrichon sempervirens*, which makes a dense rounded clump of narrow, arching, pale gray-green leaves that are hard and spiky to the touch. As it is evergreen, the clump is a striking feature throughout the seasons. In summer the dainty flower heads are borne well above the foliage, making an attractive secondary feature. Later, they dry well for flower arrangements.

The naturally rounded form of this plant makes it an obvious candidate for a corner position in a border, where it will serve the architectural function of a pivot or cornerstone. If you have a blue or silver border so much the better, because the metallic quality of the grass makes it an ideal companion to plants in this color range. Like many grasses, it also looks good growing in gravel or among pebbles.

• The foliage makes a mound about 36in/90cm high and 4ft/1.2m across, and the flowers reach about 5ft/1.5m. *H. sempervirens* does not have runners and so it is not invasive. It needs full sun and well-drained soil though it is not particular whether the soil is acidic or alkaline. The clump does not die back in winter, but individual leaves do die and so they need to be combed out to keep the plant tidy. Propagate by division of the clump in spring; as with all grasses, if division is attempted in fall the clump may rot with winter damp. Zones 5–8

OTHER GRASSES TO GROW

Carex elata 'Aurea' Of all grasslike plants, Bowles' golden sedge is probably the brightest yellow. An attractive plant, it is named after the English horticulturist E.A. Bowles, who discovered it as a mutant of an undistinguished wild sedge grass. The narrow, arching leaves are golden yellow with the narrowest margin of green. This is variable and there is a form that some gardeners would find preferable, with golden leaves lacking the green margin. The flowers are black tufts, covered with golden-brown anthers. The foliage makes a clump up to 24in/60cm in height and spread, with the flowers a little taller.

Carex elata 'Aurea' colors up best in full sun; in shade it is bright green. However it likes plenty of moisture, and does well in a poolside planting. Here it would provide a delightful contrast of textures with the same-colored bog-loving *Iris pseudacorus* 'Variegata'. Propagate by division. Zones 5–8

Cortaderia selloana Queen of all the grasses, pampas grass is so often grown in the wrong place that it has got a bad name. Its hulking tussocks, 6ft/1.8m in height and spread, consisting of sharply serrated leaves, are simply not suitable for the small garden. On a grand scale, however, there is nothing to beat them as eye-catchers. I have seen pampas grasses grown *en masse* beside the huge lake at Sheffield Park in Sussex, England, their great plumes like sails

Carex elata 'Aurea'

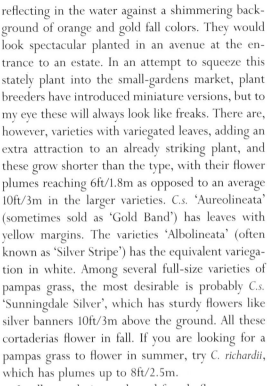

reflecting in the water against a shimmering background of orange and gold fall colors. They would look spectacular planted in an avenue at the entrance to an estate. In an attempt to squeeze this stately plant into the small-gardens market, plant breeders have introduced miniature versions, but to my eye these will always look like freaks. There are, however, varieties with variegated leaves, adding an extra attraction to an already striking plant, and these grow shorter than the type, with their flower plumes reaching 6ft/1.8m as opposed to an average 10ft/3m in the larger varieties. *C.s.* 'Aureolineata' (sometimes sold as 'Gold Band') has leaves with yellow margins. The varieties 'Albolineata' (often known as 'Silver Stripe') has the equivalent variegation in white. Among several full-size varieties of pampas grass, the most desirable is probably *C.s.* 'Sunningdale Silver', which has sturdy flowers like silver banners 10ft/3m above the ground. All these cortaderias flower in fall. If you are looking for a pampas grass to flower in summer, try *C. richardii*, which has plumes up to 8ft/2.5m.

In all cortaderias, male and female flowers grow on separate plants. The females are preferable, having the more bushy flower plumes. All cortaderias demand an open site in full sun, and well-drained soil. They will not do well in clay. Although the plant could be described as evergreen, a substantial number of leaves do die each season, and the

Planting on a grand scale. This "hedge" of *Cortaderia selloana* 'Sunningdale Silver' stretches for over 350ft/100m. The plumes, 10ft/3m high, are bending under a heavy burden of hoar frost. This enormous pampas grass looks quite wonderful in winter, though strong winds and heavy snows will take their toll of the feathery plumes. A double row of pampas grass, on either side of an entrance drive, is a feasible alternative to an avenue of trees.

center of the plant can become clogged with dead material. The best way to deal with this is to cut back all the foliage in early spring; be sure to wear strong gloves. Some gardeners counsel setting fire to the old foliage, but this is risky as it is impossible to avoid damaging the new growth. To propagate, divide the clump with a spade in early spring. Zones 8–9

Festuca glauca The blue fescue has silvery blue foliage, making a tuft of 12in/30cm height and spread. The flower heads are the same silvery color when they appear in midsummer, though they fade and dry to a pale creamy brown. A classic ingredient of the silver border, it looks marvelous when grown with plants of a similar color but contrasting texture, such as lamb's ears, *Stachys byzantina* (syn. *S. lanata*), which has soft velvety leaves of silver-gray.

This grass needs full sun and well-drained soil to attain its silvery blue color; it is much more green when grown in shade, and in soggy ground the plant will rot and die. Propagate by division in spring, removing any dead central parts. Zones 5–8

Milium effusum 'Aureum' The fresh lime-green of Bowles' golden grass brings a glow of light to a shady corner of the garden. It has flat tapering leaves that are slack and bend gracefully under their own weight. They make a loose mound, about 18in/15cm in height and spread, with a wispy halo of delicate yellow flower heads reaching perhaps 12in/30cm above the foliage in summer. Use this grass as an underplanting for green-flowered shrubs or perennials, such as euphorbias. It also makes a wonderful foil for purple flowers such as those of *Viola* 'Huntercombe Purple'.

In the wild *M. effusum* is a woodland plant and the golden version also prefers dappled shade, although it will thrive on any soil. It will spread by seeding itself, if you allow it, and you can also propagate it by division in spring. Zones 6–8

Miscanthus sinensis A grass for a sunny site at the back of the border, Japanese maiden grass makes a graceful clump of 8ft/2.5m or more in height, 4ft/1.2m in spread. The leaves are up to 36in/90cm long, fanning out from bamboolike stalks. They whisper among themselves in the slightest breeze. If you are waiting for a hedge to grow behind a border, a few clumps of this grass will be a temporary expedient to tide you over. It reaches its full height in a season, and dies back in winter. The dead winter foliage, veiled with hoar frost, is perhaps even more beautiful than the plant in full fling in summer. It would be a crime to cut it back until the cycle of new growth begins again in spring.

There are some interesting variegated varieties of miscanthus. 'Cabaret' is perhaps the most striking white-edged cultivar. 'Zebrinus' and 'Strictus' both have irregular patterns of horizontal cream stripes across the leaves. Propagate by division in spring. Zones 5–8

Pennisetum orientale A delightful small grass for the front of a border, P. orientale produces a mass of pink tufted flower heads, rather like the tails of small squirrels. The flower heads appear in the late summer and last well into fall, and so this grass is a good accompaniment for hardy asters or dahlias. Its feathery texture would also make a fitting contrast with the flat slabs of sedum flowers. And it looks striking when grown in quantity as a specimen plant. Pennisetum reaches up to 30in/75cm in height and spread. The leaves are dark green, flat, and arching.

Clumps of *Pennisetum orientale* make a fringe at the front of a fall border of dahlias, Michaelmas daisies and salvias. Grasses, with their neutral-colored flowers, make good partners for almost any border plants. Most grasses put on their peak performance in summer, but pennisetums flower in fall.

A sturdy clump of *Phalaris arundinacea* var. *picta* (gardener's garters) with a fringe of *Alchemilla mollis*

This grass is a perennial for any soil, but it must have full sun. It is not reliably hardy, so it is a good idea to take some offsets in fall and keep them under the protection of a cold frame over winter.

Another attractive pennisetum is *P. villosum*, known as feathertop. Its diaphanous flower heads are like loose stubby feathers that bounce back the light. Height and spread 24in/60cm. *P. orientale* is best in zones 6–9, *P. villosum* in zones 8–9.

Phalaris arundinacea* var. *picta Gardener's garters is one of the most commonly grown grasses, but none the worse for that. The loosely arching leaves are strongly patterned with dark green and white stripes that run along their length. The plant forms a clump 30in/75cm high with flowers 24in/60cm higher. It will thrive in any soil, in full sun or part-shade, and it is a useful plant to provide a touch of light to a dim corner of the border, but be warned – it can be very invasive. 'Feesey' is a good creamy white variegated variety, paler than *P.a.* var. *picta* and less invasive. Propagate by division. Zones 3–8

Helleborus argutifolius
Bold evergreen foliage, green flowers in early spring

You can become addicted to hellebores. Grow a few and you will crave more. The more familiar you become with them, the more you will appreciate the distinctions between the different species and varieties. As your taste for them becomes increasingly refined you will enjoy the most modest and subtle varieties – those with small flowers in shades of green – which you would probably never even have noticed in the early stages of your gardening career. At some time fairly early in the process of hellebore addiction you may become aware of one of the tallest and most striking plants of the group, *Helleborus argutifolius*, also called *H. corsicus* after the Mediterranean island which is its place of origin.

Helleborus argutifolius is the best of the genus for foliage. The evergreen leaves are held high on thick, arching stalks. They are gray-green in color and smooth to the touch. Each leaf is divided into three leaflets which have serrated edges like a fine saw. The plant has a two-year cycle, with each stem producing only foliage in its first year, and flowers developing on the mature stems in the spring of the second year. After flowering the stems die back to make room for new growth. Replacement stems will arise from the base, and so the plant counts as a herbaceous perennial rather than a biennial. The same plant will survive for many years.

The flowers are inconspicuous in color but perfect in form. They are cups of the palest green, with yellow anthers that radiate from the center and arch across the bowl of each cup. The flowers are long-lasting on the plant, but it is difficult to preserve hellebores as cut flowers. Some flower arrangers advocate plunging the base of the stems in boiling water. Others make 3–4in/8–10cm slits in the stems and soak the flowers up to their necks in water overnight before arranging them.

• Height to 36in/90cm, spread to 4ft/1.2m. The top-heavy foliage may need discreet staking. Hellebores like shade or part-shade and rich, well-drained, moist soil. They seed themselves readily, and if you have several different species and varieties of hellebore in the garden they are bound to interbreed, to give you a whole range of unpredictable hybrids. Zones 6–8

OTHER HELLEBORES TO GROW

Helleborus foetidus Another green hellebore, with arching racemes of hooded pale lime-colored flowers, usually edged with a thin rim of crimson. They appear first in late winter and last well into the spring. Finely cut leaves of the darkest green. Height 24in/60cm, spread 18in/45cm. Useful ground cover, particularly beneath shrubs of winter interest, such as coppiced willows or the rubus species with striking stems. Zones 5–9

Helleborus niger The Christmas rose is not a rose and only rarely flowers in time for Christmas, but it is otherwise perfectly named. Its Latin name of *niger* refers to its black roots, but it would have been more appropriate for it to have been given a name that celebrates its pure white flowers. These are large, about 2½in/6cm across, but the plant is relatively small, rarely reaching more than 12in/30cm in height and spread. The variety 'Potter's Wheel' has larger flowers and more of them. Zones 4–8

A sturdy plant of *Helleborus argutifolius* fills a border in spring. The flowers open from midwinter onward and last for about three months. The stiff evergreen foliage gives good value for the rest of the year. This garden is laid out for year-round interest. The infrastructure of boxwood hedges, punctuated with terracotta amphorae, is decorated with unusual standard forsythias, pruned into bobbles.

Helleborus niger in early spring

Helleborus orientalis Among the loveliest of early spring flowers, the Lenten rose has received a great deal of attention from plant hunters and breeders. They have produced strains with flowers which range in color from pure white, through cream to primrose-yellow, pink, and plum-crimson verging on black. Whatever color takes your fancy you can be sure to enjoy exquisitely beautiful cup-shaped flowers. Some recent cultivars have upward-facing flowers, but I still prefer those that are demurely downward-nodding, though you have to turn them up to appreciate the delicate markings on their faces – some varieties are plain but many are freckled with patterns of crimson dots. To highlight the flowers in spring it is best to cut away the tired old foliage. Fresh young foliage will grow up from the base. Height and spread 18in/45cm. Propagate by division or by seed – but if you want seed to come true to type you need to choose the parents carefully. Left to their own devices these hellebores are totally promiscuous and will interbreed with abandon. Zones 4–9

Helleborus orientalis in spring

Hosta sieboldiana elegans

PLANTAIN LILY

Architectural foliage from spring to fall, summer flower spikes

Grown primarily for their succulent and graceful foliage, hostas also produce elegant spikes of flowers reminiscent of lilies. Some of them give, in addition, good (though brief) fall color. Another virtue of hostas is the discreet way in which they die back in winter. The first frost of fall transforms the leaves into a pathetic mound like melted plastic, with hardly any unsightly dead stubs to wither and rot. Above ground the plant vanishes almost completely, except perhaps for a seed head or two. Below, the roots remain, poised to deliver a new crop of succulent young crowns in spring.

There are several hundred named species and varieties of hosta, and it is difficult to limit a recommendation to only a few. In choosing hostas you need to think about your preferences for leaf color and shape, plain or variegated leaves, tall or short plants. If you have sufficient room, why not consider one of the largest and most dramatic among them, *Hosta sieboldiana* var. *elegans*?

This hosta produces a magnificent mound of blue-green foliage up to 39in/1m high if it has room, with a spread of 5ft/1.5m in an unrestricted space. The leaves are enormous – about 18in/45cm long and 12in/30cm wide, splaying out from a fleshy leaf stalk about 24in/60cm long. Heart-shaped in silhouette, they are scalloped and folded into sculptural forms. Numerous veins radiate from the midriff to follow the curved shape of the leaf, and between them are prominent ridges that give a crinkled texture. After rain, droplets of water collect in the veins or run off the leaves like balls of mercury. The delicate blue-gray tone of the leaf comes from a white bloom that covers its upper and lower surfaces. This bloom comes off easily to reveal

Hosta sieboldiana 'Frances Williams' in summer

RIGHT Yellow echoes between *Hosta fortunei aureomarginata* and the yellow-leaved *Choisya ternata* 'Sundance' further back in the border. The pink flower between them is *Geranium endressii.*

OPPOSITE In a shaded border, *Hosta sieboldiana* var. *elegans* dominates a group of ferns, a large clump of *Geranium × magnificum,* and a blue-leaved *Sedum rhodiola rosea,* cleverly planted as a companion.

the dark green surface below, so the leaves are quickly spoiled by fingering.

In midsummer the flower spikes protrude just above the foliage. The narrow, funnel-shaped flowers are lilac-gray in color, and open from the bottom of the spike upward. Although they are a fitting complement to the foliage, they do have one inherent disadvantage. By the time the flowers at the top of the spike have opened, those lower down have faded and died. Unfortunately, they do not die gracefully. The first shower of rain will knock off the dead flowers, which then proceed to stick to the leaves below. This can ruin the appearance of the foliage and you may make it worse if you attempt to pluck off the decaying flowers, thus marking the leaf surfaces. The best way out, sadly, is to remove the

flower heads altogether as soon as the first flowers begin to go over.

One of the best gray-leaved foliage plants, *H.s.* var. *elegans* is a star turn in the silver border, provided it can be accorded part-shade and plenty of moisture. In this respect it differs from the majority of silver plants, which prefer full sun, and it is a test for the gardener's ingenuity to provide suitable conditions for different neighboring plants. Gray foliage is useful in other contexts too, and this hosta provides an excellent neutral foil for plants whose colors might otherwise appear too strident, such as the magnificent magenta *Geranium psilostemon*. Again, it takes its place as one of the mainstays of a corner of the garden devoted to foliage. The hosta's great wavy dinner-plate leaves make a marvelous contrast with the filigree foliage of larger ferns, such as *Matteuccia struthiopteris* – and they both favor the same conditions of moist part-shade. Hostas are also ideal plants for underplanting with spring flowers – celandines, wood anemones, snowdrops all grow marvelously with them and start to die back as the leaves of the hostas unfurl.

• This hosta will thrive in a shaded or part-shaded position in any fertile soil, but it must be kept moist; the edge of a pond or boggy area is ideal. It will survive in full sun, but the gray bloom on the leaves will be less effective and they will appear a darker green. It needs to be fed regularly. It shares its favored damp conditions with its worst pests, snails and slugs, which find the juicy leaves and stems irresistible. Uncontrolled, they will devastate the leaves with unsightly holes and if you love hostas you will have to wage war on these molluscs without sentimentality. Propagate hostas by division: the best way is simply to cut a slice out of the mature clump with a spade as if you were cutting a cake. This should be done in spring as the crowns are just appearing above the soil. Zones 3–8

Companionable foliage. *Hosta crispula* makes a centerpiece in a green and white composition that includes *Dicentra spectabilis alba, Brunnera macrophylla* 'Dawson's White' (with blue flowers), and a single white star of *Ornithogalum umbellatum.*

OTHER HOSTAS TO GROW

***Hosta sieboldiana* 'Frances Williams'** Also known under the name of 'Gold Edge', this hosta is a sport of *H.s.* var. *elegans,* first noticed by Mrs Frances Williams in a nursery bed in Connecticut in 1936. She recognized the value of this oddity with glaucous leaves and broad yellow margins. This pattern is most marked in young growth, and by the end of the season the two tones are much less distinguishable. Unfortunately, the leaves tend to decay earlier in the fall than those of other hostas. They may be somewhat unstable as a result of the plant's origin as a sport. This hosta reaches a height and spread of 39in/1m. Zones 3–8

Hosta crispula An elegant hosta with narrow leaf stalks and wavy, white-edged leaves that taper to a point. The leaves have pronounced leaf veins that add to the complexity of the surface pattern. Height to 30in/75cm, spread 36in/90cm. Zones 3–8

Hosta fortunei This graceful hosta has finely pointed, fresh green, wavy-edged leaves. It makes a mound of up to 30in/75cm high with a spread of 36in/90cm. The lilac-colored flowers are held on tall spikes well above the foliage. There are several attractive variegated varieties, including *H.f.* var. *albopicta*, in which the central segments of the leaves are variably patterned with light green and cream. *H.f.* 'Albomarginata', as its name suggests, has white margins to its leaves, and, similarly, *H.f. aureomarginata* has yellow margins. Zones 3–8

Hosta plantaginea An exception among hostas in its preference for full sun, this is one of the few hostas to flourish in a Mediterranean climate. It has broad, shiny, lime-green leaves, but its flowers take on more importance than those of other hostas by virtue of their sweet scent. The flowers, produced in late summer, are pure white and open fully at night, when they release maximum scent. This hosta is a good candidate for growing in a pot, which can be moved to nosing distance when the flowers appear. Height 24in/60cm, spread 30in/75cm. Zones 3–9

Hosta ventricosa An excellent hosta with heart-shaped midgreen leaves, making a graceful mound 30in/75cm high with a spread of 4ft/1.2m. The flower tubes are a bulging bell shape, and they are a deep lilac color. There are two excellent variegated forms of the same dimensions, *H.v.* var. *aureomaculata,* in which the young leaves are strikingly marked with yellow, and *H.v.* 'Aureomarginata' (syn. *H.v.* 'Variegata'), which has leaves edged with cream. Zones 3–9

Iris foetidissima

GLADWYN OR STINKING IRIS

Evergreen leaves, summer flowers, orange fall berries
lasting through the winter

As a general rule irises are ephemeral flowers. The most glamorous types, the bearded irises, take up a lot of space in the garden for the sake of three weeks of glory in early summer. So any iris that extends its season with a double act is especially welcome. *Iris foetidissima* does just that.

It has to be said that the first part of the performance is somewhat modest. The flowers are characteristically iris-shaped, but compared with their bearded cousins they are dingy in color. Though there is considerable variety among them, all have tones of creamy yellow and dull purple mixed in different proportions. The most attractive are to be found in a variety called *citrina*, in which the yellow element predominates.

The chief glory of *I. foetidissima* is in the seed heads. The parts of an iris flower come in threes, and the seed heads are no exception. They are formed of three separate lobes which swell throughout the summer until in fall they split along their seams.

Iris foetidissima in winter

Iris foetidissima in summer

The flamboyant orange berries do not spill out but remain attached, come wind, rain, and snow, for much of the winter.

This iris has yet another interesting feature, in its dense clump of evergreen leaves. It is the foliage that earns the plant its name of *foetidissima*, or "stinking iris", because when crushed it gives off an acrid smell (said, by those who have imagination in these matters, to be reminiscent of roast beef).

● Height and spread 30in/75cm. This plant is a great survivor, tolerant of sun or shade and damp or dry conditions. Propagate by division or by seed. Zones 7–9

Lamium maculatum roseum

PINK DEAD-NETTLE

Silver-patterned leaves, pink flowers in
late spring and summer

The dead-nettles, so called because they lack the sting of their pestilential lookalikes, are quintessential ground-cover plants. Put them under trees and shrubs where hardly anything else will grow and they will perform for you with little further trouble. They will also thrive in part-shade at the feet of herbaceous perennials and bulbs. You only need to intervene when they begin to encroach upon your prime border plantings.

There are countless varieties of dead-nettles, named for their flower color or leaf pattern, and *Lamium maculatum roseum* is one among several favorites. The flowers are pale pink and appear first in late spring and again intermittently throughout the summer. The first flush coincides with the last of the tulips and an effective treatment is to grow the pink peony-flowered tulip 'Angélique' through a carpet of pink lamium. If you are lucky there will still be flowers on the plants to accompany pink and magenta geraniums and roses at midsummer.

The lamium's leaves are crossed by a multiplicity of ribs, giving them a wrinkled texture. They are dark green and marked with a variable broad silvery gray stripe down the center. This attractive variegation gives the plant the sparkle that makes it ideal to brighten up a shady corner under a tree.

Other attractive varieties of *L. maculatum* include *L.m. album*, which has pure white flowers. 'Beacon Silver' has leaves in which the variegation has taken over the whole surface so that they are pure silver, with just a suggestion of pink at the edges; the

No bare soil to be seen. *Lamium maculatum roseum* makes a thick carpet around the feet of *Knautia macedonica* and annual larkspurs.

flowers are dark pink. *L.m.* 'White Nancy' has similar leaves but white flowers. The variety *L.m.* 'Aureum' has yellow-variegated leaves; it needs to be in shade or part-shade because, as with yellow-leaved cultivars of many plants, the sun tends to brown the leaves.

• Height 9in/23cm, spread 15in/40cm. Any soil. Shade or part-shade. The plant propagates itself by putting out roots at points where the stems touch the ground, and it will also set seed. Zones 4–9

ANOTHER LAMIUM TO GROW

Lamium galeobdolon 'Florentinum' A more vigorous and invasive ground cover than *L. maculatum*, *L. galeobdolon* 'Florentinum' (syn. 'Variegatum') is nevertheless to be recommended for a wild area on account of its exceptionally beautiful foliage. Each leaf is like a heart-shaped artist's palette, marked with a central dab of green, with freehand swashes of pure silver on either side. The flower spikes are yellow. Zones 4–9

Lamium maculatum 'White Nancy'

Making effective ground cover beneath a Rugosa rose, *Lamium maculatum album* intermingles with *Geranium sanguineum.* This should be the limit of its spread – if the lamium encroaches further and threatens to strangle the geranium it will need to be suppressed.

Planted beside a house wall, *Lavatera* 'Barnsley' receives some protection from winds that could snap its brittle stems. Next to the lavatera a container holds a selection of tender perennials and annuals, planted for a single season. Chosen to harmonize with the pale pink of the lavatera, they include the tender *Verbena* 'Silver Anne' and two pink forms of annual cosmos, as well as an ornamental cabbage tucked in beneath them.

Lavatera 'Barnsley'

TREE MALLOW

Shell-pink flowers all summer, persisting
until the first fall frosts

There is a story behind most of the named cultivars with which we populate our gardens. Some of the names have become blurred by history, but with *Lavatera* 'Barnsley' we have a new plant of our own time, named after the village of Barnsley in Gloucestershire, England, where the distinguished garden designer and writer Rosemary Verey has created her unique garden at Barnsley House. The story goes that Mrs Verey spotted the plant growing in the garden of a friend. She took a few cuttings and grew plants on at Barnsley House.

The feature that distinguishes 'Barnsley' from other lavateras is the delicate shell-pink color of its flowers. Their shape is typical of mallow flowers, cup-shaped with wavy-edged petals – somewhere between a hibiscus and a hollyhock. At the throat of the flower, where each petal tapers to a narrow base, the color darkens to deep rose, giving the flowers an attractive bicolored effect. The flowers line the many-branching stems and in a good season the plant is covered with a mass of blooms for some five months from midsummer to early fall. Individually the flowers do not last long, but no sooner has one withered and dropped than another bud has opened to take its place. They die gracefully, and drop to the ground, where they can be swept up if necessary.

A versatile filler for the end of the season. Easily grown from seed sown in spring, annual *Lavatera trimestris* 'Mont Blanc' is useful for filling spaces left by earlier-flowering bulbs or perennials. Here a mass of it has been planted to fill an area of the garden that had been left fallow.

Alcea rosea in summer

The plant does present problems, however, in the brittleness of its stems. It tends to grow bigger and faster than is good for it. It can put on over 6ft/1.8m of growth in a single season, with stems the size of a man's wrist at their base. The weight of the branches may split the stems, and strong winds will make this problem worse. I favor planting it against a wall or fence for support. You can tie hoops of strong twine at different heights around the plant to hold the branches in (but don't tie them so tightly as to restrict its natural growth). In cold areas the wall will give some winter protection too. This lavatera is vulnerable to heavy frosts, which may cut it back to the ground. This is not necessarily the disaster that it sounds, because pruning right back in spring is recommended practice (see below).

• Height and spread to 8ft/2.5m. Full sun in any well-drained soil. Feed well for best results. To prevent the main stems splitting, support the plant with a stake, or tie against a wall; thin the branches if they become too top-heavy. The plant has a tendency to revert to its dark pink ancestral form: cut out any reverting branches. In winter, I recommend tying up the plant with protective burlap, against winds and frosts. The upper growth will itself give some frost protection to the base of the plant. In spring, cut right back to within 18in/45cm of the ground. This plant does not have a long life expectancy – four or five years at the most – so take cuttings in late summer to ensure that you have replacements if needed the following spring. Propagation can only be achieved by cuttings; seeds will not grow true to type. Zones 8–10

OTHER MALLOWS TO GROW

The family Malvaceae includes several distinct genera, some of them perennials, some biennials or annuals, some (like *Lavatera* 'Barnsley') capable, in a favored climate, of growing as shrubs, but all plants having the distinctive mallow flower shape. The following are among the best.

Lavatera maritima An attractive tree mallow that has pale pink flowers with magenta centers. Its gray-green leaves have serrated edges, but are soft to the touch. It is smaller than *Lavatera* 'Barnsley', reaching a height and spread of 5ft/1.5m, and it begins flowering later in the summer. Unfortunately, being a plant from the Mediterranean, it is not reliably hardy in colder regions, and needs to be overwintered as cuttings under glass. Zones 9–10

***Lavatera trimestris* 'Mont Blanc'** A bushy annual, of height 30in/75cm, spread 20in/50cm, with

Lavatera maritima in summer

trumpet-shaped flowers of purest white. Easily grown from seed sown in spring in the site where it is to flower, or grown under glass and transplanted. Thrives in pure sun. Collect the nobbly seed heads when ripe and the seeds should come true. *L. trimestris* is available in other colors, notably 'Silver Cup', but do not be deceived by this name; it is not silver at all, but an aggressive shade of pink. Zones 8–9

Alcea rosea One of the delights of traditional cottage gardens, hollyhocks produce tall spires up to 2.5m/8ft high of flowers in a range of colors from white, through pale yellow to pink to mauve to deep purplish black. Hollyhocks are biennials, easily grown from seed. Zones 3–9

Malva moschata The musk mallow, so called because of the scent given off by the leaves when crushed, is a short-lived perennial. This means that plants are best replaced every other year by new stock grown from seed. Growing to a height of 36in/90cm and spread of 20in/50cm it is a delicately pretty plant, with fine-cut, fernlike leaves and frilly-edged pink flowers. There is a white form, *M.m. alba*, also highly desirable. Like other mallows, *M. moschata* needs full sun, but it will not tolerate poor soil. Zones 3–5

Sidalcea malviflora One of the most elegant of the mallows, with spikes up to a height of 4ft/1.2m and spread of 18in/45cm of clean-cut, saucer-shaped, clear pink flowers, like miniature hollyhocks. The cultivar 'Loveliness' lives up to its name, with flowers of a delicate shell-pink. The plant has two kinds of foliage; the leaves at the base grow in clumps and are broad and rounded, whereas those attached to the stems are narrow and lobed. A perennial, requiring full sun, it can be propagated by division or from seed. Zones 5–7

Sidalcea malviflora in summer

Lunaria annua

MONEY PLANT

Spring flowers, followed by silvery seed heads
that last all winter

Money plant must have earned its name from the coin-shaped seedpods that it extends so generously in the winter months. The seed cases glow silver in the low winter light, looking especially good with a sprinkling of snowdrops beneath them, a colorless frosty picture that sums up the season.

Lunaria pays its dues in spring too, and for my money I prefer the form with white flowers and variegated leaves, *Lunaria annua* 'Alba Variegata'. The flowers add a touch of brilliance to the spring border, bringing light to a shady corner and combining happily with tulips of any color. The mature leaves have a sprinkling of white around their heart-shaped edges, as if their rims have been dipped in thick cream. This leaf pattern complements the white flowers to give a plant that positively sparkles.

Flower arrangers value lunaria for dried flower displays, and they commonly spruce up cut stems by picking off the outer seed cases. The seeds are sandwiched between three paper-thin layers of transparent tissue. The two outer layers can easily be stripped off, releasing the seeds and leaving the central partition still attached to the stem to make a far brighter display than the full three-layered seedpods. I would counsel gardeners to do the same to plants *in situ*. It is a time-consuming business, but it is the only way to collect seed, and you are improving the winter display into the bargain. I find that it is a task that I can give to my children without the fear of putting them off gardening for life. They have a satisfying harvest of seeds and they can see at the end that they have enhanced the appearance of the plant.

● Height up to 30in/75cm, spread 15in/40cm. Sun or part-shade, any soil. Obtain seed from a reliable

Lunaria annua 'Alba Variegata' in spring

source, to ensure that you get the right color. Once you have lunaria in the garden it will readily seed itself but, as it is a biennial, you will need to make a second sowing of seed one year after the first, to guarantee an annual succession of plants. The white-flowered and variegated forms come true from seed, but only when the plants are completely isolated from other types. Do not be discouraged if the young plants show no variegation in their first year; the patterning will be distinct by the time they come to flower. Zones 4–8

ANOTHER LUNARIA TO GROW

Lunaria rediviva The perennial lunaria has white flowers similar to those of *L. annua*, with the added virtue of a delicate scent. Height and spread to 30in/75cm. Zones 5–8

In late fall, the seed heads of money plant *(Lunaria annua)* accompany the berries of the Oregon grape *(Mahonia aquifolium)*. The money plant will seed itself and the mahonia will spread by suckers. The two plants need little attention, and will keep their piece of ground decoratively covered for many a year.

Matteuccia struthiopteris in winter

Matteuccia struthiopteris

SHUTTLECOCK FERN, OSTRICH FERN

Attractive foliage from spring to fall, with decorative plumes lasting through the winter

There are few more potent symbols of spring than the sight of fern fronds uncurling. They seem to contain the potential energy of watch springs. Add a sprinkling of daffodils to the fresh sap-green of the ferns and you have the very image of spring.

From the vast range of ferns available, *Matteuccia struthiopteris*, the shuttlecock fern, is a good choice to begin with, because it has something to offer in every season, including winter. In spring each clump is renewed by a circle of young fronds, facing inward. As they unfurl they bend outward, so that the plant assumes a hollow shuttlecock shape.

In summer matteuccia produces reproductive fronds which are very distinct from its other foliage. These fronds, which produce spores, rise, upright and bushy, from the center of the fern. Although they go brown they remain through the winter, after the rest of the foliage has died back.

• Like most ferns, matteuccia needs moist conditions. It thrives beside ponds and streams and is an ideal candidate for the bog garden. It prefers sunny sites, but will survive full shade. Zones 4–8

Matteuccia struthiopteris unfurling in spring

Osmunda regalis fronds

Asplenium scolopendrium

Dryopteris filix-mas in spring

OTHER FERNS TO GROW

Asplenium scolopendrium (syn. *Phyllitis scolopendrium*) The evergreen hart's-tongue fern, with its characteristic strap-shaped fronds, makes a plant of height 30in/75cm. Prefers neutral or acidic soil and will grow in crevices or rock gardens. Zones 4–8

Asplenium trichomanes The maidenhair spleenwort is a small creeping fern, with a spread of only 12in/30cm, which readily colonizes walls and rocky crevices. It has delicately divided fronds. Sun or part-shade, tolerant of seaside conditions. Zones 3–8

Dryopteris filix-mas The male fern is a robust deciduous woodland fern, common in the wild over a wide range of Europe and northern parts of the United States, but none the worse for that. Tufts of elegantly divided fronds reach a height and spread of 4ft/1.2m. Requires moist soil rich in humus, in shade or part-shade. Zones 4–8

Osmunda regalis One of the tallest and most stately ferns, the royal fern has broad fronds with finger-sized divisions. It produces plumes of brown-colored fertile fronds. The foliage turns golden brown in fall. Prefers neutral or acidic soil, and likes damp conditions. Ideal for a waterside planting, where it may reach a height of 6ft/1.8m and a spread of 10ft/3m. Zones 3–9

Polystichum setiferum The semievergreen soft shield fern is among the most elegant of the hardy ferns, with intricately divided arching fronds which tend to make a ground-hugging shield-shaped tuft of height 20in/50cm and spread 36in/90cm. There are countless varieties, among the best of which is 'Divisilobum', which has fronds that are especially finely divided. Shade or part-shade, any soil with plenty of humus. Zones 5–8

Meconopsis cambrica

Meconopsis cambrica

WELSH POPPY

Yellow flowers appearing over summer and fall

Not to be confused with its stately blue cousins from the Himalayas, which can be very difficult to grow, the Welsh poppy is disarmingly easy. Simply beg a seed head or two from a gardener who has the plant, scatter some seed in odd corners of the garden and off you go. Once established, it will seed itself at the edge of paths and in undisturbed corners of beds to give an informal "lived-in" look to the garden. The flower comes in two colors, lemon-yellow and orange, and both come true from seed. I strongly urge you to choose the yellow and dispense with the orange, which is rather a strident color and diffi-cult to associate with other plants. The yellow variety fits in well with herbs and vegetables, and makes a cheerful contrast with low blue plants, such as the veronicas and blue omphalodes. However, being a self-seeder it is not a flower for careful plantsmanship, but rather for informal general effect. It is particularly effective for lighting up dark corners under trees or in shaded areas of the garden; not grown *en masse* but as an accent plant, springing up here and there.

● Height 12in/30cm, spread 8in/20cm. Any soil, sun or shade. Seeds scattered in spring should flower the same summer and reseed for a further show. Fall sowings will produce flowers in late spring. Zones 6–9

Morina longifolia

Handsome foliage, white and pink summer flowers persisting as seed heads

Morina is one of those perfect perennials – attractive in all its parts and at all stages of its growth. The foliage is thistlelike, making a rosette of narrow, prickly leaves near ground level. Rising from the center of the rosette in midsummer are spires of delicate white flowers arranged in whorls around the stems. The flowers are tubular and change in color in the course of their development from almost pure white to varying shades of pink.

Being predominantly white, the flowers look good with almost any companion colors, including blues, lilacs, and yellows. You might choose to high-light the pink touch to the flowers by partnering them with a pink geranium such as *Geranium endressii* 'Wargrave Pink', whose softly rounded habit will contrast satisfyingly with the morina's spiny erect form.

The flowers die off without any fuss, simply drop-ping discreetly to the ground and leaving the strik-ing, spiny seed heads to mature. Their tall sil-houettes make a valuable contribution to the fall bounty in the border. Then they can be gathered, dried off, and kept as everlasting flowers.

• Height 30in/75cm, spread 45cm/18in. Needs a mild climate, full sun, and well-drained soil; will do well in sandy conditions. Propagate by division after flowering or by seed. Zones 8–9

Morina longifolia seed heads

Adding height at the front of a colorful border, a clump of *Morina longifolia* dominates potentillas, mimulus, and *Geranium endressii*. After the other, brighter flowers have passed over, the morina will still be giving value with its attractive seed heads.

Paeonia mlokosewitschii
in early spring

Paeonia mlokosewitschii
in midspring

Paeonia mlokosewitschii
in fall

Paeonia mlokosewitschii in late spring

Paeonia mlokosewitschii

Attractive foliage, primrose-yellow flowers
in late spring, fall fruits

As far as flowers go, the herbaceous peonies are among the prima donnas of the border, most of them giving a sensational but short-lived display, which often coincides with that of those other shooting stars, the old-fashioned roses. However, all have attractive cut-leaved foliage which makes up for the ephemeral appearance of the flowers. Aristocrat among this large group is the peony with the unpronounceable name *Paeonia mlokosewitschii*, often memorized by despairing gardeners as "Molly the Witch." For sheer quality of flower, foliage, and fall fruits, she stands head and shoulders above the rest, with something to offer for every season. In early spring the first shoots appear – dark crimson spears of unfolding leaves. These look good with hybrid red primroses and polyanthus – an appropriate association because later the peony leaves will give welcome shade to the primroses. The maturing foliage retains a pink tinge in the leaf stalks but the rounded lobes of the leaves become an attractive pale gray-green. The cupped flowers appear in late spring, earlier than those of most hybrid peonies, and, provided the sun is not too hot, they may last for up to two weeks. They are a tender shade of primrose-yellow, with a crown of golden stamens at the center.

To my eye the pale yellow of the peony flower

looks best in the company of blues and I would like to see it underplanted with bluebells, or with the lovely shade-loving *Omphalodes cappadocica* with its bright caerulean eyes.

At the end of summer, the peony has another gift in store: the seed heads split to reveal brightly colored berries which remain attached as the seed case peels wide open. The mature berries are shiny black but the immature ones and those that have shriveled are blood-red. This two-toned effect will stop you in your tracks.

• Height and spread to 36in/90cm. Peonies like rich, well-drained soil in sun or part-shade. The thick, fleshy roots are said to resent disturbance; left unmolested the plant may survive for decades. However, one method of propagation is by division of the roots in fall. Alternatively grow from seed, but plants will take four years to mature to flowering size. Zones 4–8

Paeonia lactiflora 'Emperor of India'

Paeonia lactiflora 'Bowl of Beauty'

OTHER PEONIES TO GROW

***Paeonia officinalis* 'Rubra Plena'** The common cottage garden peony, with flowers that are fluffy deep crimson balls up to 6in/15cm in diameter. These appear fleetingly in early summer. Good, deeply cut dark green leaves. Height and spread to 24in/60cm. The tuberous roots are easily divided. There are pink and also white varieties, less attractive than the common form. Zones 3–8

***Paeonia lactiflora* varieties** For centuries *Paeonia lactiflora* was an obsession with Chinese gardeners who bred countless varieties, ranging from whites through pinks to deep crimson. Some are single in form; some are exotic doubles. In many of the doubles the central anthers have mutated into numerous thin ribbons, usually of the same color as the petals. Among the most sensational flowers are

Paeonia lactiflora 'Barrymore'

Paeonia lactiflora 'Bridal Veil'

'Bowl of Beauty', with pink petals surrounding a central "explosion" of cream. 'Colonel Heneage' has petals and central frills that are magenta throughout. 'Duchesse de Nemours' is frilly white and deeply scented. 'Bridal Veil' is pink with cream anthers. 'Barrymore' is a paler pink. 'Emperor of India' (sometimes called 'Empress') is perhaps the most exotic, with deep rose petals surrounding a central crown of burnished gold. Height and spread to 36in/90cm. Zones 3–8

Pulmonaria saccharata

LUNGWORT

Spotted leaves for ground cover, pink and blue flowers in early spring

The pulmonarias are among the earliest of the herbaceous plants to flower. They come soon after the first spring bulbs, the snowdrops, and in advance of all but the earliest of the daffodils. *Pulmonaria saccharata* gives an attractive bicolored effect in the

bare borders of early spring. The flower buds open pink, but within a day or two they have changed to a pastel blue. The flower heads are a loose gathering of tubular flowers arranged on a short stalk rather in the manner of a cowslip.

Only when the flowers have dropped do the leaves reach any size. They are elliptical and pointed, soft and slightly furry to the touch. Their background color is dark green, but they are mottled with silvery gray spots to a very variable extent – in some plants the leaves have small spots while in others the patterns merge to give an almost entirely silver leaf.

This is a well-behaved plant which seeds itself readily but does not become unduly invasive. It makes good ground cover, especially under trees and shrubs where few plants can put up with the dim light. It is most effective under deciduous shrubs, such as philadelphus or weigela, as long as there is enough moisture. The pulmonaria flowers will give

A dual-purpose perennial. *Pulmonaria saccharata* makes a compact and colorful companion for narcissi in early spring (BELOW LEFT). By midsummer (BELOW RIGHT) decorative foliage has spread to cover the bare ground, with *Alchemilla mollis* behind it.

pleasure before the shrub's leaves appear and its leaves will provide continuing interest at ground level later.

• Height 9in/23cm, spread 18in/45cm. Grows in shade or part-shade, any soil. Propagate by seed or division. Zones 3–8

OTHER PULMONARIAS TO GROW

Pulmonaria angustifolia This species has narrow leaves without the variegated patterns found in *P. saccharata*, but there are several varieties with superior flower color. These include *P. angustifolia azurea* and *P. angustifolia* 'Mawson's Blue', both of which have gentian-blue flowers, the latter with chocolate-colored calyces. Zones 3–8

Pulmonaria officinalis rubra A lungwort with flowers of a deep salmon-pink – a color that I personally find a little aggressive in the bare borders of early spring. I prefer *P. officinalis* 'Sissinghurst White', with pure white flowers. Both varieties have spotted leaves, though they are not so richly marked as those of *P. saccharata*. Zones 3–8

Pulsatilla halleri

PASQUE FLOWER

Silvery foliage, lilac-colored spring flowers, followed by seed heads in summer

The Pasque flower is lovely in all its parts. Tufts of foliage push above the ground in early spring and open to reveal fernlike leaves, covered with soft white hairs which give an overall silvery effect. The flowers follow soon. Resembling anemones, they are also covered with fine hairs which give them the texture of soft felt. They are lilac-colored with a mass of yellow stamens at the center. This plant is an asset to any rock garden or alpine bed in spring. It would

be difficult to imagine any plant of softer appearance, or more inviting to the touch.

When the petals drop, you should resist deadheading this plant, as it has another treat in store. The round seed heads are covered with hairy wisps which catch the light, rather like "old man's beard," the seed heads of the wild clematis.

Pulsatilla vulgaris is a relation and looks very similar, although the flowers are more variable in color, ranging from purple through pink to white.

• Height 9in/23cm, spread 12in/30cm. Like other alpines, it prefers a gritty, well-drained soil such as may be incorporated into a rockery, raised bed, or sink garden. Zones 5–7

Pulsatilla halleri in spring

Pulsatilla halleri in summer

Salvia officinalis

SAGE

Ornamental foliage, summer flowers

As a cooking herb, sage has relatively limited uses, but it has great value as an ornamental plant, by virtue of its several varieties with distinctive leaf color. The purple sage, *Salvia officinalis* 'Purpurascens', is perhaps the most useful. It has attractively soft, felty leaves, dull purple in young growth, becoming green and lighter in tone when mature. With young and old leaves on the same plant, the two-tone effect of the foliage is attractive in itself, so it is a bonus when spikes of purple flowers appear in summer. The purple sage makes an effective contrast with silver-leaved shrubs. I have seen it well used as an underplanting to a massive cardoon, *Cynara cardunculus*, and underplanted, in turn, by the low-growing, gray-leaved *Stachys byzantina* (syn. *S. lanata*).

Another lovely sage is the yellow-variegated *S. officinalis* 'Icterina', the patterns on whose leaves are particularly subtle. Plant this beside the purple sage to make a contrast; the leaf shape and texture are the same, but the colors, yellow and purple, are at opposite ends of the spectrum. A third variety, *S. officinalis* 'Tricolor', has leaves with bolder variegation. Here the leaf edges are creamy white, the centers green, and the younger shoots are dabbed with pink. Less vigorous and less hardy than the other varieties, it looks a little sickly to my eye, but every gardener must follow his or her own taste.

• Height 24in/60cm, spread 36in/90cm. Originating in the Mediterranean, sage likes a sunny position in any well-drained soil. It looks most attractive as a young plant, and it can become woody after a year or two. For best results, then, prune back strongly in spring; there is a risk that the plant will not survive this treatment, in which case replace it with a young

plant. Propagate by cuttings. *S.o.* 'Purpurascens', 'Icterina', and 'Tricolor' are all best in zones 7–9.

Salvia officinalis 'Purpurascens'

OTHER SAGES TO GROW

The genus *Salvia* is a vast and diverse one, with some seven hundred species, many of which are useful in the garden. Among those that qualify for this book, the following have very different virtues from each other, and from *S. officinalis*, although a certain family likeness can be detected in the shapes of the flowers of all sages.

Salvia sclarea in summer

Salvia horminum (now correctly *S. viridis*) This sage has long-lived flowers consisting of brightly colored bracts of white, red, or blue. These keep their color when dried, and so this makes a good plant for winter decoration. Height 18in/45cm, spread 10in/25cm. Grow as an annual, from seed.

Salvia patens A perennial with intensely blue flowers which appear for many weeks in late summer. Standing some 18in/45cm in height, with a spread of 12in/30cm, *S. patens* makes a valuable ingredient for an all-blue border. If you prefer a pale version, *S.p.* 'Cambridge Blue' is the one for you. This salvia is quite tender and will only survive the winter in mild areas. Zones 9–10

Salvia sclarea This is a biennial plant. In summer tall and dramatic sprays of long-lived lavender-pink flowers surmount its broad, furry leaves. These flowers are surrounded by bracts of a matching lavender, creating an overall shimmering effect. Height 30in/75cm, spread 24in/60cm. Zones 6–8

Salvia uliginosa Flowering over a long period toward the end of summer, *S. uliginosa* has small flowers, but many of them, on tall, open sprays of height 5ft/1.5m. They are sky-blue and look marvelous in the company of the mauve *Verbena bonariensis*, which is about the same height. Unfortunately this salvia is fairly tender and needs winter protection in many areas. Zones 8–9

Salvia patens in late summer

Grown from seed in a shaped bed within a restored nineteenth-century garden, a clump of *Salvia horminum* displays its color range of white and pink through purple. It is boldly underplanted with red and purple verbenas.

Sedum 'Autumn Joy'

STONECROP

Blue-green leaves from spring, flowers in fall, seed heads for winter

This perennial emerges from dormancy very early in the spring, with fleshy blue-green leaf buds appearing at the base of last year's flower stems. It then proceeds to grow steadily and to look promising throughout the summer months. Other border perennials come and go – phlox, geraniums, campanulas all reach maturity and decline as the sedum plods on. Its fleshy leaves swell, and the plant forms an attractive clump, but only in late summer do the flowers mature. In flower it retains its good compact shape, and never becomes straggly unless forced to

compete with its neighbors for light. Coinciding with dahlias and hardy asters, the pink flower heads are flat and fluffy and are totally irresistible to butterflies. I have counted twenty tortoiseshell butterflies on a single plant.

Sedum 'Autumn Joy' (correctly called 'Herbst-freude') has the added virtue of aging gracefully through the seasons. The subtle, slightly biscuit-pink flowers deepen in color to a dull burgundy and the stems remain hard enough to stay upright through the winter. A clump of sedum looks magical with a covering of frost, and will provide interest in the winter garden until new growth begins at the base in spring.

- Height and spread 18in/45cm. Any soil, preferably in full sun. Propagate by division, but it will also seed itself. It is advisable to lift and divide plants every three years in spring, or else they are liable to become bare at the center. Zones 4–9

OTHER SEDUMS TO GROW

Sedum kamtschaticum 'Variegatum' A succulent for the rock garden, with striking cream-variegated foliage and a prostrate habit. The flower buds are red, opening to yellow star-shaped flowers. Height 6in/15cm, spread 20in/50cm. Zones 4–9

LEFT TO RIGHT *Sedum* 'Autumn Joy' makes a good rounded shape at the front of the border in midsummer. Hardy geraniums and roses dominate the scene, but they are over by early fall when the sedum comes into its own. The shrub behind the sedum is *Berberis thunbergii* 'Rose Glow'. This gives good color from spring to fall but is bare in midwinter when the dried flower heads of the sedum are still excellent value, providing flat perches on which hoar frost settles.

Sedum spectabile 'Meteor'

Sedum spectabile One of the parents of *S.* 'Autumn Joy', of the same dimensions, with similar biscuit-pink flower heads. *S. spectabile* 'Carmen' and *S. spectabile* 'Meteor' have fluffier flower heads of a brighter pink. Zones 4–9

Sedum 'Ruby Glow' A sprawling plant of height 10in/25cm and spread 18in/45cm, with gray-blue succulent foliage and heads of rose-red flowers in late summer and lasting well into fall. Makes a useful edging plant for a fall border. Zones 4–9

Sedum 'Vera Jameson' A sedum with succulent purplish-bronze leaves and dark pink flowers in late summer. It has a prostrate habit, with a height of 8in/20cm over a spread of 20in/50cm. Zones 5–8

Sedum 'Ruby Glow'

Silybum marianum

· OUR LADY'S MILK THISTLE ·

Variegated foliage in spring, thistlelike flowers
in summer

One plant above all others inspires curiosity among visitors to my garden. This is *Silybum marianum*, a highly decorated form of thistle that can be an annual or a biennial. Like most thistles, *S. marianum* has undulating leaves with barbarous spines along their edges. The feature that distinguishes this plant and earns it the enchanting name of "Our Lady's milk thistle" is the pattern of silver veining on the leaves. In its early growth the plant forms a broad rosette (about 30in/75cm diameter) of leaves that appear to glitter with this silver decoration. I find its broad, horizontal presence in the spring border the perfect companion for the vertically oriented tulips, particularly pale pink ones, such as 'Angélique', and the whites, 'Purissima' and 'White Triumphator'.

Silybum marianum in spring, with *Centaurea montana*, violas, tulips, and forget-me-nots

A word of warning though. Wonderful as it is in young growth, this plant becomes a hulking and aggressive monster. Within a few weeks the tight rosette opens up, branches, and expands upwards to a height of 5ft/1.5m. You are faced with a hazard in your border, for its spines will penetrate your flesh as if you were made of butter. The stiff expanding leaves, up to 36in/90cm wide, will edge out the neighboring plants. I have absolutely no qualms about heaving out this cuckoo in the nest, long before it reveals its unpleasant nature. Yet equally I have no hesitation in continuing to grow it, as I cherish its young beauty.

There remains the problem of propagation. *S. marianum* is very easy to grow from seed, but of course you can only obtain seed from a mature plant that has been allowed to flower. For this purpose I grow one plant hidden away in a corner of the garden, so that I can save seed for the coming year.

• Height and spread at maturity 5ft/1.5m. Sunny position, any soil. Propagate by seed. Seeds sown inside in early spring and planted out when big enough will flower the same year. To obtain a sizeable rosette by tulip time, plant the seeds straight into the ground in early fall. Zones 6–10

Vinca major 'Variegata'
VARIEGATED PERIWINKLE
Variegated evergreen foliage for ground cover,
with lilac summer flowers

The periwinkles make extremely useful ground cover – provided you do not put them with more fragile plants. The more delicate perennials will stand little chance against the thuggish advance of the vinca. This is a virtue when you have waste ground that you would like to see screened by foliage, but the periwinkle will not be appropriate for your more subtle planting designs.

Vinca major 'Variegata'

There is a wide choice of periwinkles available, varying in their size of leaf and color of flower. My own favorite is the large-leaved variegated form, which has lilac flowers in early summer. With its brightly patterned leaves it can bring a little light to a shady corner under trees. Personally, I find it effective in a raised bed above a terrace, where its long shoots trail over the side, finding no purchase for new roots in the stone slabs below. It will also soften the austerity of raised beds made from bricks or railroad ties, and its great virtue is that it remains equally effective in winter. It is worth cutting the plant right back in spring as the new growth will look much neater than the old.

• This vinca is unfussy in its requirements – it will grow in any soil and is content in sun or shade. It puts out long shoots of mottled green leaves, edged with creamy yellow, that grow up to 4ft/1.2m long. Where a shoot tip meets the soil it will take root and so the plant will "leapfrog" across the ground if it is left undisturbed. Wherever it takes root it makes a bushy growth of new shoots. Zones 7–9

Viola cornuta
HORNED VIOLET
Flowers from late spring to fall

Here is a plant that will flower for you from late spring to fall with hardly a pause for breath. Sometimes it will flower so persistently that it runs out of energy and dies of exhaustion. However, it will have produced so much seed beforehand that you will be very unlucky if a new generation does not spring up to take its place the following season.

Compared with its highly bred cousins the pansies, this species viola has flowers that are restrained in color and modest in size. They are pure lilac without any patterning, and shaped like large and flattened violets. There is also a pure white form which comes true to seed. In the right conditions this viola is a prodigious performer, with a dense display of flowers which are constantly replaced, especially if you are able to deadhead the plants.

Viola cornuta is an ideal plant to line the edge of a border. It also looks good as an underplanting in the bare area under roses. The lilac hue associates well with the broken pinks and purples of old-fashioned roses such as *R.* 'Cardinal de Richelieu'.

• Makes a mound up to 15in/40cm high, spreading to 24in/60cm. It likes sun or part-shade, but is intolerant of dry conditions. Zones 6–9

Viola cornuta, planted under a gleditsia

Zone chart
Approximate range of average annual minimum temperatures
  1 below −50°F/−45°C
  2 −50°F/−45°C to −40°F/−40°C
  3 −40°F/−40°C to −30°F/−34°C
  4 −30°F/−34°C to −20°F/−29°C
  5 −20°F/−29°C to −10°F/−23°C
  6 −10°F/−23°C to 0°F/−18°C
  7 0°F/−18°C to 10°F/−12°C
  8 10°F/−12°C to 20°F/−7°C
  9 20°F/−7°C to 30°F/−1°C
  10 30°F/−1°C to 40°F/4°C
  11 40°F/above 4°C

The usefulness zones quoted at the end of each plant entry represent the range of zones in which the plant may be successfully grown. The lowest figure is the coldest zone in which the plant will be hardy without winter protection; the highest is the limit of its tolerance of hot summer weather.

ACKNOWLEDGMENTS

AUTHOR'S ACKNOWLEDGMENTS

Rosemary Verey was an inspiration from the outset. Sue Dickinson was generous with advice on cultivation. I was very privileged to be able to call on Tony Lord, distinguished Editor of *The Plant Finder* for authentication of plant names.

At home, my tangled texts were patiently unravelled by Gillian Naish, Judy Dod and Carolyn McNab, who word-processed them and served them up to the publisher on a disk. On this my first venture into writing about gardening I count myself especially fortunate to have worked with Frances Lincoln's outstanding publishing team. Jo Christian has been the most painstaking of editors, so thorough and so self-effacing that she is bound to cut out this sentence unless I put my foot down. Serena Dilnot backed her up admirably, and Sandra Raphael meticulously compiled the index. On the design front, Louise Tucker and James Campus were very sensitive in the linking of text and pictures and were most tactful with an opinionated author.

My only disagreements have been with the photographer. Seeing us at work, people might think that we are inseparable. The truth is that we are firm rivals and it is my contention that his pictures distract people from reading my text.

PUBLISHERS' ACKNOWLEDGMENTS

The publishers would like to thank Joanna Chisholm, Margaret Crowther, Sarah Mitchell, Ray Rogers and Caroline Taylor for their help in the production of this book.

PHOTOGRAPHER'S ACKNOWLEDGMENTS

I am most grateful to the garden owners who have generously allowed me to take pictures in their gardens. They include the following:

Mr and Mrs Bill Baker; Mrs Gerda Barlow; Batsford Arboretum; Mrs Gwen Beaumont; M. Raymond Blanc; the late Humphrey Brooke; Mr & Mrs Martin Caroe; The Hon. C. & Mrs Cecil; Mr & Mrs J. Chambers; Mr & Mrs Leo Clark; Mrs Anne Dexter; Mr & Mrs Mike Elliott; Fibrex Nurseries; Mr & Mrs Thomas Gibson; Mr & Mrs Harry Hay; The Hon. Mrs E. Healing; Mr & Mrs David Hodges; Mr & Mrs John Hubbard; Lady Mary Keen; Mr C. Laikin; Mr & Mrs David Langton; Mr & Mrs L. Lauderdale; Miss Joan Loraine; Mr & Mrs Peter Maclaren; Mr & Mrs Ralph Merton; Mr & Mrs Jeremy Naish; Dr Julia Trevelyan Oman; Norrie and Sandra Pope; Mrs J.H. Robinson & John Brookes; Lord & Lady Saye and Sele; Mr & Mrs Kurt Schoenenberger; Mrs Shuker & Mrs Pollitt; Dr James Smart; Ron Spice; Rosemary Verey; Mr & Mrs Robin Wade; Mr & Mrs Geoff Walton; Mr & Mrs Whittington; Mr & Mrs John Williams.

Horticultural Consultant   Tony Lord
Editor   Jo Christian
Art Editor   Louise Tucker
Designer   James Campus
Picture Editor   Anne Fraser
Production   Adela Cory
Editorial Director   Erica Hunningher
Art Director   Caroline Hillier
Production Director   Nicky Bowden